THY GRACE RESTORE, THY WORK REVIVE

Revival, Reform, and Revolution in Global Methodism

Essays from the 14th Oxford Institute of Methodist Theological Studies

SARAH HEANER LANCASTER,
General Editor

Thy Grace Restore, Thy Work Revive: Revival, Reform, and Revolution in Global Methodism

The General Board of Higher Education and Ministry leads and serves The United Methodist Church in the recruitment, preparation, nurture, education, and support of Christian leaders—lay and clergy—for the work of making disciples of Jesus Christ for the transformation of the world. Its vision is that a new generation of Christian leaders will commit boldly to Jesus Christ and be characterized by intellectual excellence, moral integrity, spiritual courage, and holiness of heart and life. The General Board of Higher Education and Ministry of The United Methodist Church serves as an advocate for the intellectual life of the church. The Board's mission embodies the Wesleyan tradition of commitment to the education of laypersons and ordained persons by providing access to higher education for all persons.

Wesley's Foundery Books is named for the abandoned foundery that early followers of John Wesley transformed, which later became the cradle of London's Methodist movement.

Thy Grace Restore, Thy Work Revive: Revival, Reform, and Revolution in Global Methodism

Essays from the 14th Oxford Institute of Methodist Theological Studies

ISBN 978-1-953052-14-8

GBHEM Publishing is an affiliate member of the Association of University Presses.

Manufactured in the United States of America

Contents

Introduction

Sarah Heaner Lancaster

JOHN WESLEY'S METHODISM BEGAN AS a renewal movement to call people to a fuller experience of being Christian so that through their revival both the nation and the church could be reformed. He expressed this purpose for Methodism by recording in the "Large Minutes" (1763), "What may we reasonably believe to be God's design in raising up the preachers called 'Methodists'? A. To reform the nation and, in particular, the Church; to spread scriptural holiness over the land."[1]

Wesley was not the first to recognize the need for revival and renewal in England, and he made good use of practices that were already familiar. Religious Societies, where people could come together under the leadership of a priest to pursue disciplined holiness, had existed in the Church of England since the seventeenth century. These societies were largely located in London, and John's father, Samuel, actively encouraged their organization in less populated areas.[2] Even if he was not himself the originator of revival and reform, John Wesley certainly was

1 John Wesley, "The Large Minutes, B, 1763," in *The Methodist Societies: The Minutes of Conference*, ed. Henry Rack, *The Bicentennial Edition of the Works of John Wesley* [hereafter *Works*] (Nashville: Abingdon Press, 2011), 10:845.

2 Geordan Hammond, "The Revival of Practical Christianity: The Society for Promoting Christian Knowledge, Samuel Wesley, and the Clerical Society Movement," in *Revival and Resurgence in Christian History: Papers Read at the 2006 Summer Meeting and 2007 Winter Meeting of the Ecclesiastical Historical*

a successful and central figure in its implementation in the eighteenth-century evangelical revival in England.

Although Methodism began as a renewal movement, over time it became church, and it inevitably took on the structure of an institution. With a deep sense of the energy and focus that can be lost in institutionalization and with sensitivity about the fragility of existing institutions in our time, the theme "Thy Grace Restore, Thy Work Revive: Revival, Reform, and Revolution in Global Methodism" invited the Fourteenth Oxford Institute to explore ways that Methodism can regain a spirit that seeks and participates in renewal. Held in 2018, the Fourteenth Oxford Institute met just one year after global celebrations of the five hundredth anniversary of the Reformation. This meeting, then, provided opportunity to consider Methodism in light of other efforts for reform among Protestants and to consider what specifically Methodist reform might look like.

Revival, Reform, and Revolution

As a central figure in the evangelical revival in England, Wesley interacted with other leaders, and his own ideas and practices were influenced by them. His engagements (both positive and negative) with George Whitefield and the Moravians in England shaped his own view of what was needed for revival. Positively, George Whitefield influenced Wesley to consider field preaching. The Moravians drew him to heart religion that helped him understand faith as reliance on Christ. Their community structure also informed Wesley's system for organizing Methodists. However, the antinomian tendencies of both Whitefield's and the Moravians' theology forced Wesley to think carefully about the role of holiness in Christian life. His own approach to revival was to call people not only to lively experience of God's forgiving love (justification), but also to a more disciplined life before God that would

Society, ed. Kate Cooper and Jeremy Gregory (Woodbridge, UK: The Boydell Press, 2008), 116–27.

allow them to become renewed as the holy people God had created them to be (sanctification).

Differences in theology as well as personal differences eventually led the evangelical revival to split into groups. Wesley's Methodists thrived under his organizational leadership and theological vision. Despite Wesley's belief that God had raised up Methodist preachers to reform the nation and its established church, Methodism eventually took ecclesial form itself. The break between the American colonies and England in the American War of Independence led to Methodism becoming a church in North America. Methodists in Britain and Ireland also established themselves as churches.

With this change, Methodism had to organize ecclesially, incorporating the practices and lay leadership of the societies with an order of ministry and sacraments. The driving purpose to spread the gospel and scriptural holiness propelled Methodists outside of their own lands to mission around the globe. Methodist churches now exist in many cultures and contexts. This expansion of Methodist churches into other lands means that revival and reform may take different shapes in different Methodist churches.[3]

It may seem odd to associate the word *revolution* with the words *revival* and *reform* in the theme of the Fourteenth Institute. The oddness may be especially apparent in light of Wesley's opposition to the American Revolution (in "A Calm Address to Our American Colonies") and Élie Halévy's thesis that Wesley's Methodism was the primary factor for preventing in England violent political revolution that was suffered elsewhere in continental Europe in the late eighteenth and nineteenth centuries.[4] The suggestion to add "revolution" came not in connection with violent revolution, but rather because the pursuit of

3 This point is made clear by the variety of topics and points of view presented in the working groups of the Fourteenth Oxford Institute. Although this book cannot include all the papers presented on the theme, many of them are available on the Oxford Institute of Methodist Theological Studies website, https://oxford-institute.org/.

4 Élie Halévy, *A History of the English People in the Nineteenth Century*, trans. E. I. Watkin (New York: P. Smith, 1952).

scriptural holiness in this life has sometimes led to changes in social systems that seem revolutionary. The word opens reflection not only on the personal and the ecclesial, but also on the social relevance of Methodism.

The Plenary Papers from the Fourteenth Oxford Institute

Because the Fourteenth Oxford Institute named three dimensions of renewal in its theme, the plenary presentations engaged the theme in different ways. The presentations included not only lectures by a single speaker, but also panels that explored an aspect of the theme from different perspectives. All of the presentations are concerned with the way Methodists may be enlivened to make a difference where they are.

This book begins as the institute itself did with the panel that locates Methodism in relation to the Protestant Reformation. This volume's first chapter, consisting of three panel presentations, examines Wesley's reform in light of other reformers. Prof. Dr. Ulrike Schuler, a Methodist in Germany, reflects on the celebrations in Germany of the five hundredth anniversary of the Protestant Reformation. Although her paper covers Martin Luther's influence on Wesley, it also reconsiders history's focus on the Reformation as a period with towering figures. When the church is in need of reform, reformers rise to do God's work, even though they may be forgotten by others. Looking closely at the way Scripture was understood in the period of the Protestant Reformation, Dr. G. Sujin Pak compares Wesley's understanding of the soteriological message in Scripture to that of Luther and Calvin. She finds common commitments but suggests that Wesley was "protestant" in a different way. The Rev. Dr. Jonathan Dean looks at Wesley in relation to the English Reformation. He reminds us that the Church of England itself contains many elements from many reformers and Wesley's thinking about which elements the Church of England needed to recover changed over time.

The next five chapters were given as lectures. In chapter 2, the Rev. Prof. Pablo Andiñach considers the challenges of being faithful to the gospel. He highlights the lives of four women from very different backgrounds and from different times and places in order to fire our imaginations to face new challenges. These women can serve as models for Methodists as we seek an identity that helps us to be faithful so we can take our place in what he describes as the "unfinished" Bible.

In chapter 3, Prof. Priscilla Pope-Levison also looks to women as models, in this case Methodist deaconesses. She sees in the deaconess movement an unrealized potential that might still provide a map for revival in global Methodism. Her work identifies five core elements in the movement that could spark revival if put into practice across Methodism today.

To seek revival in global Methodism, we must bear in mind the needs of different contexts. In chapter 4, the Rev. Dr. Albert Jebanesan considers how mission might be reformed in light of global, contextual realities. The spread of Methodism provides an opportunity to think in fresh ways about how we share the gospel, and he focuses on Sri Lanka as an example of how we can rethink mission. He sees the need for a theology of mission that can allow for Indigenization, or contextualization.

In chapter 5, the Rev. Prof. Nichole R. Phillips pursues questions about self-understanding. If Methodism wants to bring life to people, it must understand how those people understand themselves, and Rev. Prof. Phillips's work provides insight into how people frame the narrative of their collective identity. She uses three examples (two involving working-class whites in East London and Youngstown, Ohio, and one involving working-class Blacks in the United States) to explore how people remember, respond, and interpret their collective experiences. Concepts of "selective forgetting" and "disremembering" illumine how these groups understand and tell their group history. If Methodism wants to respond to the plight of traumatized and marginalized groups, it would do well to consider the role of memory in shaping collective identity.

With a focus on The United Methodist Church in chapter 6, the Rev. Prof. Sarah Heaner Lancaster considers how revival might be different for a church than for early Methodism as a movement. Using

Wesley's image of "spiritual respiration," this paper thinks about the importance of constantly calling people who are marked by baptism to life with God, not just to dramatic conversion experiences.

Chapter 7 also consists of three panel presentations that examined connexionalism in flux. Connexionalism is such a deeply Methodist way of being that pressures on the connexion can either threaten the life and work of Methodism or present an opportunity for revival and reform. The Rev. Nicola V. Price-Tebbutt examines the way connexionalism is embodied in British Methodism, as explained in the report adopted by the Methodist Church in Britain titled *The Gift of Connexionalism in the 21st Century*. Her description shows that the understanding of connexionalism has changed over time in the face of challenges, but the importance of connexion has always been affirmed. The Very Rev. Dr. Chinonyerem Ekebuisi gives an account of how the principle of connexion took unique form in the Methodist Church Nigeria after it gained autonomy from the British Conference. The Methodist Church Nigeria shares the value of connexion but expresses it in distinctly African ways. Bishop Kenneth H. Carter Jr. reports on the state of connection (the US spelling) in The United Methodist Church as of the time of the meeting of the Fourteenth Oxford Institute. Speaking from his position as a moderator for the Commission on a Way Forward, Bishop Carter explains the process the Commission used to explore possible ways to address the threat to connection posed by different views within The United Methodist Church on the issue of same-sex relations.

Chapter 8 is the sermon preached at the close of the Oxford Institute in Wesley Memorial Methodist Church. The Rev. Prof. Peter Storey calls us to be the revolutionary church that breaks itself open so that the world can be mended.

The publication of these presentations from the Fourteenth Oxford Institute invites others into further reflection on revival, reform, and revolution so that this tradition may continue to pursue God's design for raising up the people called Methodist.

Reflections on the Reformation

Relation of Methodism to the Protestant Reformation

Ulrike Schuler

Some Preliminary Remarks from a Methodist in a German Context

When in an ecumenical setting in Germany we have to describe ourselves as United Methodists, the first point we make is that Methodists stand on the foundation of the Reformation. What this means is that our theology centers on the doctrine of justification by God's unconditional love, grace that is received by faith alone. Nevertheless, despite all the ecumenical progress of the last seventy years (taking the landmark foundation of the World Council of Churches in 1948 as the start), which includes both growth in knowledge and mutual understanding, as well as official agreements with the Protestant churches in Germany and worldwide, we always need to explain that Methodists are really Protestants.[1] We have to explain that we—as other Free Churches in

1 German agreements: e.g., with the Evangelische Kirche in Deutschland (today twenty Lutheran, Reformed, and United regional churches—"Landeskirchen"—that form the Evangelical Church in Germany): Full Communion of pulpit and sacrament (since 1987); *Magdeburger Erklärung* (2007, Magdeburg Declaration: mutual recognition of baptism, adopted by those member churches of the National Council of Churches in Germany that practice infant baptism); *Charta Oecumenica* (signed in Europe by the Conference of European Churches in 2001, guidelines for the growing

Germany—arose from renewal movements inside the mainline Protestant churches (Reformed, Lutheran, or Anglican), that we are Christian communities who practice reception into membership in which testimony in a congregation is included.[2] Although Methodism spread from a revival movement within the Church of England two hundred years after the so-called Reformation era, theological roots, connections, and relationships to the Reformation always need to be defined. That is also true with regard to the relationship between Methodism and pietism in the eighteenth century, with Methodism seen as an Anglo-American variety of the German pietism in the times of the Enlightenment in the Western European cultures.[3] With regard to Protestantism shaped by Lutheran confessions, the primary tenets of the *Confessio Augustana* guide the conversation as a kind of a threshold (definitions on baptism, Eucharist, ministry, and ecclesiology). Reformed theology—shaped by multiple confessions—is generally much more open to different interpretations of the Bible.

---

cooperation among the churches in Europe, and signed again by National Council of Churches in Germany 2003). Worldwide agreements: Dialogues of the World Methodist Council with final reports and decisions, with The Lutheran World Federation (1979–1984); The World Alliance of Reformed Churches (1987); The Anglican Communion (since 1992); The Salvation Army (2003–2011); The Baptist World Alliance (2014–2018).

2 In recent years, I explained these difficulties in several lectures in ecumenical settings as well as in articles, e.g., Ulrike Schuler: "'. . . ich liebe die Wahrheit mehr als alles' (John Wesley) Das Reformationsjubiläum aus der Sicht evangelischer Freikirchen—Einblicke aus evangelisch-methodistischer Perspektive," in *Theologie für die Praxis* 39 (2013): 82–111. In the following footnotes, I mention my articles of recent years in the German context in view of the Reformation in which I note publications in German as well as English on a respective topic.

3 See, for instance, *Geschichte des Pietismus*, 4 vols., ed. Martin Brecht and Klaus Deppermann (Göttingen: Vandenhoeck & Ruprecht, 1993–2004); Thomas Kraft, *Pietismus und Methodismus. Sozialethik und Reformprogramme von August Hermann Francke und John Wesley im Vergleich* (Stuttgart: EmK Geschichte, 2001).

The Five Hundredth Anniversary of the Reformation Celebrated in Germany in 2017

The five hundredth anniversary of the Protestant Reformation in its core country, Germany, in 2017 became a huge challenge to ecumenical togetherness. The anniversary was anticipated by several years of preparatory events. In 2008, a Reformation Decade was initiated by the Lutherans with an annual focus on a special topic related to the Reformation: 2009 Confession, 2010 Education, 2011 Freedom, 2012 Music, 2013 Tolerance, 2014 Politics, 2015 Image and Bible, 2016 the One World,[4] and 2017 the anniversary of the Reformation itself as "Christus-Fest" that began with a church congress (Evangelischer Kirchentag) in Berlin and smaller simultaneous events in so-called *Luther-Stätten*, places where Luther was active, such as Eisenach, Erfurt, Leipzig, Halle, Eisleben, and Wittenberg. The final service with about 200,000 participants took place in Wittenberg followed by programs for ninety-five days (to reflect ninety-five theses), segmented in weeks with special topics. At the end of 2016, a truck began a journey for the five hundredth anniversary of the Reformation to reach sixty-eight stations in nineteen countries by May 2017 in order to connect people and collect Reformation stories. The truck ended its route in the Wittenberg World's Fair "Gates of Freedom." It was a huge spectacle; millions of people from all over the world attended.

The focus on Luther has touched and agitated minds very differently. In 2013, Roman Catholics asked the question at the ecumenical church congress (Ökumenischer Kirchentag) in Munich, "To whom do the Reformation and even Luther belong?"[5] Although Luther of course had a central influence on the breakthrough of reforming efforts

4 For reflection on all these topics from a Methodist perspective, see Ulrike Schuler, "'Reformatorische' Impulse aus evangelisch-methodistischer Perspektive," in *Freikirchenorschung*, vol. 26 (Münster: i.W., 2017), 176–204.

5 See Deutsches Historisches Museum, dem Verein für Reformationsgeschichte und der Staatlichen Geschäftsstelle "Luther 2017," in *Wem gehört Luther?* (Halle, Germany: Mitteldeutscher Verlag, 2015); Matthias Matussek, "Wem gehört Luther?" *FOCUS Magazin* 42 (2016), https://www.focus.de/magazin/archiv/geschichte-wem-gehoert-luther_id_6069655.html.

that had already been attempted for centuries, to limit attention to him personally around the fabled posting of his ninety-five theses at the portal of the Schlosskirche in Wittenberg is—as several scholars have shown—historically an inappropriate reduction of what happened.[6] Also, there was public criticism by other churches, atheists, and agnostics because the German state invested heavily (annually €5 million) to support preparations of this event, with conferences, publications, renovations, and the facilities around the final celebration itself. All this finally forced a broader perspective on the sixteenth century, including reforming events as well as the reforming actors.

The open accusations of other churches related to the monopoly of the Reformation by Lutherans finally launched many projects of the twenty German Landeskirchen (territorial churches—Reformed, Lutheran, and United who constitute the Protestant church in Germany) in an ecumenical outreach. That extension became a huge challenge for the small Free Churches in Germany (Baptists, Mennonites, Methodists, and others) who now were involved, although they often did not have enough professional scholars to participate in conferences or publications reflecting on the main theological topics of interest from a mainly Lutheran perspective.[7] Others frequently criticized the topics themselves because they were often not in the center of interest for congregations and churches that focus on the believer's scriptural readings and faithful right conduct. But finally, a lot of very inspiring ecumenical projects and publications came out of this and—last but not least—a common statement of the member churches of the Council of Christian Churches in Germany, titled "Reconciled with One Another." The common guilt for the division of the church, "the

---

6 See Wolfgang Marchewka, Michael Schwibbe, Andreas Stephainski, *Zeitreise. 800 Jahre Leben in Wittenberg. Luther. 500 Jahre Reformation* (Göttingen: Zeit Reise, 2008), 39.

7 I explained this challenge and dilemma for German Free Churches in the following article: Ulrike Schuler, "Das Reformationsjubiläum aus der Sicht evangelischer Freikirchen. Einblicke aus evangelisch-methodistischer Perspektive," in *Ökumenische Rundschau* 3 (Leipzig: Evangelische Verlagsanstalt, 2017), 325–42.

alienation of Christians from one another in the individual denominations" that "gave rise to many prejudices and assumptions," and its painful consequences were confessed: the common responsibility for obfuscating the liberating power of the gospel that hindered the spread of the gospel.[8]

From my perspective, for Methodism to be involved in multiple projects was a fruitful challenge to reflect on and define our opinion, relationship, and perspective on central topics of Protestantism. It was also a chance to bring up our specific emphasis on scriptural understanding and add topics that are meaningful from the Methodist point of view and that were not so much in the center (e.g., the personal relationship to God and the process of holiness in its three dimensions: relation to God, myself, and others—in other words, the focus is theologically on holiness and social holiness and, finally, on faithful discipleship).

John Wesley and Martin Luther

I do not want to repeat all the insights of scholars such as Albert Outler, Gordon Rupp, Richard Heitzenrater, or Martin Schmidt and others about Luther and Wesley—their respective age when experiencing their conversion; their character, thinking, theological approaches to central theological questions; their roots of influences; and so on.[9] It is

---

8 Ulrike Schuler, "Reconciled with One Another: Commemorating the Reformation Ecumenically in Germany," *Holiness* 3 (2017): see especially 262, https://www.wesley.cam.ac.uk/wp-content/uploads/2014/09/08-schuler.pdf. Originally published in 2016 as "Versöhnt miteinander. Ein ökumenisches Wort der Mitgliederversammlung der ACK in Deutschland zu 500 Jahre Reformation," https://www.oekumene-ack.de/ueber-uns/struktur/geschaeftsstelle-oekumenische-centrale/.

9 See this selection of German publications about Wesley and Luther: Philip S. Watson, *Die Autorität der Bibel bei Luther und Wesley*, Beiträge zur Geschichte der EmK, vol. 14 (Stuttgart: Christliches Verlagshaus, 1983); Gordon E. Rupp, *John Wesley und Martin Luther. Ein Beitrag zum lutherisch-methodistischen Dialog*, Beiträge zur Geschichte der EmK, vol. 16 (Stuttgart: Christliches Verlagshaus, 1983); Roland Gebauer, "Rechtfertigung und

of no question that theologically Luther's preface to the Epistles of the Galatians and to the Romans were of central importance for Charles's and John's spiritual conversions. Luther reintroduced the Wesleys to justification by faith alone. And they also rediscovered this central message in their own tradition—in the Thirty-Nine Articles of Religion (Articles IX–XVIII) as well as in the *Books of Homilies* of the Church of England (III. Of the salvation of all mankind; IV. Of the true and lively faith). That liberating scriptural knowledge had been overshadowed by a strong puritan tradition in the century before.

John Wesley's relationship to Martin Luther was mixed. He was thankful and absolutely convinced that Luther's insight on the centrality of justification by grace through faith was the theological cornerstone of the Reformation. The Wesleys also shared the Reformation's commitment to Scripture and to the priesthood of all believers. But John Wesley did not agree with all of Luther's interpretations, such as the relation of justification and holiness, the question of free will, and the impact of original sin.[10] He was sure that Luther erred by downplaying or ignoring sanctification, that is, God's gift of healing sinners by transforming them to saints who are able to live holy lives. But all these different emphases did not separate him from Luther or Lutherans.

The theologian Franz Hildebrandt spoke of Wesley's more emotional than analytical analysis of Luther.[11] Wesley also seemed to be repelled by Luther's rough character. In 1749, Wesley wrote of Luther: "But O! what pity that he had no faithful friend! None that would, at all hazards, rebuke him plainly and sharply, for his rough, intractable spirit, and bitter zeal for opinions, so greatly obstructive of the work of

---

Heiligung bei Luther und Wesley. Eine Verstehensbemühung mit biblisch-theologischem Ausblick," in *Luther und die Reformation aus freikirchlicher Sicht. Kirche – Konfession – Religion*, vol. 59, ed. Volker Spangenberg (Göttingen: V & R Unipress, 2013), 89–106.

10 See Ulrike Schuler, "Was tun mit 2017? Die ökumenische Herausforderung des Jubiläums aus methodistischer Perspektive," in *Luther und die Reformation aus freikirchlicher Sicht. Kirche – Konfession – Religion*, 129–52.

11 Franz Hildebrandt, *From Luther to Wesley* (London: Lutterworth Press, 1951).

God!"[12] In his correspondence with Mrs. Elizabeth Hutton (August 22, 1744), Wesley wrote, "I love Calvin a little; Luther more; the Moravians, Mr. [William] Law, and Mr. [George] Whitefield far more than either. But I love truth more than all."[13] This statement characterizes him in a striking way: his deep interest in striving for truth while staying in a constant relationship with God. Wesley's approach is more pragmatic than it is legal or confessional in nature. This attitude of life distinguishes him—and Wesleyan Methodism after him.

Wesley does not seem to have dealt too much with Luther's theology. Rather, he was inspired by Luther to find his bearings about the interpretation of the Pauline doctrine of justification in various teaching traditions. He found it, as said before, in his own church but also among the church fathers of the old church. According to the God–man relationship, he discovered among the Greek church fathers (e.g., Makarios, Gregory of Nyssa, Ephraim the Syrian) the relational relevance—the interaction of God and human beings, which brings about a changed life in sanctification, in salvation, and even makes possible the promise of Christian perfection in Scripture.[14] Wesley believed that with God's guidance, humans could achieve Christian perfection during life. He understood Christian perfection as a final goal, as perfection in relation, as participation in the love of God or perfecting of that love in the human being who remains in relationship with God, the Creator. He also learned from the Greek church fathers and adopted their holistic therapeutic understanding of holiness.[15] All these scripturally rooted

---

12 John Wesley, "July 19, 1749," *Journals and Diaries*, in *The Bicentennial Edition of the Works of John Wesley*, ed. W. Reginald Ward and Richard P. Heitzenrater (Nashville: Abingdon Press, 1991), 20:285.

13 J. Ernest Rattenbury, *The Conversion of the Wesleys: A Critical Study* (London: Epworth Press, 1938), 171.

14 See Walter Klaiber and Manfred Marquardt, *Gelebte Gnade. Grundriss einer Theologie der Evangelisch-methodistischen Kirche* (Göttingen: Ruprecht, 2006), 347.

15 For the influence of Eastern Orthodoxy on John Wesley, see S. T. Kimbrough Jr., ed., *Orthodox and Wesleyan Spirituality* (Crestwood, NY: St. Vladimir's Seminary Press, 2002); S. T. Kimbrough Jr., ed., *Orthodox and Wesleyan Scriptural Understanding and Practice* (Crestwood, NY: St. Vladimir's

and experienced ideas are hard to believe for a Lutheran or Moravian as Lutheran pietism. This view on Eastern Orthodoxy is from my perspective most evident in the ecumenical process of communication today whereby Methodists can bridge between confessions that lost track of each other (especially to Eastern Orthodoxy).

Something else seems to be important: Lutheran theology was mediated to the Wesleys by German Lutheran pietists from Herrnhut and Halle, with a strong emphasis on the concrete everyday relevance of the doctrine of justification by faith. Wesley (ideally) believed he could find this emphasis reflected most likely among the Lutheran pietists of his time. Thus, Wesley made a trip to Germany to the centers of life of the Moravians around Count Nikolaus von Zinzendorf as well as the pietists in Halle, inspired by August Hermann Francke. Wesley had conversations with Zinzendorf and also met Gotthilf August Francke, the son of the then-deceased August Herrmann Francke. He participated in services, feasts, gatherings for guests, gatherings of various small congregations, and singing lessons of the Moravians—but he seems to have remained at the critical distance of an observer, and he had been evaluated as a restless man (*homo perturbatus*), so he was not admitted to the Lord's Supper. Wesley also made empirical surveys of conversion experiences of members of the communities.[16] He was interested in the question of Christian experience, which for him, along with Scripture, tradition, and reason, was a criterion of theological reflection and still belongs to the hermeneutic method of Scripture interpretation of the Methodists. That theological method

---

Seminary Press, 2005). Summarizing the Orthodox influence on Methodism according to a therapeutic aspect of holiness, see Ulrike Schuler, "Heiligung als Gestaltungsprozess," in *Die Frage nach Gott heute. Ökumenische Impulse zum Gespräch mit dem "Neuen Atheismus" Beiheft zur Ökumenische Rundschau*, vol. 11, ed. Ulrike Link-Wieczorek and Uwe Swarat (Leipzig: Evangelische Verlagsanstalt, 2017), 195–207.

16 Especially Martin Schmidt describes these meetings and relationships in much detail in his three volumes about John Wesley's life and work: *John Wesley. Leben und Werk* (Zürich: Gotthelf Verlag, 1987–1988). See also Sung-Duk Lee, *Der deutsche Pietismus und John Wesley* (Gießen: Brunnen Verlag, 2003).

of interpretation also bridges other confessional theological interpretations and can be mentioned fruitfully when participating in dialogue.[17]

A Broader View on the Reformation

Wesley's way of "doing theology" by validating theological statements in Scripture as well as in other church traditions is exemplary for our reflections on the Reformation. We have to remember that limiting reformation to the sixteenth century is misleading. Renewal movements have been around since Christianity assumed its privileged position as the imperial church in the Holy Roman Empire. In the center of renewal (reform) was always the question of the Christian's way of life—according to the scriptural core values of Christian living and the consistency of faith and action. Along with different monastic ascetical movements and then again their renewals during the Middle Ages, Petrus Valdus, John Wycliffe, and John Hus led the most successful reform efforts. Each tried to put the Bible into the vernacular and emphasized individual conversion. Also, the sixteenth-century reformation did not occur in a vacuum. There were revivals of religious feelings like the Brethren of the Common Life, who accomplished renewal in Western Christianity. They stressed the connection of mystical experience and subjectivism. These examples bring to mind several reformations. All these have always attempted to address the troubling area of being a Christian, namely, the lack of consistent seriousness, the authenticity of the faith, and the missed holistic penetration of Christian life in faith and action. It was always about the connection between a deep relationship with God, which permeates the daily life and leads to action, the so-called fruits of the faith.

Let me now add some important rediscoveries and extensions to the focus on the Reformation in the sixteenth century by sharing a few examples from a variety of motivating and inspiring movements,

---

17 See Ulrike Schuler, "Die Autorität der Heiligen Schrift allein. Die Notwendigkeit der hermeneutischen Reflexion—das Wesleyanische Quadrilateral," in *Die Bibel im Leben der Kirche*, ed. Walter Klaiber and Wolfgang Thönissen (Göttingen/Paderborn: Ruprecht, 2007), 105–26.

reformers, and theological understandings as well as ascertainment of what it means to be justified by God's grace through faith. In this way we rediscover those who first seemed to have been forgotten in the five hundredth anniversary: the radical reformers, those who were pursued and who were, for centuries after the Peace of Augsburg (1555), by law condemned to death. Among them were the Anabaptists (like Balthasar Hubmaier and others),[18] who shifted the believer's baptism to the center for the beginning of Christian life, and the Spiritualists, such as Thomas Müntzer.[19] In the former German Democratic Republic, the territory in which all Lutheran places of action are located, it was Müntzer who was remembered as the original true reformer of the sixteenth century and fought for justice, for the influence and freedom of peasants. Luther compromised with feudal authority and finally handed the responsibility for the Reformation over to the aristocracy so that the movement became a reformation from above. In opposition to this, the revolt of the peasants at the grassroots level, supported and partly led by Müntzer, was brutally quelled. The Peasants' War in 1525 was Europe's largest and most widespread popular uprising prior to the French Revolution (1786).

Two examples of forgotten women reformers also must be remembered. First, we remember the remarkable dispute of the abbess of a monastery of the Poor Clares in Nuremberg, Caritas Pirckheimer.[20] She had a successful dispute with Philipp Melanchthon in 1525 when she argued that justification by faith does not consistently mean to obligatorily discharge all nuns from their monastic vows and to leave

---

18 E.g., Andrea Strübind, *Eifriger als Zwingli. Die frühe Täuferbewegung in der Schweiz* (Berlin: Duncker und Humblot, 2003).

19 E.g., Hans-Jürgen Goertz, *Thomas Müntzer. Revolutionär am Ende der Zeiten. Eine Biografie* (München: Beck, 2015); Günter Brakelmann, *Müntzer und Luther* (Bielefeld: Luther-Verlag, 2016).

20 About important women in the Reformation, see Martin H. Jung, *Nonnen, Prophetinnen, Kirchenmütter. Kirchen- und frömmigkeitsgeschichtliche Studien zu Frauen in der Reformationszeit* (Leipzig: Evangelische Verlagsanstalt, 2002); *Frauen mischen sich ein. Katharina Luther, Katharina Melanchthon, Katharina Zell, Hille Feicken und andere* (Wittenberg: Evangelisches Predigerseminar Lutherstadt Wittenberg. Drei Kastanien Verlag, 2004).

the monastery. Caritas Pirckheimer biblically argued for her right to decide on a life consecrated to God by living celibately in a monastery. Finally, the aldermen in Nuremberg had to embrace the nun's decision in a city that had as one of the first in the Holy Roman Empire implemented Protestantism and had decided to dissolve all monasteries. But it needs to be said that this freedom of conscience for the nuns in Caritas Pirckheimer's care was very limited: the nuns no longer received pastoral care by their father confessors, and they also were unable to receive the sacraments because they lost the presence of their priests.[21]

The second example of an influential woman of the Reformation time is Katharina Zell. She was the wife of a reformer, Matthäus Zell, in Strasbourg. She was very well educated, and as a reformer's wife she corresponded with a lot of other reformers, such as Martin Bucer, who celebrated the Zells' marriage, as well as with others whom the couple knew well. Katharina wrote a huge number of letters, most remarkably to wives of persecuted Anabaptists. Finally, against opposition she preached at her husband's funeral. She can be seen as a groundbreaker for female ministry.[22]

There are many more women of the Reformation time who can be identified because, as a result of being reformers' wives and well educated, they left written sources.

I conclude with some final theses:

- The Reformation cannot be reduced to a century or to special persons. A reform or renewal is a process that never ends and is certainly not tied to individual groups, congregations, churches, or denominations.
- The Reformation as an era of church history offers more meaningful and inspiring central developments and rudiments of renewals to us than only the focus on Luther and Calvin. For

21 Jung, *Nonnen, Prophetinnen, Kirchenmütter*, 77–120.

22 Jung, *Nonnen, Prophetinnen, Kirchenmütter*, 121–68; Gabriele Jancke, "Publizistin–Pfarrfrau–Prophetin: Die Straßburger 'Kirchenmutter' Katharina Zell," in *Frauen mischen sich ein*, ed. Peter Freybe (Wittenberg: Ev. Predigerseminar, 1995), 55–80.

our Methodist roots in the Church of England, there was also Martin Bucer, a continental reformer from Strasbourg who finally went to Cambridge and who reconciled opposing views in his time. But there were also the Anabaptists, Spiritualists, and women (some of whom were reformers' wives and who were writers), those who interpreted central Reformation topics in different ways—by word (writing), life (living according to the Reformation), and education (particularly of the next generation).

- As Methodists, we can be convinced by John Wesley to open perspectives on scriptural interpretations by studying the church fathers, especially those from the Eastern Orthodox tradition whose view had less influence on Western theology and who take a different approach by adding spirituality to rational text interpretations of the Bible.
- There is a broader wealth of renewing movements before and after the Reformation. Wesley reflected on them and used writings of mystics, puritans, and pietists for his *Christian Library*. Of course, after Wesley there were lots of important awakening movements in the holiness and Pentecostal movement as well.
- Finally, "re-formation" also means to be open to changes in life and perspective, including atonement where needed. The topic of the Reformation has shadow sides: Luther's harsh and disastrous writings and sayings about Jews that were used as arguments in the Third Reich; the persecutions of Anabaptists (in 2012 the process of a Lutheran–Mennonite dialogue ended with a moving service, begging for forgiveness); and the numerous people in renewing movements who had to leave Europe to find their home in the colonies that became the United States to live with a freedom of conscience.
- Re-formation is, from a Methodist perspective, a holistic transformation that begins with each single person and his or her deepening relationship with God, which is a faithful renewal into God's image as new creation.

- Reformation is a constant challenge. The church must renew itself constantly. This is a principle that goes back to St. Augustine and was revived by Karl Barth in 1947: *ecclesia semper reformanda*—the church is always in need of renewal by the power of the gospel of Christ.

Appendix

As further background of my statement, here are three other publications written in the ecumenical context in Germany during the discussions and preparations of the Reformation anniversary in 2017.

- Schuler, Ulrike. "Christliche Einheit in Zeugnis und Dienst. Eine evangelisch-methodistische Perspektive." In *Heillos gespalten? Segensreich erneuert? 500 Jahre Reformation in der Vielfalt ökumenischer Perspektiven*, ed. Uwe Swarat and Thomas Söding, 93–115. Quaestiones Disputatae 277. Freiburg im Breisgau: Verlag Herder GmbH, 2016.
- Schuler, Ulrike. "Freiheit: Verbindung und Verantwortung. Wesleyanisch-methodistische Akzente und Fallstudie." In *Kontroverse Freiheit: Die Impulse der Ökumene*, ed. Thomas Söding and Bernd Oberdorfer, 237–65. Quaestiones Disputatae 284. Freiburg im Breisgau: Verlag Herder GmbH, 2017.
- Schuler, Ulrike. "Religionsfreiheit aus freikirchlicher Sicht." In *Religionsfreiheit, Meinungsfreiheit und christlicher Glaube*, ed. Jürgen Schuster and Volker Gäckle, 35–61. Interkulturalität & Religion 5. Berlin: LIT Verlag, 2017.

Bibliography

Brakelmann, Günter. *Müntzer und Luther.* Bielefeld: Luther-Verlag, 2016.

Brecht, Martin, and Klaus Deppermann, eds. *Geschichte des Pietismus.* 4 vols. Göttingen: Vandenhoeck & Ruprecht, 1993–2004.

Deutsches Historisches Museum, dem Verein für Reformationsgeschichte und der Staatlichen Geschäftsstelle "Luther 2017." *Wem gehört Luther?* Halle: Mitteldeutscher Verlag, 2015.

Evangelisches Predigerseminar Lutherstadt Wittenberg. *Frauen mischen sich ein. Katharina Luther, Katharina Melanchthon, Katharina Zell, Hille Feicken und andere.* Wittenberg: Drei Kastanien Verlag, 2004.

Gebauer, Roland. "Rechtfertigung und Heiligung bei Luther und Wesley. Eine Verstehensbemühung mit biblisch-theologischem Ausblick." In *Luther und die Reformation aus freikirchlicher Sicht. Kirche – Konfession – Religion*, vol. 59. Edited by Volker Spangenberg. Göttingen: V & R Unipress, 2013.

Goertz, Hans-Jürgen. *Thomas Müntzer. Revolutionär am Ende der Zeiten. Eine Biografie.* München: Beck, 2015.

Hildebrandt, Franz. *From Luther to Wesley.* London: Lutterworth Press, 1951.

Jancke, Gabriele. "Publizistin–Pfarrfrau–Prophetin: Die Straßburger 'Kirchenmutter' Katharina Zell." In *Frauen mischen sich ein*, ed. Peter Freybe, 55–80. Wittenberg: Evangelische Predigerseminar, 1995.

Jung, Martin H. *Nonnen, Prophetinnen, Kirchenmütter. Kirchen- und frömmigkeitsgeschichtliche Studien zu Frauen in der Reformationszeit.* Leipzig: Evangelische Verlagsanstalt, 2002.

Kimbrough, S. T., Jr., ed. *Orthodox and Wesleyan Scriptural Understanding and Practice.* Crestwood, NY: St. Vladimir's Seminary Press, 2005.

———, ed. *Orthodox and Wesleyan Spirituality.* Crestwood, NY: St. Vladimir's Seminary Press, 2002.

Klaiber, Walter, and Manfred Marquardt. *Gelebte Gnade. Grundriss einer Theologie der Evangelisch-methodistischen Kirche.* Göttingen: Ruprecht, 2006.

Kraft, Thomas. *Pietismus und Methodismus. Sozialethik und Reformprogramme von August Hermann Francke und John Wesley im Vergleich.* EmK Geschichte, vol. 47. Stuttgart: Druckhaus West, 2001.

Lee, Sung-Duk. *Der deutsche Pietismus und John Wesley.* Gießen: Brunnen Verlag, 2003.

Marchewka, Wolfgang, Michael Schwibbe, and Andreas Stephainski. *Zeitreise. 800 Jahre Leben in Wittenberg / Luther. 500 Jahre Reformation.* Göttingen: Zeit Reise, 2008.

Matussek, Matthias. "Wem gehört Luther?" *FOCUS Magazin* 42 (2016). https://www.focus.de/magazin/archiv/geschichte-wem-gehoert-luther_id_6069655.html.

Rattenbury, J. Ernest. *The Conversion of the Wesleys: A Critical Study.* London: Epworth Press, 1938.

Rupp, Gordon E. *John Wesley und Martin Luther. Ein Beitrag zum lutherisch-methodistischen Dialog.* Beiträge zur Geschichte der EmK, vol. 16. Stuttgart: Christliches Verlagshaus, 1983.

Schmidt, Martin. *John Wesley. Leben und Werk.* 3 vols. Zürich: Gotthelf Verlag, 1987–1988.

Schuler, Ulrike. "Die Autorität der Heiligen Schrift allein. Die Notwendigkeit der hermeneutischen Reflexion—das Wesleyanische Quadrilateral." In *Die Bibel im Leben der Kirche*, ed. Walter Klaiber and Wolfgang Thönissen, 105–26. Göttingen/Paderborn: Ruprecht, 2007.

———. "Heiligung als Gestaltungsprozess." In *Die Frage nach Gott heute. Ökumenische Impulse zum Gespräch mit dem "Neuen Atheismus,"* edited by Ulrike Link-Wieczorek and Uwe Swara, 195–207. Vol. 11 of *Beiheft zur Ökumenische Rundschau*. Leipzig: Evangelische Verlagsanstalt, 2017.

———. "'. . . ich liebe die Wahrheit mehr als alles' (John Wesley). Das Reformationsjubiläum aus der Sicht evangelischer Freikirchen—Einblicke aus evangelisch-methodistischer Perspektive." *Theologie für die Praxis* 39 (2013): 82–111.

———. "Reconciled with One Another: Commemorating the Reformation Ecumenically in Germany." *Holiness* 3, no. 2 (2017): 257–70, https://www.wesley.cam.ac.uk/wp-content/uploads/2014/09/08-schuler.pdf.

———. "Das Reformationsjubiläum aus der Sicht evangelischer Freikirchen. Einblicke aus evangelisch-methodistischer Perspektive." *Ökumenische Rundschau* 66, no. 3 (2017): 325–43.

———. "Reformatorische Impulse aus evangelisch-methodistischer Perspektive." In *Freikirchenforschung*, vol. 26. Münster i.W: Verein für Freikirchenforschung, 2017, 176–204.

———. "Was tun mit 2017? Die ökumenische Herausforderung des Jubiläums aus methodistischer Perspektive." In *Luther und die Reformation aus freikirchlicher Sicht. Kirche – Konfession – Religion*, vol. 59. Edited by Volker Spangenberg. Göttingen: V & R Unipress, 2013.

Strübind, Andrea. *Eifriger als Zwingli. Die frühe Täuferbewegung in der Schweiz*. Berlin: Duncker und Humblot, 2003.

Watson, Philip S. *Die Autorität der Bibel bei Luther und Wesley.* Beiträge zur Geschichte der EmK, vol. 14. Stuttgart: Christliches Verlagshaus, 1983.

Wesley, John. *Journals and Diaries*. Vol. 20 of *The Bicentennial Edition of the Works of John Wesley*, edited by W. Reginald Ward and Richard P. Heitzenrater. Nashville: Abingdon Press, 1991.

John Wesley and the Protestant Reformers on Scripture

G. Sujin Pak

WHAT DID JOHN WESLEY HOLD in common with the leading sixteenth-century Protestant reformers—most notably Martin Luther and John Calvin—concerning the nature and purpose of Scripture and its interpretation, and in what ways is Wesley distinctive? Studies of Wesley's views of and approaches to Scripture often note that he shared several central commitments with the Protestant reformers.[23] At least six shared affirmations can be identified. First, Wesley and the Protestant reformers affirmed Scripture as divine revelation, as the divinely inspired Word of God.[24] As the divinely inspired Word of God, a second affirmation immediately follows: Scripture functions

23 See, for example, Larry Shelton, "John Wesley's Approach to Scripture in Historical Perspective," *Wesleyan Theological Journal* 16, no. 1 (1981): 23–50; Scott J. Jones, "The Rule of Scripture," in *Wesley and the Quadrilateral: Renewing the Conversation*, ed. W. Stephen Gunter et al. (Nashville: Abingdon Press, 1997), 43, 55–56; and Scott J. Jones, *John Wesley's Conception and Use of Scripture* (Nashville: Kingswood Books, 1995), 121–27.

24 For studies that discuss Wesley's view of Scripture as revelation and divinely inspired, see Jones, *John Wesley's Conception and Use of Scripture*, 17–36; Jones, "The Rule of Scripture," 50–51; Duncan S. Ferguson, "John Wesley on Scripture: The Hermeneutics of Pietism," *Methodist History* 22, no. 4 (1984): 240; and Shelton, "John Wesley's Approach to Scripture in Historical Perspective," 37–38. For concise descriptions of Luther's and Calvin's affirmation of Scripture as revelation and divinely inspired, see Mark Thompson, "Biblical Interpretation in the Works of Martin Luther," in *A History of Biblical Interpretation: The Medieval through the Reformation Periods*, vol. 2, ed. Alan J. Hauser and Duane F. Watson (Grand Rapids, MI: Eerdmans, 2009), 299–302; and Wulfert de Greef, "Calvin's Understanding and Interpretation of the Bible," in *John Calvin's Impact on Church and Society, 1509–2009*, ed. Martin Ernst Hirzel and Martin Sallmann (Grand Rapids, MI: Eerdmans, 2009), 69–70.

for both Wesley and the Protestant reformers as the *prime* authority for all Christian faith and practice. Indeed, Wesley, Luther, and Calvin each clearly stated that Scripture is the primary authority above and beyond the authority of the church.[25] Third, Wesley and the Protestant reformers together maintained that the primary purpose of Scripture is to communicate the message of salvation. They strongly upheld the *soteriological* function and purpose of Scripture: that Scripture is given by God to reveal God's path of salvation for humanity. They further agreed that this soteriological message of Scripture is *clear*. Consequently, as a fourth shared commitment, Wesley and the Protestant reformers together affirmed the principle of Scripture's clarity and located the content of that clarity precisely in Scripture's teachings concerning salvation.[26] These affirmations of Scripture's primacy of

---

25 See John Wesley, "Roman Catechism and Reply," in *The Works of John Wesley*, ed. Thomas Jackson (Grand Rapids, MI: Zondervan, 1958), 10:91, 94. In "Letter to 'John Smith'," Wesley wrote, "What is scriptural in any church, I hold fast; for the rest, I let it go," *Letters of the Rev. John Wesley*, ed. John Telford (London: Epworth Press, 1960), 2:46, hereafter cited as "*Letters*." Similarly, in a letter to James Hervey, he exclaimed, "If by catholic principles you mean any other than scriptural, they weigh nothing with me. I allow no other rule, whether of faith or practice, than the Holy Scriptures," *Journal*, in *Works* 19:67. See also Jones, *John Wesley's Conception and Use of Scripture*, 31–35. For clear examples of Luther's and Calvin's assertions of Scripture's prime authority above that of the church, see Martin Luther, *Luther's Works*, ed. J. Pelikan and H. Lehman, 55 vols. (Philadelphia: Fortress Press, 1957–86), 36:145, hereafter cited as "LW"; and John Calvin, *Institutes of the Christian Religion*, ed. John T. McNeill, trans. Ford Lewis Battles (Philadelphia: Westminster, 1960), 1.7.2, hereafter cited as "*Institutes*."

26 Luther wrote, "The proper subject of theology is the human guilty of sin and condemned and God the Justifier and Savior of the human sinner. . . . All Scripture points to this . . . the God who justifies, repairs and makes alive and the human who fell from righteousness and life into sin and eternal death. Whoever follows this aim in reading the Holy Scriptures will read holy things fruitfully" (LW 12:311). Calvin made similar statements; see *Institutes* 2.10.1–2. Scholars of John Wesley point out that Wesley also affirmed Scripture's prime soteriological purpose and directly identified this with Scripture's clear content (i.e., Scripture's clarity). See Don Thorsen, *The Wesleyan Quadrilateral: Scripture, Tradition, Reason and Experience as a Model of Evangelical*

authority, soteriological purpose, and clarity can be seen as culminating for both Wesley and the Protestant reformers in their common appeal (the fifth shared commitment) to the hermeneutical principle of the *analogia fidei* ("analogy of faith"). Wesley and the Protestant reformers counseled that any faithful reading of Scripture must be according to the analogy of faith (Rom. 12:6), in which the clear central content of Scripture (its teachings on salvation) serves as the standard by which to gauge all faithful interpretation. More specifically, in practice this means that any faithful interpretation of Scripture should resonate with and certainly not conflict with Scripture's clear soteriological teachings concerning original sin, justification, new birth, and sanctification.[27]

Lastly, a sixth point of agreement between John Wesley and the Protestant reformers pertains to their mutual assertion of the necessity of the Holy Spirit's guidance in any faithful interpretation of Scripture. Wesley wrote, "We need the same Spirit to understand the Scripture

---

Theology (Lexington, KY: Emeth, 1990, 2005), 82, 86; Jones, "The Rule of Scripture," 49, 53; Ferguson, "John Wesley on Scripture," 241; Timothy L. Smith, "John Wesley and the Wholeness of Scripture," *Interpretation* 39, no. 3 (1985): 253; Mack B. Stokes, "Wesley on Scripture," in *Basic Methodist Beliefs: An Evangelical View*, ed. James V. Heidinger II (Wilmore, KY: Good News Books, 1986), 13; and Robert W. Wall, "Toward a Wesleyan Hermeneutics of Scripture," *Wesleyan Theological Journal* 30, no. 2 (1995): 63–65.

27 For example, Wesley instructed, "Have a constant eye to the analogy of faith—the connection and harmony there is between those grand, fundamental doctrines [of] original sin, justification by faith, the new birth, [and] inward and outward holiness" (Preface, *Explanatory Notes Upon the Old Testament*, 1). Likewise, in his comments on Romans 12:6, Wesley defines the "analogy of faith" as expounding Scripture "according to the general tenor of them; according to that grand scheme of doctrine which is delivered therein, touching original sin, justification by faith, and present inward salvation. . . . Every article therefore concerning which there is any question should be determined by this rule [and] every doubtful scripture interpreted according to the grand truths that run through the whole" (*Explanatory Notes Upon the New Testament*, Romans 12:6). These notes to both Old and New Testaments are available at *Wesley's Notes on the Bible*, accessed January 22, 2021, https://ccel.org/ccel/w/wesley/notes/cache/notes.pdf. One might note the similarities with Luther's description of Scripture's clear soteriological content quoted in note 4.

which enabled the holy men of old to write it."[28] He defined the "testimony of the Spirit" as an "inward impression on the soul, whereby the Spirit of God directly witnesses to my spirit that I am a child of God, that Jesus Christ loves me and has given himself for me, and that all my sins are blotted out, and I, even I, am reconciled to God."[29] In other words, the witness of the Holy Spirit testifies to the truth of Scripture's central salvific message—a sentiment that is much in line with Luther's and Calvin's appeals to the inner testimony of the Holy Spirit to authenticate Scripture, as well as to aid in its proper interpretation. For example, Luther wrote, "No one perceives one iota of what is said in the Scriptures unless [one] has the Spirit of God."[30] Moreover, Calvin pointed to the work of the Holy Spirit to testify to the truth of Scripture's soteriological message, stating that the "Spirit is the inner teacher by whose effort the promise of salvation penetrates into our minds, a promise that would otherwise only strike the air and beat upon our ears."[31] In these ways, Wesley affirmed, alongside the Protestant reformers, the necessity of the Holy Spirit both to authenticate the truth of Scripture in the hearts and minds of believers and to guide faithful interpretation of Scripture.

It should be recognized, on the one hand, that all of these central commitments concerning Scripture resonate with the larger commitments of Christian antiquity (Christian tradition) though, of course,

---

28 As quoted by Randy L. Maddox, "The Rule of Christian Faith, Practice, and Hope: John Wesley on the Bible," *Methodist Review* 3 (2011): 14. Wesley, "Letter to Bishop of Gloucester," II.10; *Works* 11:509. Similarly, he wrote in his preface to *Explanatory Notes upon the Old Testament*, "Scripture can only be understood through the same Spirit whereby it was given," in *The Works of John Wesley*, ed. Thomas Jackson (repr., Grand Rapids, MI: Baker, 1979), 14:253. In *An Address to the Clergy*, Wesley pointed to the promise of the Holy Spirit by which they are "assured of being assisted in all their labor by [God] who teaches knowledge [and] . . . gives wisdom to the simple" (*Works* 10:486).

29 Wesley, Sermon 10, "The Witness of the Spirit (I)" §I.7, in *Works* 1:254.

30 LW 33:28. Similarly, Calvin exclaimed that the Word of God "cannot penetrate into our minds unless the Spirit, as the inner teacher, through illumination, makes entry for it" (*Institutes* 3.2.34).

31 Calvin, *Institutes* 3.1.4.

with some notable variations of emphasis particularly concerning questions of church authority in relation to Scripture.[32] One might then ask, "What is distinctive about the Protestant reformers, let alone John Wesley?" In another article, I have argued that the Protestant reformers set themselves apart from prior tradition concerning their views of Scripture exactly in the intersection of four of their key teachings: (1) Scripture's primacy of authority, (2) Scripture's clarity, (3) the necessary aid of the Holy Spirit, and (4) the pivotal doctrine of justification by faith alone, the latter of which serves as the glue that holds these together in a distinctively Protestant way.[33] The Protestant reformers staunchly challenged the authority of the Roman Catholic Church and asserted the primacy of Scripture. Alongside this, they declared that Scripture is clear, thereby negating the necessity of the church's authoritative oversight of Scripture's interpretation. Rather, since Scripture is clear, any person who has been justified by faith alone receives the Holy Spirit, who—as the only true interpreter of Scripture—enables the believer to interpret Scripture faithfully. Consequently, the doctrine of justification by faith alone is exactly what holds together the early Protestant reformers' assertions of Scripture's primacy and clarity and the necessary aid of the Holy Spirit in a distinctly Protestant fashion. Justification by faith alone is both the clear *content* of Scripture according to the Protestant reformers—a content that is sufficiently clear to act as the authoritative guide for Christian life above and beyond the authority of the church—and it is the very *principle* that operationalizes Scripture's authority and clarity. That is, for the Protestant reformers, "Scripture is clear solely because of *God's* actions, because of God's *gifts* of faith and the Holy Spirit to the believer. [In other words,] Scripture is clear only

---

32 Larry Shelton offers a very good, concise account of this, so there is little need to make this case again. See Shelton, "John Wesley's Approach to Scripture in Historical Perspective," 23–50.

33 G. Sujin Pak, "The Perspicuity of Scripture, Justification by Faith Alone, and the Role of the Church in Reading Scripture with the Protestant Reformers," *Covenant Quarterly* 75, no. 2 (2017): 3–23.

through the effective working of justification by faith alone in the life of the believer."[34]

If justification by faith *alone* is the crucial, distinctive element of the Protestant reformers' views of Scripture, then this immediately underscores the source of Wesley's divergence from them. Namely, Wesley's and the Protestant reformers' descriptions of the soteriological character and purpose of Scripture—and thus, its clear content—differ in a key substantive manner. Luther and Calvin located the clear content of Scripture specifically in the doctrine of justification by faith alone and its corollary teachings—specifically teachings concerning original sin, the human will in bondage to sin, the necessity of Christ, the necessity of faith as 100 percent gift in which works play no role, and so on. More specifically, the sixteenth-century reformers' conception of justification by faith alone entailed a corollary affirmation of some form of a doctrine of predestination—whether one that is viewed as necessary but unfruitful to talk about (Luther) or a doctrine of double-predestination seen as a source of comfort (Calvin). For Luther and Calvin, if one is justified by faith alone, which is a pure gift of God and in which human will or works play absolutely no role, then it follows that *only God* acts in justification; salvation is solely in the hands of God with no space of even an iota of human cooperation. Wesley, on the other hand, identified the clear soteriological content of Scripture with the overarching principle not of justification by faith *alone*—and certainly not a teaching on predestination—but with the conviction of God's universal love.[35] Wesley affirmed a doctrine of justification by faith, but not one of faith

34 Pak, "The Perspicuity of Scripture," 14.

35 See especially Mildred Bangs Wynkoop, "A Hermeneutical Approach to John Wesley," *Wesleyan Theological Journal* 6, no. 1 (1971): 13–22; Maddox, "The Rule of Christian Faith, Practice, and Hope," 26–30; Thorsen, *The Wesleyan Quadrilateral*, 84–86; Ferguson, "John Wesley on Scripture," 235; Shelton, "John Wesley's Approach to Scripture in Historical Perspective," 41; and Jones, "Rule of Scripture," 54–55. Wesley defined a Methodist, as well, in terms of love: a Methodist is one who has "the love of God shed abroad in his heart by the Holy Ghost given unto him" and one who loves the Lord his God with all his heart, soul, mind, and strength. "The Character of a Methodist," §5, in *Works* 9:35.

alone. He also affirmed a form of the primacy of God's action, but he identified divine action first and foremost as the act of *divine universal love*—a love given to all without distinction—rather than an act of divine election oriented to only particular, chosen persons.

Indeed, Wesley directly argued that a belief in the total bondage of the human will that leads to an assertion of a doctrine of predestination is directly contrary to the clear teachings of Scripture. In his sermon "Free Grace," Wesley affirmed that grace is indeed "free"—it "does not depend on any power or merit of [humanity]"; "it does not in anywise depend on the good works or righteousness of the receiver"; it does not depend on good purposes or intentions. These, insisted Wesley, "are the *fruits* of free grace and not the root. They are not the cause but the effects of it."[36] Yet Wesley went on to add that this grace is free *for all* and *in all*. Pointing to the universal offering of God's love and grace, he immediately countered the view that this grace is free "only for those whom God has ordained to life" (i.e., the decree of predestination).[37] He proffered five arguments why predestination cannot be a scriptural doctrine or doctrine of God. I summarize these briefly: first, predestination makes void the ordinance of God's love and sets God against God's self; second, it undercuts the very holiness God ordains; third, it destroys the peace, joy, and comfort God ordains; fourth, it destroys zeal for good works; and fifth, it overthrows Christian revelation and makes it contradict itself. This last point is of most interest to our concerns here, because Wesley ultimately argued that the doctrine of predestination is contrary to "the whole scope and tenor of Scripture."[38] In this statement, we see Wesley's appeal to the clear "scope and tenor" of Scripture—its central soteriological teachings. In a similar fashion, he appealed to the "analogy of faith" in another sermon, in which he proclaimed that the "real religion" of God's love "runs through the Bible from the beginning to the end, in one connected chain; and the agreement of every part of it, with every other, is, properly the analogy of faith." Wesley then exhorted, "Beware of taking anything else or anything less than this for

36 Wesley, Sermon 110, "Free Grace," ¶3, in *Works* 3:545.

37 Wesley, Sermon 110, "Free Grace," ¶4, in *Works* 3:545.

38 Wesley, Sermon 110, "Free Grace," ¶2, in *Works* 3:552.

religion! . . . Do not take part of it for the whole! What God has joined together, put not asunder! Take no less for his religion than the 'faith that worketh by love' all inward and outward holiness."[39]

In these statements, we begin to see Wesley's alternative conception of the role of works and the human will from that of the Protestant reformers. Wesley affirmed the necessity of faith as the only condition of justification and sanctification.[40] Yet, even as he affirmed that faith is most certainly *God's* work, he also maintained that there is no opposition between the statement that "God works; therefore, do we work." Indeed, these are not only *not* in opposition, Wesley insisted that they have the "closest connection," arguing that because "God works, therefore you *can* work" and, secondly, because "God works, therefore you *must* work."[41] He thus concludes, "Therefore inasmuch as God works in you, you are now able to work out your own salvation"—pointing to both the primacy of God's action and the responding, cooperative role of the human will.[42]

John Wesley emerges as distinctive from the Protestant reformers' understanding of Scripture exactly in how he identified the chief elements of Scripture's central soteriological message. Wesley's prioritization of the love of God and the identification of "faith that works inward and outward holiness by love" as the scope and tenor of all Scripture have immediate implications for the role of the will in salvation. It is a "faith that *works*," and the overarching purpose of that working is toward *inward and outward holiness*, which speaks directly to Wesley's profound emphasis upon *sanctification* as equally (if not more so) a clear teaching at the heart of Scripture's soteriological message.[43] These scriptural convictions of the cooperative role of the will

39 Wesley, Sermon 62, "The End of Christ's Coming," §III.5–6, in *Works* 2:482–83.

40 Wesley, Sermon 43, "The Scripture Way of Salvation," §III.1, in *Works* 2:162.

41 Wesley, Sermon 85, "On Working Out Our Own Salvation," §III.2, in *Works* 3:206.

42 Wesley, Sermon 85, "On Working Out Our Own Salvation," §III.5, in *Works* 3:207–8.

43 To be more careful, sanctification is a key emphasis of John Calvin, though Luther tended to emphasize justification (by faith alone) quite profoundly at

alongside Scripture's sanctifying purposes culminate in Wesley's championing Christian *perfection* as a core scriptural teaching.[44] Even as Wesley, together with the Protestant reformers, affirmed the authoritative, clear, soteriological message of Scripture, *different* components of that message emerged as pivotal in his reading of Scripture—namely, sanctification, perfection, and the will redeemed by divine grace.

It seems quite possible that Wesley's conviction that the clear teaching of Scripture includes an understanding of a human will aided by God's grace that is able to work toward and reach perfection has additional implications for more positive conceptions of the roles of experience and reason in the Christian life.[45] While Wesley maintained a clear primacy of Scripture, in which Scripture serves as a rule or

---

the expense of sanctification. Yet, as scholars have pointed out, Luther was a situational theologian; he believed the church of his day knew plenty about sanctification but misunderstood justification.

44 There is not space here to go into detail about Wesley's doctrine of perfection or its contrast to the Protestant reformers' teachings. It is sufficient to point out its clear implications for conceptions of sin, particularly sin in the Christian's life. For example, in interpreting Proverbs 24:16 ("A just man falls seven times and rises up again," NASB), Wesley insisted that the text does not say that a just person "sins." He asserted, "Here is no mention of falling into sin at all." Rather, the text is about "falling into temporal affliction"—a reading that Wesley supported through appeal to the larger literary context. See Wesley, Sermon 40, "Christian Perfection," §II.9, in *Works* 2:108–9.

45 Comparing Wesley with Luther and Calvin on the topics of reason and experience is a much trickier task. On the one hand, Luther (given his aim to critique the nominalism of the schools of his day) spoke very harshly against any trust in reason. For example, in his debate with Erasmus over the will, Luther insisted on the necessary aid of the Holy Spirit in contrast to a trust in reason, pointing to the example of David: "he wants to lay hold of the real teacher of the Scriptures so that he may not seize upon them pell-mell with his reason and become his own teacher" (LW 34:286). Calvin is much more positive toward reason while simultaneously affirming total human depravity. As to experience, both Luther and Calvin seemed to carve a positive place for experience, yet they were much less explicit about it than Wesley. Thus, it is a difference of whether the appeal is more explicit or implicit. Yet, on a few occasions Calvin invoked experience to verify Scripture. See *Institutes* 1.7.5, 1.13.14, 2.4.7, 3.20.12, and 3.22.1.

standard for all Christian belief and practice, he also held a significantly optimistic view of the role of experience and reason as useful, necessary, and powerful tools for engaging Scripture and understood the Spirit's work as operating alongside them.[46] On the one hand, clarified Wesley, it is true that no right Christian doctrine or practice can be founded on reason or experience alone, for it must first be founded on Scripture. On the other hand, he maintained that experience *confirms* Scripture's teaching and that reason is given by God to provide additional guidance.[47] Furthermore, Wesley often identified experience exactly with the experience of the Holy Spirit in one's life. In his two-part sermon "The Witness of the Spirit," he equated Christian experience with the experience of the Spirit, as seen most clearly in his assertion that the conviction that we are children of God is a "conclusion drawn partly from the Word of God and partly from our own experience."[48] He immediately thereafter pointed to the joint roles of Scripture, experience, and reason: "The *Word of God* says that everyone who has the fruit of the Spirit is a child of God; *experience* or inward consciousness tells me that I have the fruit of the Spirit and hence I *rationally* conclude, 'Therefore I am a child of God.' "[49] He thus appealed to the joint

---

46 In a letter to Thomas Whitehead, Wesley distinguished between the role of Scripture as a rule and the Spirit as the guide, writing, "For though the Spirit is our principal leader, yet [the Spirit] is not our rule at all; the Scriptures are the rule whereby [the Spirit] leads us into all truth. . . . Call the Spirit our guide, which signifies an intelligent being, and the Scriptures our rule, which signifies something used by an intelligent being, and all is plain and clear." Wesley, "Letter to Thomas Whitehead," in *Letters* 2:117.

47 Wesley, Sermon 11, "The Witness of the Spirit (II)," §III.6, in *Works* 1:290; Sermon 70, "The Case of Reason Impartially Considered," §II.6, 10, in *Works*, 2:596, 598; Sermon 45, "The New Birth," §I.1, in *Works* 2:188; and "A Plain Account of Christian Perfection," §25, *Works* 11:429. See also the discussions of Thorsen, *The Wesleyan Quadrilateral*, 88–89, and Jones, *John Wesley's Conception and Use of Scripture*, 65–80, 176–83. Most clearly, Wesley maintained that if it is established that a doctrine is founded on Scripture, then experience can most certainly serve to confirm it. See Wesley, Sermon 11, "The Witness of the Spirit (II)," §IV.1, in *Works* 1:293.

48 Wesley, Sermon 11, "The Witness of the Spirit (II)," §II.6, in *Works* 1:287–88.

49 Wesley, Sermon 11, "The Witness of the Spirit (II)," §II.6, in *Works* 1:287–88.

work of Scripture, experience, and reason within the larger purpose of describing "the witness of the Spirit."

In sum, Wesley shared common commitments with the Protestant reformers, but he offered a distinctive way of holding those Protestant commitments. In his rejection of the twin doctrines of justification by faith *alone* and predestination, Wesley is not "protestant" in the manner of the sixteenth-century Protestant reformers. Yet, Wesley is "protestant" in his insistence on Scripture's clarity as a principle that can function authoritatively above and beyond the authority of the church. Distinctively, he located that clarity not in the doctrine of justification by faith alone, but in the doctrine of God's universal love. Similarly, in his conception of the cooperative role of the human will in salvation and the corresponding implications for potentially more expansive roles of human reason and experience, Wesley is not "protestant" in the way of the sixteenth-century Protestant reformers. Yet, he is "protestant" in the ways he carefully outlines Scripture as the prime authority and standard by which to regulate the proper bounds of experience and reason—that only insofar as experience and reason confirm and resonate with what is already clearly taught in Scripture are they to be trusted.

I conclude with some brief reflections on some of the implications of this for the church today. Wesley, the Protestant reformers, and much of Christian tradition (both premodern and modern) have often claimed that Scripture is clear in its core teachings, its teaching concerning salvation. A favorite saying is that Scripture is sufficiently clear concerning salvation. Yet, what happens when we define and identify the key components of Scripture's clear soteriological message differently? This is exactly the bane of Protestant existence. The appeal to the clear teachings of Scripture (and thus to its authority) falls apart when the actual content of such clarity is not shared. To this, though, Wesley had a profound response for the church—which makes me proud to be a Methodist. Wesley and the Protestant reformers both pointed to the necessity of humility—recognizing the limits of human knowledge and the posture of humility necessary to actually receive and follow the

Spirit's guidance.[50] But Wesley advocated an important step beyond humility; he pointed to the character to which Christians are called—a character distinctly shaped by divine love. In this, he asks us, "Though we cannot think alike, may we not love alike? May we not be of one heart, though we are not of one opinion?" That is, though we may not think alike, can we not *walk alike*? Can we not walk alike in bearing the fruits of the Spirit even in the midst of difficult, passionate disagreements? To this he unwaveringly responds, "Without all doubt we may!"[51] As Tom Greggs, in a recent article on Wesley's little-"c" catholicity so eloquently summarizes, "Catholicity for Wesley is not brought about by a negative denial of the significance of doctrines and practices, but it is brought about by a positive loving enactment of fellowship in the context of disagreement."[52] In the midst of sharp divides and disagreements today, Wesley poses the important question, "Is not right and holy ethics—how we act and behave—equally, if not more, important than right and holy doctrine?" And he would insist such a question—such a teaching of the overarching call to such loving, holy living together even in our brokenness—is exactly the clear call of Scripture on the life of the faithful Christian.

Bibliography

Calvin, John. *The Epistles of Paul the Apostle to the Romans and to the Thessalonians*. Translated by Ross Mackenzie. Edited by David Torrance and Thomas Torrance. Grand Rapids, MI: Eerdmans, 1995.

---

50 See LW 10:332 and Calvin, *The Epistles of Paul the Apostle to the Romans and to the Thessalonians*, trans. Ross Mackenzie, ed. David Torrance and Thomas Torrance (Grand Rapids, MI: Eerdmans, 1995), 4. In his preface to *Notes upon the New Testament*, Wesley began with a "deep sense of his own inability" (§1). Likewise, the necessity of "serious and earnest prayer" was one of the key steps in his instructions on how to read Scripture well (*Explanatory Notes upon the Old Testament*, Preface §18).

51 Wesley, Sermon 39, "Catholic Spirit," §I.4 and §I.3, in *Works* 2:83–84.

52 Tom Greggs, "The Catholic Spirit of Protestantism: A Very Methodist Take on the Third Article, Visible Unity, and Ecumenism," *Pro Ecclesia* 26, no. 4 (2017): 357.

———. *Institutes of the Christian Religion*. Translated by Ford Lewis Battles. Edited by John T. McNeill. Philadelphia: Westminster, 1960.

de Greef, Wulfert. "Calvin's Understanding and Interpretation of the Bible." In *John Calvin's Impact on Church and Society, 1509–2009*, edited by Martin Ernst Hirzel and Martin Sallmann, 67–89. Grand Rapids, MI: Eerdmans, 2009.

Ferguson, Duncan S. "John Wesley on Scripture: The Hermeneutics of Pietism." *Methodist History* 22, no. 4 (1984): 234–45.

Jones, Scott J. *John Wesley's Conception and Use of Scripture*. Nashville: Kingswood Books, 1995.

———. "The Rule of Scripture." In *Wesley and the Quadrilateral: Renewing the Conversation*, edited by W. Stephen Gunter, Scott J. Jones, Ted A. Campbell, Rebekah L. Miles, and Randy L. Maddox, 39–62. Nashville: Abingdon Press, 1997.

Luther, Martin. *Luther's Works*. Edited by J. Pelikan and H. Lehman. 55 vols. Philadelphia: Fortress Press, 1957–86.

Maddox, Randy. "The Rule of Christian Faith, Practice, and Hope: John Wesley on the Bible." *Methodist Review* 3 (2011): 1–35, https://www.methodistreview.org/index.php/mr/article/view/45.

Pak, G. Sujin. "The Perspicuity of Scripture, Justification by Faith Alone, and the Role of the Church in Reading Scripture with the Protestant Reformers." *Covenant Quarterly* 75, no. 2 (2017): 3–23.

Shelton, Larry. "John Wesley's Approach to Scripture in Historical Perspective." *Wesleyan Theological Journal* 16, no. 1 (1981): 23–50.

Smith, Timothy L. "John Wesley and the Wholeness of Scripture." *Interpretation* 39, no. 3 (1985): 246–62.

Thompson, Mark. "Biblical Interpretation in the Works of Martin Luther." In *A History of Biblical Interpretation: The Medieval through the Reformation Periods*, vol. 2, edited by Alan J. Hauser and Duane F. Watson, 299–318. Grand Rapids, MI: Eerdmans, 2009.

Thorsen, Don. *The Wesleyan Quadrilateral: Scripture, Tradition, Reason and Experience as a Model of Evangelical Theology*. Lexington, KY: Emeth, 2005.

Stokes, Mack B. "Wesley on Scripture." In *Basic Methodist Beliefs: An Evangelical View*, edited by James V. Heidinger II, 12–18. Wilmore, KY: Good News Books, 1986.

Wall, Robert W. "Toward a Wesleyan Hermeneutics of Scripture." *Wesleyan Theological Journal* 30, no. 2 (1995): 50–67.

Wesley, John. "Roman Catechism and Reply." In *The Works of John Wesley*, edited by Thomas Jackson. Grand Rapids, MI: Zondervan, 1958.

———. *Letters of the Rev. John Wesley*. Edited by John Telford. London: Epworth Press, 1960.

———. *The Works of John Wesley*. Edited by Thomas Jackson. Reprint, Grand Rapids, MI: Baker, 1979.

———. *The Methodist Societies, History, Nature, and Design*. Edited by Rupert E. Davies. Vol. 9 of *The Bicentennial Edition of the Works of John Wesley*. Nashville: Abingdon Press, 1989.

———. *Sermons*. Edited by Albert C. Outler. Vols. 1–4 of *The Bicentennial Edition of the Works of John Wesley*. Nashville: Abingdon Press, 1984–1987.

Wynkoop, Mildred Bangs. "A Hermeneutical Approach to John Wesley." *Wesleyan Theological Journal* 6, no. 1 (1971): 13–22.

Articles, Homilies, and Liturgies: John Wesley and the English Reformation

Jonathan Dean

THE QUESTION OF JOHN WESLEY'S commitment to his own national Church of England and of the measures he took that made separation from it more and more inevitable, even as he trumpeted his loyalty to it, is a well-trodden path in Wesleyan scholarship.[53] There is not room here to explore these issues in greater depth, but it may be worth a brief consideration, in the five hundredth anniversary season of the Protestant Reformation, of a more basic issue. To *which* Church of England was this loyalty expressed?

Perhaps it seems a strange question to ask. It is certainly worth remembering the varieties of what we might anachronistically call *Anglicanism* in the eighteenth century—a strange collection of

53 Still one of the finest accounts remains Frank Baker's *John Wesley and the Church of England* (London: Epworth Press, 1970).

approaches and ecclesiologies that had become even stranger than the hybrid Settlement under Elizabeth I because of the upheavals, challenges, personalities, and vicissitudes of the English Civil War a century later. John Wesley's own sense of where he located himself on the wide map of English-established Christianity shifted over time, as he himself attested—and that is at the heart of some of the difficulty. But, amid his own struggles and his evolution as regards his own self-understanding and that of the people called Methodists, Wesley increasingly looked to the rock from which all English Christianity was hewn: the Reformation Church under Edward VI and the key statements of its faith and practice. These statements certainly underpinned subsequent iterations of the Church of England, but there may be evidence to suggest that John Wesley came to the view that they needed more faithful recovery. Indeed, he seems to have seen Methodism itself as a renewal of the Reformation's most radical phase in England, an urgent summons to recover the renewing fire and the theological passion that the reign of the boy king had offered.

There is not time here either for an adequate survey of the English Reformation. We ought simply to recall that the death in 1547 of Henry VIII, who separated English Christianity from papal oversight but never intended anything like a Protestant Reformation, inaugurated a six-year period of the most dramatic and remarkable change. Matters in Henry's turbulent and unpredictable court, and among his courtiers, were so set when he died that a Protestant ascendancy was the result. The young king's uncle, Edward Seymour, became Lord Protector. Archbishop Thomas Cranmer was finally liberated from the constraints of Henry's conservatism and his enemies at court to unleash the full version of his newfound radical zeal on the English people.[54] The king himself, with precocious confidence, asserted his Protestant theological convictions with assurance.

---

54 The publication of the "Great" Bible in 1539–40, for instance, is often seen as a great high point in the Henrician reforming agenda, and Cranmer's preface emphasized the fact. But it was soon undercut, and its progress undermined, by the fall of Cromwell and the publication of the Six Articles, which were of a far more conservative character and bent.

It is now thought unlikely that Cranmer did indeed call Edward the new Josiah at his coronation, but it is abundantly clear that something very similar was in his mind.[55] Hoping for a long reign, he clearly envisaged a root and branch cleansing of the Church, and he dreamed of establishing it as the beacon of Reformed Christianity across Europe, even as in some areas Catholicism reasserted itself again. To that end, some of the finest minds in continental Protestantism were offered refuge in England, including those who came to prestigious chairs at Oxford and Cambridge.[56] Cranmer actually hoped for a great General Council of Protestant Europe to be held in England, rivaling the Council of Trent, which was just beginning, in scope and influence.

This was all more than mere window dressing. But the substance of the publishing output in Edwardian England is the most important testament to the scale and ambition of the project. Just months after Henry's death, in July 1547, Cranmer oversaw the publication of a set of official *Book of Homilies*, for possession by and the use of every parish church in the land. They were designed to help a church without much of an established or flourishing preaching ministry by giving local clergy set pieces, which echoed official and Reformed doctrine, to read aloud. The *Homilies* had a long history—the archbishop had been trying unsuccessfully to gain permission to publish a set for years, but Henry had always resisted. Now, given his head at last, they radically reshaped the landscape of public theology in England. Unashamedly espousing the "full" Lutheran doctrine of salvation by faith alone, they

55 See Diarmaid MacCulloch, *All Things Made New* (London: Allen Lane, 2016), 91, for his latest thinking on this, a correction of his earlier work, for instance, in *Thomas Cranmer* (New Haven: Yale University Press, 1996). But it is clear also that the *Book of Homilies* saw biblical parallels like Josiah and Nehemiah as helpful ones in the Edwardian project.

56 Martin Bucer, the Strasbourg reformer, came to Cambridge as Regius Professor of Divinity; Peter Fagius came to the same university as professor of Hebrew but died unexpectedly before achieving much; Peter Martyr Vermigli went to Oxford as Regius Professor of Divinity. Bucer in particular was a source of advice for Cranmer and the leading English clergy on issues of doctrine and polity, and he was valued for his own "middle way" approach to issues of *adiaphora* in the English Reformation.

represented the English Reformation in full cry and good heart at last. Cranmer himself almost certainly wrote the three central homilies, on salvation, faith, and good works. They are the heart and soul of the set and of the revolution in English church life he was steering.[57]

The other main plank of all this, of course, was a new liturgy. Not one new liturgy, in fact, but two: the rather conservative Book of Common Prayer of 1549 was very swiftly replaced by the much more radical version of 1552. It abolished the Mass and thoroughly refashioned the theology of public worship in a profoundly reformed direction. Altars were destroyed, icons whitewashed, rood screens removed, simple tables set lengthwise down the aisles, all undergirded with language that very clearly echoed the emphases of the *Homilies*, asserting the believer's dependence on the grace of God alone, and the place of worship as a response to and encounter with that grace but by no means a way to increase it.

Then, finally, just as the boy king lay dying, early in 1553, a very Tudor way of doing theology was introduced: a set of forty-two "Articles of Religion." Unreservedly Reformed in their tone and content, assertive and confident in their expression of an undiluted Protestant church, and avowedly Lutheran on the key doctrines as reflected in the *Homilies*, they were meant to herald the end of the beginning of the great Edwardian project of national renewal. In the end, of course, they were its death rattle. Edward died on July 6, 1553, to be succeeded by a Catholic half-sister, Mary, who swept away his reforms, his liturgies, and his official public theology.

The English Reformation never recovered this moment, this zeal, or this poise. What emerged under Elizabeth in 1558 was an intentional compromise, a step back from what Cranmer and his circle had achieved by 1553, and from which they no doubt intended to go on to

---

57 See, e.g., Alec Ryrie, *The Age of Reformation* (London: Routledge, 2013), 155–57, and MacCulloch, *Tudor Church Militant* (London: Penguin, 1999), 147–49. It is also worth noting Cranmer's own long and losing battle with Henry VIII on the question of justificatio, and the late king's refusal to embrace anything that felt Lutheran in its tenor; cf. Jonathan Dean, *God Truly Worshipped* (Norwich, UK: Canterbury Press, 2012), 10–11, 27–31.

better things. For Elizabeth, the compromise seems to have matched her instincts and her preferences.[58] But, while there was no room in the English religious landscape for unrepentant Catholics, nor was there the possibility of the kind of continued reform that many, some of whom had spent the Marian years in exile in the Reformed cities and states of Europe, yearned for. Some compromised with the compromise: Bishop John Jewel of Salisbury set to, writing his magnificent *Apology of the Church of England*, which sought to show how Elizabeth's church was in fact genuinely Protestant.[59] But the divisions the Settlement engendered, hardened by poor leadership into schism and violence, produced a civil war, a disastrous experiment with non-episcopal forms of governance, and a Restoration of Religion in 1660 that established the Elizabethan compromise again as the Church of England's final form. For many, however, the heady days of the Edwardian reforms, and the radical direction of their ecclesiology, were never forgotten, even as they passed into distant memory.

If there is little time to properly chart the course of the English Reformation, there is even less adequate time to track the evolution of John Wesley's own ecclesiology and evolving relationship to the Church of England. His curious and multifaceted inheritance from his parents, reflecting the divisions and disagreements of the seventeenth

---

58 The subject of the Elizabethan Settlement and its theological and ecclesiological character is complex and sometimes fraught. Good, if older, accounts remain those of MacCaffrey and Haugaard; more recently Alec Ryrie's *The Age of Reformation* (London: Routledge, 2013) has offered a nuanced view. Chapter 7 of my own *To Gain at Harvest* (London: SCM Press, 2018) is an effort to penetrate a little into the mind and heart of Elizabeth herself, who was responsible for much of the strangeness and hybridity of the Settlement.

59 The other great scholarly apologist for Elizabethan Anglicanism is Richard Hooker, whose work represents in some ways a more moderate view than that of Jewel; there is not space here to analyze his distinctive contribution, from which much of the subsequent character of the Church of England drew its wisdom, and he seems not to have been especially important to Wesley. But my colleague Andrea Russell has recently produced her own perspicacious volume on his work: *Richard Hooker, Beyond Certainty* (London: Routledge, 2017).

century, is one obvious factor.[60] He emerged from these conflicting influences, and from his education, something of what we might call a "high churchman," especially in his attitude toward the Church's governance. In all things, as he said himself, he was in his youth "as regular a clergyman as any in the three kingdoms."[61] It is interesting to note, however, the debt he owed to his father, who had written to his son in 1725, repeating advice he had previously given to a curate about the books one ought to read early in public ministry. Foremost on the list were the Edwardian *Homilies*, which "should be often and carefully read," along with Jewel's *Apology*, described as "neat and strong."

Assuming that John Wesley read these works at the time or soon afterward, there is every reason to suppose that they were increasingly important to him later. By his own description of events, the searing failure of his years in Georgia led to a soul-searching and a reevaluation of much of the basis of his former confidence in the Church in which he was ordained. When we survey the writings and utterances of his middle and later years, once the Methodist revival was well underway and its existence more secure, it is fascinating to note the shift in emphasis. Wesley certainly echoed the concerns of Bishop Jewel, whose *Apology* had been largely an appeal to the first centuries of the Church and to their doctrine and practice, in order to demonstrate the vitality and fidelity of Queen Elizabeth's odd creation. Wesley's own works were liberally scattered with patristic sources, and the *Christian Library* included versions of many ancient authors.

By the 1740s, Wesley had become more and more intent on proving the rectitude of the Methodists' adherence to Anglican doctrine and law. The *Earnest Appeal to Men of Reason and Religion* of 1744 cited several canons in their defense. The much longer *Farther Appeal to Men of Reason and Religion* of the following year strove to assert Methodist credentials by quoting extensively from the *Homilies*, the Articles (under Elizabeth reduced to a mere thirty-nine), and the Book

60 See, e.g., Henry Rack's *Reasonable Enthusiast* (London: Epworth Press, 1992), 43–61.

61 From the *Arminian Magazine* of 1790, quoted by Baker, *John Wesley and the Church of England*, 138.

of Common Prayer itself. In all of this, it became his fervent concern simply to prove the inevitability of Methodism's rise, once members of the Church of England took their own doctrines seriously. As he put it to Lord Dartmouth in 1761, "The doctrine of the Established Church, which is far the most essential part of her constitution, [we] manifestly confirm."[62]

Such quotations as these identify the nature of his evolution: toward a deeper love for the Church's doctrines, as established in those radical Edwardian years, and further away from some of the matters of order that his younger self, along with the successors of the Elizabethan and Carolinian establishments, had so cherished. He believed less in the authority of priests and more in the necessary ministry of gifted laypeople; he became more dismissive of any canon that prevented the proper preaching of the gospel by anyone with the ability to do so; he even came to see episcopal authority as a convenient framework but by no means a guarantor of ecclesial integrity and authenticity. In all this, he identified himself increasingly with the more radical end of the English Reformation and even with those of a puritan bent who had wished for better things.

In 1755, addressing the Conference on the question "Ought we to separate from the Church of England?," Wesley nailed his colors to the mast with a keen sense of this history. In the address, he very clearly identified adherence to the *Homilies*, Articles, and liturgies of the Prayer Book as essential marks of belonging to the Church of England, and he affirmed again that Methodists "keep closer thereto than any other body of people in England." As I reflect on Professor Pak's work earlier in this chapter, I'm actually more convinced that in large measure he saw in Cranmer's homilies on salvation, faith, and good works exactly the kind of Protestant theology, espoused by the infant Reformed Church of England, which he believed also to lie at the heart of Methodism's own success and appeal. It embraced Luther's insistence on the absolute sovereignty and priority of God's action but resisted his caution, shared with other leading reformers, about insisting on works

62 Letter to the Earl of Dartmouth, *The Letters of John Wesley*, ed. John Telford (London: Epworth Press, 1960), 4:152.

as the fruit of that salvation.[63] Indeed, it is interesting to note that Wesley himself in the early years of the revival spoke only of "salvation by faith," as Cranmer did; only later did he feel it increasingly important to distinguish justification from sanctification as phases or stages of the *via salutis*, the more he sought (I would argue) to espouse this distinctively English soteriology, as expounded in the *Homilies*.[64]

Where some in 1755 would have added to this list of the marks of allegiance to the Church of England "submission to its laws," Wesley demurred. He could not allow such submission, when contrary to Scripture, and thus when limits were placed on universality of preaching, extempore prayer, the commitment to social holiness, or the preaching ministry of the laity.[65] Echoing Thomas Cranmer, Wesley clearly identified what he had come to view as the radical driving force for English Christianity, a period that ought still to inform and inspire and energize the national Church over two centuries later:

> King Edward the Sixth required several priests in the then Church of England to "search into the law of God and teach it to the people"; . . . afterwards he restored the scriptural worship of God to the utmost of his knowledge and power, and (like Josiah and Nehemiah) gave several rules for the more decent and orderly performance of it—if you mean this only by saying "the church is a creature of the state"—we allow it is, and praise God for it![66]

63 See the extracts from the *Homilies* in Dean, *God Truly Worshipped*, 57–74.

64 See also Richard P. Heitzenrater, *Wesley and the People Called Methodists* (Nashville: Abingdon Press, 1995), 83–84 and 220–22, and Wesley's great 1765 Sermon 43, "The Scripture Way of Salvation," in *Works* 2:153–69.

65 Wesley also spelled out the areas of his necessary disobedience in his 1789 sermon "The Ministerial Office" or Sermon 121, "Prophets and Priests," in *Works* 4:72–84; they were: (1) open-air preaching, (2) extempore prayer, (3) the societies and associated class and band systems, (4) regular meetings of the preachers, and thus (5) the Conference and its task of assigning the stations.

66 Address to the Conference of 1755, reproduced in Baker, *John Wesley and the Church of England*, 330–31.

This gets to the crux of the mature view to which Wesley came, his frustration, as again expressed to Lord Dartmouth, about those around him who had "deliberately engaged to defend [the Church's] orders to the destruction of her doctrine."[67] His own historical investigations led him further in these directions, toward his own decision to ordain ministers for America and to an increasingly self-confident assertion of the calling of his "extraordinary messengers," in a tone and spirit that matched the debates of the English Reformation, in which the *Homilies* had been produced by Cranmer to foster and encourage preaching in a time of want and not, as Elizabeth I fiercely and erroneously insisted, to subdue it altogether. In his *A Concise Ecclesiastical History* of 1781, drawing from the work of Mosheim, Wesley sided with those moderate puritans such as Bishop Jewel and Archbishop Grindal, who bridled at the Queen's conservatism. It is worth noting Jewel's somewhat subversive language too: frequently in his published polemic he chose to refer to England's bishops as "superintendents" in a nod to continental purity.

So much more could and needs to be said—about the precise nature of Wesley's construction of a "new" form of Anglicanism for the nascent United States of America, about his confrontations with episcopal authority and his own reevaluation of his debt to and unfinished business with his beloved Church of England, and about his ongoing spats with his brother about their ecclesial identity. But he does seem to have valued increasingly the radical simplicity and gospel zeal of the early period of the Reformation in England, the brief years under Edward, the boy king, in which the life blood of English Protestantism was infused with a vitality, a clarity, and a theological acuity that marked for him a high point toward which Methodism sought to restore the national Church, in very different times. Professor Schuler wrote earlier in this chapter of the dynamics of the Reformation as leading to a process of renewal that is continual; Wesley, drawing on the wellsprings of the English Reformation, would surely have agreed.

67 Letter to the Earl of Dartmouth, *The Letters of John Wesley*, vol. 4, *January 16, 1758 to February 28, 1766*, ed. John Telford (London: Epworth Press, 1960), 148.

Bibliography

Baker, Frank. *John Wesley and the Church of England.* London: Epworth Press, 1970.

Dean, Jonathan. *To Gain at Harvest.* London: SCM Press, 2018.

———. *God Truly Worshipped.* Norwich, UK: Hymns Ancient and Modern Ltd., 2012.

Heitzenrater, Richard P. *Wesley and the People Called Methodists.* Nashville: Abingdon Press, 1995.

MacCulloch, Diarmaid. *All Things Made New.* London: Allen Lane, 2016.

———. *Tudor Church Militant.* London: Penguin, 1999.

Rack, Henry. *Reasonable Enthusiast.* London: Epworth Press, 1992.

Russell, Andrea. *Richard Hooker, Beyond Certainty.* London: Routledge, 2017.

Ryrie, Alec. *The Age of Reformation.* London: Routledge, 2013.

Wesley, John. *The Letters of John Wesley.* Edited by John Telford. London: Epworth Press, 1960.

———. *Sermons.* Vols. 2 and 4 of *The Bicentennial Edition of the Works of John Wesley*, edited by Albert C. Outler. Nashville: Abingdon Press, 1985, 1987.

Being Methodist in Argentina: To Be or Not to Be

Pablo R. Andiñach

Introduction

Allow me to start with a modest and sincere homage to the host country and to its contribution to universal culture. By this I am referring to the subtitle of this presentation: "To be or not to be." These famous words written by someone who lived near here enclose in a kernel the question of identity, the search for the meaning of life. The first part of my title expresses my condition of Argentine Methodist. And here arises also the question of identity.

Therefore, before we pose the question about what it means to be a Methodist, I think I must ask myself what the meaning is of being Argentine. A very common joke in Latin America mentions that all the people descend from the monkeys (another important British contribution to universal culture!), but we Argentines descend from ships. Most of our literature, art, and music express the difficulty of defining our identity. We are a country where millions of men and women arrived between 1870 and 1930. Argentina was a huge territory, with a scarce native population and without the solid Indigenous cultures that existed in places like Mexico or Peru—an area quite similar in size to the subcontinent of India but that had very little population. And these people arrived from a variety of latitudes, buying the cheapest passage in those ships—women and men traveling third class because there was no fourth class. They arrived with no money but with eyes full of hopes and dreams. Buenos Aires was at the time a Tower of Babel. There were churches, but the people preferred other places. There were bars where women and men met to have fun after their long day's labor. At the end of the nineteenth century these were dark establishments by the port where Poles, Italians, Russians, Spaniards, Welsh, Germans, Greeks, Jews, Arabs, Turks, and French met. And among this confusion of languages and flavors they perceived that the melancholic sound of an instrument created in Germany, the bandoneon, brings them together. Its box and its notes are as foreign to the Argentine soil as every single one of those women and men, but maybe that fact is what generates their claim for ownership. In Buenos Aires the bandoneon does not belong to anyone in particular, and for that reason it belongs to everyone. The same as these women and men, on the shores of the River Plate the bandoneon is an orphan; much like the instrument, they have no history or they have lost it or have strived to get rid of it. Therein a profound and complex music is born, that decades later will be known all over the world and acquire fame and fortune. Its name is enigmatic and African: tango—a music that expresses nostalgia for a lost land, the search for an identity still diffuse, the certainty that nothing is assured.

You are probably asking yourselves why I am providing this description of a slice of South American culture in this theological talk. As it happens, the Methodist Church has been in Argentina for quite a long time. In 1836, the First Methodist Church was established by an English-speaking community whose members were British and American businessmen and traders. Thirty years later, this community would define itself as a faith community with a commitment for Spanish-language missionary work among the local Argentine population.

It is in that social context that Methodism grew and expanded in Argentina. And it was in that Protestant and evangelical church that the immigrants and their sons and daughters discovered the gospel, which became the light that illuminated their lives. Those immigrants were looking for a faith and they found it in our Church, maybe because Methodism did not demand that they abandon their gifts and their dreams. On the contrary, Methodists preached that the faith of Jesus and the presence of the Holy Ghost did not reject what they were, but rather enhanced their gifts and directed them in another direction (what we call *conversion*, from the Hebrew *shub*, from the Greek *metanoia*). Their lives were now called to tune in with God's plan and to work for the transformation of the world. They were socialists, anarchists, liberals; they carried libertarian dreams that instigated them to dignify women, to educate their children, to think and to work for a just and fraternal world. In the Methodist Church nobody condemned their social and political ideas, but instead, apart from a strong anticlericalism (anti-Catholicism) typical of the period, they found a community that boosted education, progress, the culture of work, and the ethics of personal and social solidarity.

It was in this quest for social identity that Argentina was striving for (and in a certain sense still is) that Methodism grew and developed through those values and added its own search for identity. Although it was not the first Protestant church in Argentina, it was the first missionary church that was trying to take hold among Argentines. And in order to become Argentine, Methodism had many identity problems: it was a church English in origin that had arrived to the country as a US missionary endeavor; that had to preach in a Catholic land, in Spanish, a language until then foreign to the evangelical and Protestant denominations; and it was a church that was growing due to the conversion of members who were Argentine but also "foreigners" of a variety of nationalities.[1] Therefore, it was in this missionary context that the Argentine Methodist Church constructed its theology and its identity.

Allow me to make a brief digression in order to comment in regard to what we call *theology*. I teach at a university where we have departments called "Theological Sciences" and "Biblical Sciences." I must

1 It is interesting to know that even today the office of the national government related with the non-Catholic churches and other religions (Oficina para el Culto no Católico) is located under the Foreign Office (Ministerio de Relaciones Exteriores). This office was created in 1853 and remains in that structure.

confess that I teach in these departments, but I do not know the meaning of these disciplines. I do not understand the word *science* added to "theology" or "Bible." Is a scientific reading of *Hamlet* possible? Does anybody know how to read Walt Whitman scientifically? In my own field (Hebrew Bible) the best introductions to the Old Testament start with a description of the ancient history of Israel, some of them with elements of archaeology and others with a history of the canon. It is clearly crucial to know these things in order to be able to read the Bible in depth. But before that, it is necessary to be aware of what a text is, and I consider the Bible to be a text. It is essential to know what a poem or a myth is, because a psalm is a poem, and the creation narratives are profound and very rich myths that must be analyzed and studied. By this I mean that my approach to theology and to biblical studies is closer to artistic discourse rather than scientific discourse. For my theological thinking I find more inspiration in my readings of Charles Dickens or Daniel Defoe (and of course also in the ample variety of works of the rich Latin American literature) than in those books about theology or the Bible that have scientific pretensions. Nevertheless, I enjoy reading Kazoh Kitamori, Rasiah S. Sugirtharajah, Elisabeth Schüssler Fiorenza, and also my colleagues from Latin America. But theology grows from the experience of faith. The primary place of theology is a world where faith is present and where the gospel is proclaimed, and from there on, questions will arise that will provoke our reflection. It is in a second instance that theology becomes academic and a college subject, and we, as academics, should never forget that first point of reference for our task. The *loci theologici* are life itself and its challenges.

Therefore, in this chapter, we will reflect theologically with reference to four examples of life that move us. In them, humanity shines, and they become food for thought. They are four women whose lives were transformed due to an imperative of faith and life. They searched and found their identity in the trial the Lord set forth in their lives. Three of the women were Methodists, and the fourth one was a Jew. Two are from the eighteenth century, one is from the twentieth century, and one died in this century. Two are from the Caribbean, one is German, and one is Argentine.

Two Enslaved Persons in Antigua, Island in the Caribbean

Sophia Campbell and Mary Alley, enslaved persons[2]

On November 29, 1758, John Wesley wrote in his diary, "I rode to Wandsworth and baptized two Negroes belonging to Mr. Gilbert, a gentleman lately come from Antigua." The baptism was a result of the three of them having participated in Wesley's preaching and having a strong conversion experience.

Upon his return to the island of Antigua, in the Caribbean, Nathaniel Gilbert resigned his post in the local parliament and began to preach the gospel among those around him: enslaved persons who worked in his sugar cane plantation. After a few years, he formed a congregation of two hundred members. Later, Nathaniel Gilbert eventually died. He was succeeded for a short time by his brother Francis, who followed his brother's work, but he also died. The community was left without mentors, without those who took the gospel to it.

The Bible has duos of famous women. There were the midwives Shiphrah and Puah in Egypt; Naomi and her daughter-in-law Ruth; the cousins Elizabeth and Mary, mothers of John and Jesus, respectively; Martha and Mary, the sisters of Lazarus who received Jesus in their home. Now we would like to rescue from the bottom of the barrel of history and add to this distinguished list the enslaved persons Sophia Campbell and Mary Alley.

We know little about them—so little that it is not possible to attempt a biography or even a short summary of their lives. We know that they had both gone to London with their master to hear the preacher everyone was talking about. We know that they were baptized there and also that when the Gilberts died, without titles or pomp, they took up the conduction of the church in Antigua, a congregation of enslaved persons who had discovered that the gospel gave them the freedom denied to them by the world.

---

2 From P. Andiñach, *The Book of Gratitudes: An Encounter between Life and Faith* (Eugene, OR: Wipf and Stock, 2016), 168–69; cf. Michael N. Jagessar, "Early Methodism in the Caribbean: Through the Imaginary Optic of Gilbert's Slave Women—Another Reading," *Black Theology* 5, no. 2 (2007): 153–70.

They were pastors and preachers; they celebrated the arrival of babies in the church and gave thanks at funerals for the lives of those who had departed.

These two enslaved women, during a time when masters and pirates had the power, led the mission and made it grow, and were bearers of the light that shines in the darkness.

The Spirit ordained that there would be no grave for Sophia and Mary. Their remains lay somewhere on the island, already part of new life. They are sugar cane; they are the wood of a pulpit; they are the infinite sand. Somewhere in the world where beauty floods everything, we can imagine the immense loveliness of Sophia and Mary.

Sophia and Mary are considered to be the women who enabled the Methodist Church to survive in Antigua.

The first thing to point out is that a man who was cultivated, white, and rich founded the Church in Antigua. We must thank God because someone like Nathaniel Gilbert, who was powerful, accepted a mission destined for the marginalized members of society. He left his government post and spent his days sharing the gospel with the enslaved persons of the island where he lived. Although he did not give up his money, he abandoned his prestigious station in life in order to reach out to the lowly inhabitants of the island. But Nathaniel died and so did his brother Francis. The enslaved persons' new church was then without a leader.

Then Sophia Campbell and Mary Alley appeared. They were very different from Nathaniel: He was a man, they, women. He was cultivated, and we could imagine his eighteenth-century library with authors such as John Milton, John Bunyan, Thomas Hobbes, and maybe the recent and marvelous travel book of the Irishman Jonathan Swift; most probably Sophia and Mary barely knew how to read and write, and the only book they possessed was the Bible. He owned land and enslaved persons, while they had nothing. Finally, Nathaniel was a free man, while Sophia and Mary were enslaved persons; they did not even possess their own bodies.

It was then that the Holy Spirit intervened and a miracle occurred—the miracle of revealing that what appeared to be weakness was hiding an incredible strength. We should not be deceived by a superficial theological discourse that the Holy Spirit transformed the weakness of these women into strength in order to carry on with the mission. They were never weak, and they were already strong when they took over the challenge that the Lord placed in their path. They were enslaved persons and strong; they were poor but rich in intelligence; they were women with a capacity for decision-making and leadership. The miracle was not transforming what was coarse into something brilliant: they were brilliant and we, unaware.

This tale is an opportunity for posing the question, What is a miracle? In my understanding a miracle is not an act of disruption of natural law. Of course, God could do that if God so pleases, but in my experience God scarcely desires it. A miracle is the revelation that something that seems to be impossible is possible due to God's intervention. Could two Black enslaved women in the eighteenth century have the sufficient capability to lead a congregation of men and women? Common sense does not agree with that; the Holy Spirit ascertains that it is possible. Let us note that, seen from this angle, the miracle does not operate on *them* but rather on *us*. We are the ones who think that it is not possible that persons with very limited education could lead a community of faith, and the Holy Spirit operates the miracle of opening our eyes to the reality of the wealth that those two persons were hiding.

A second aspect that I wish to explore is the relationship between the world and the gospel. Personally, I grew up in a Methodist family in which I was taught since I was a child that faith did not separate us from the world. On the contrary, we had to search for the good things in the world and support them, as well as reject the ones that were against God's will. The message was not that we needed to distance ourselves from the world but rather that our challenge was to be in the world and contribute to improving it. I feel happy with that conception of the gospel, and today I still think in that manner. However, the story of Sophia and Mary helped me revise my way of thinking, and although this did not induce me to change it, it allowed me to see another dimension of the same problem.

What good can we find in the world when we look at it from the perspective of the enslaved? When society, the dominant culture, the world, tells enslaved persons that they inhabit a body that does not belong to them, that they do not own their hands, their lungs, their sex? In the case that an enslaved woman gave birth to a boy or a girl, the baby did not belong to her, because the owner might sell the child if pleased to do so or if needed. What can we say when the world offers enslavement as a way of life? Some texts in the Bible may help us to delve into this reality.

The enslaved person feels pain in the soul. Human pain is always specific and historical but is raised in the *wail* to a cosmic and universal dimension. When this happens the event of enslavement becomes a symbol, and for that reason the biblical text places in God's lips, "I have heard their cry because of their taskmasters" (Exod. 3:7, RSV). The text refers to the concrete clamor (Heb. *tzea'qa*) of the Israelites in Egypt, but their words are significant for all time and all peoples who are suffering oppression and anguish. The tale of the exodus from Egypt would be of value simply as information of an event suffered by a Semitic group of people. But the God who liberated Israel is the same that today hears the clamor of those who suffer oppression and cry for justice. The text turns a specific, passing, and forgettable event—as hundreds of acts of justice and injustice, endured by women and men that disappeared in time—in a tale of mythical characteristics and therefore with a narrative density that takes us beyond historical time. The biblical statement regarding the enslavement of Israel refers to our enslavements, our pains, and our injustices. It refers to Sophia and Mary and to their hidden anguishes.

In other passages the Hebrew expression *ne'aqah* (Exod. 2:24; 6:5) is used, which we translate as "moaning." Let us ponder for a moment the question, What is a moan? To moan is to make a sound that does not have as its primary purpose communication. A cry, in the same way as a word does, expects to be listened to and is waiting for an answer. However, a moan is something primal, and it originates before the word. It is what comes from one's innards, and it does not wait for an answer because it does not believe that there is someone who might be able to hear. It is the lament of a desperate human being, of someone who has lost all hope. What the text reveals is that God moved toward that moan and operated in an incredible way in regard to enslaved persons. God acted in a creative manner when he responded to this moan. When God came upon Moses and summoned him to the liberation feat, God created unforeseen conditions. Once again, we are facing a miracle.

We have no knowledge of what Sophia and Mary thought of miracles. But we are certain that they read with plenty of attention the story when the God of the Bible operated the miracle of Israel's liberation from enslavement. In those narratives, and in others, they found an identity and succor for their lives. Sophia and Mary discovered that the gospel provided the freedom that the world denied them.

A Woman in Germany, the Rabbi Regina Jonas

Rabbi Regina Jonas (1902–1944)[3]

She was a rabbi when no woman had ever been one before. She remained in Berlin when almost everyone else was leaving. At twenty-nine years of age she was given a book and the dedication said, "To our first preacher since Deborah . . . who is not only a talented speaker but a good preacher, and with a sense of humor as well." We can imagine the congregation smiling, happy with the rabbi that made them open up body and soul with her words.

She was one in millions, and even so, we wished to forget her. She left a text, a single text that survived a fire and was not reduced to ashes. In it she says that a woman could be a rabbi, and that she would be one, if the Lord called her to such a task. When violence and Nazism were growing and becoming intolerable, she was offered a way to leave the city. She refused, because leaving the city meant leaving her community. She decided to stay behind to preach and accompany those she most loved in their pain and anguish. The psychiatrist Viktor Frankl, who would know her later in an extermination camp, remembered her sermons. He remembered that in

---

3 P. Andiñach, *The Book of Gratitudes,* 158–59; cf. Elisa Klapheck, *Fräulein Rabbiner Jonas: The Story of the First Woman Rabbi* (San Francisco: Jossey-Bass, 2004).

them she dealt with Talmudic and biblical subjects, and she encouraged the lives of her brethren. However, Frankl did not mention her in his memoirs. A woman who shared forced labor with Regina in 1941 said, "The veil of forgetfulness must be allowed to fall over her because everything she did was forbidden."

On November 3, 1942, Regina and her mother, Sarah, made a state-mandated statement of their assets: some old furniture and a gramophone soon to be confiscated. Three days later they were both deported to the Theresienstadt Camp. Two years went by, and one of the many trains that went from Theresienstadt to Auschwitz-Birkenau took rabbi Regina Jonas and her mother to their deaths. They both died on December 12, 1944. Her brother Abraham had died one year earlier in the Łódź ghetto. Rabbi Joseph Norden had written Regina a letter a few weeks before: "Don't cry . . . there is no sense in crying; it doesn't help anyone and has a negative effect on you, especially on your eyes, your beautiful sweet eyes."

Seventy years have gone by. What can I wish for you now, Regina? For you to have embraced your mother during the last minute, the last beat of your heart.

When I became acquainted with the life story of Regina, my first impression was to understand the force of her call for a mission. And the field for that mission was the community of believers that surrounded her. From early on, Regina understood that she was not alone in the world but rather that she was living among a community that provided her with an identity and a community that she wanted to serve.

It is quite remarkable how Regina distinguished herself in her preaching. It has been mentioned that her preferred subjects were the Bible and Talmud and that she applied humor to her preaching. It is probable that the humor would be destined to comfort the Jewish community that already in the 1930s was starting to feel in Germany the oppression of anti-Semitism. Her engagement with her community of faith was so powerful that when she was offered to abandon her city for a country where her life would not be in danger, she refused and decided to stay with her flock. Who were these people? Most probably the Jews who could not leave—the old folk, the widows, the ones who had no family to go to. Regina decided to stay, although there is little doubt that her determination condemned her to death.

The example of Regina has made me think about the sense of that community that we Christians call the church. It is a community that has a double dimension, the visible one and the invisible one. The visible one is the one that each one of us makes up, with our virtues and our flaws. But there is another dimension to the church, that is, the invisibility of the church. The invisible church is the church of Christ, the one that is present whenever two or three gather in his name and that defines itself in such a way that it cannot be reduced to a mere human expression. The Holy Spirit works according to its own free will and cannot be shaped or locked into our tastes, models, and thoughts. It is not limited to buildings, cultures, denominations, languages, or any of our human barriers. The church of Christ is there, where the Holy Spirit is. It is also the church that has existed through the past centuries, the church of those who have preceded us on the path of faith and who have offered their testimonies, brothers and sisters to whom we are linked through our belonging to the people of God.

The invisible church is the church that is not present even if we are standing in the most prestigious cathedral in the city or next to the most well-known preacher, if God does not approve the work that is being done in that place. The invisible church is the "actual" church, the one that is not based on our abilities—rather, it exists despite our behavior and inabilities—but on the free and generous grace of God. Of course, I do not want to baptize Regina. She did not need to be baptized to be truly a woman of God. But I feel that she is in my church with me, in our Church.

One of the most routine, and least perceived, miracles is that God grants us his invisible presence in the visible church made up of men and women. By this we mean that the invisible church is present in the world through the visible church. When the church preaches, educates, creates links among people, and shares the faith and the sacraments, it is making visible a deeper reality that is invisible and transcends what we do. We may say that the task of each Christian is to make visible that dimension of the presence of God in the church and in the world, that is and will be invisible to our eyes.

A second thought comes to my mind when I think of the life of Regina, and that is the value of the Other (the neighbor) in her life story—the sacred value of the person she was facing. The Other was a human being, and Regina understood that her own destiny was tied to him or her. A Jewish philosopher of our time and one of the great minds of the twentieth century, Emmanuel Levinas, during the Second World War was taken prisoner, as was Regina. He lived four years in a concentration camp in Hannover, Germany. There he learned about contempt and pain. His writing will be stained by the experience of having endured a tragedy that very few were able to survive. His philosophical works exude that fundamental question of the meaning of life and of the place of ethics in human relations. In his thoughts, the Other, the neighbor, is always at the center of his concern. Levinas repeatedly mentioned that the book that left a mark in his life and thought was, in his words, "the Hebrew Bible, from my most tender age in Lithuania."

Once he gave a lecture in Paris on the Holocaust and its consequences for ethics and culture. In his talk he mentioned his experience in the concentration camp, his fears, his anguish, his loss of practically all his family. When he finished, a few Latin American students approached him and asked him what he could say about the *other* holocausts. They were referring to the fate of the original inhabitants of America during the European conquest or of the millions of persons who slowly die of hunger in the present. Levinas was silent for a moment and then answered, "It is you who must talk about that." Far from avoiding his responsibility, Emmanuel Levinas—much like Regina Jonas—brings us face to face with our own responsibility of denouncing the injustice inflicted on our neighbor, that in biblical terms would be "the destitute, the orphan, the widow and the foreigner."

Allow me to take a minute in order to reflect on the words of this other woman who met Regina in a forced labor camp. She said, "The veil of forgetfulness must be allowed to fall over her because everything she did was forbidden." It moves me profoundly to know that someone has lived and has given her own life to do forbidden things. It was forbidden to collect heads of grain on Saturday. It was forbidden to talk to a woman in public. No woman was allowed to argue in the Assembly of Rabbis of her city. It was forbidden to be a woman rabbi. The only text that survived from Regina's papers is an essay, a kind of brief dissertation to be presented at the rabbinical school, titled "Why a Woman Can Be Rabbi." It is an analysis of biblical and Talmudic texts in which she proves that, even though it is forbidden, there is nothing to be found in them that denies the right for a woman to be rabbi. She says that what defines a rabbi is not the gender but the call from God. And if the call arrives, one must respond to it. Regina did and said forbidden things, much like Jesus in many moments of his life.

A Woman in Argentina, Evangelina Rodríguez

Evangelina Rodríguez[4]

Evangelina had given birth by caesarean section and was ordered on bed rest. She lived in the Ingeniero Budge District in southern Greater Buenos Aires, where it flooded when it rained long. On the second day of her convalescence, it began to rain, and the waters rose. Her two-year-old son was home alone and, when the rising water gathered strength, it began to sweep away everything in its path. The water that took furniture and garbage also took the body of her child and, with it, also his life.

Evangelina went looking for him downstream, where everything that got dragged built up, but she could not find the child's body. She searched through the mud for two days on both sides of the stream and among the filthy remains left behind by the current. The body was not recovered, and the little angel slept forever with no wake and not even a fistful of earth to cover him, nor a gravestone to remember him.

While searching for her son in the most unsanitary places, Evangelina contracted an abdominal infection, forcing her to fight for her life for several days. Her body finally overcame death, and she was able to move forward.

4 P. Andiñach, *The Book of Gratitudes*, 118–19.

After these events, and throughout her lifetime, Evangelina knitted and put together quilts of multicolored squares that she herself designed. And while she knitted, she thought. As the yarn ran through her hands, she meditated. At night she also meditated. She knit and treasured all her thoughts and pondered them in her heart.

Evangelina is known in the neighborhood as the Methodist lady who went to funerals and prayed for the life of the deceased. She arrived and prayed, talked to the family, and consoled them. She gave a word of encouragement to those who found no consolation; she calmed the desperate with words of faith. Evangelina mourned a neighbor, a grandfather, a young mother who left little ones behind, but in secret, throughout her lifetime, she mourned for her little angel who had had no funeral.

Evangelina was a simple and poor woman. She attended a Methodist congregation in one of the poorest neighborhoods in the south of Buenos Aires. Since very early on, her life was pierced by the tragedy recounted above. The loss of her small child was present in her heart every day of her life, as is the case of any mother who loses a child. What moves me in her life story is how the Holy Spirit operated the miracle of turning her personal tragedy into a purposeful mission.

Every day people die—in fact, thousands—in a city as big as Buenos Aires. For most of the people that is only a statistical matter. But due to her experience Evangelina knew that the dead body was not a statistical figure. She knew that behind every single person who departed, there were persons who felt that their lives would not be the same, for whom the death of a loved one (an old person or a young one, a husband or a wife, a child) would leave a mark in the soul that would never heal. She knew that the loss of a loved one was a very deep pain. But Evangelina knew something else. She knew about the succor that you have when you carry Jesus in your heart. There, where she had the memory of her loved one, she also had the presence of Christ in her life. Therefore, the pain for her loss remained, but this tragedy of her past did not determine her present and her future. She faced life hand in hand with Jesus, and thus she found the strength to tackle the challenges she would find along the tracks.

Evangelina attended funerals and consoled the relatives with words of faith. She spoke of the love of God and of the gratitude they had to have for the life of the departed, who had been important for them. She told them all life is a gift from God and that we must thank God for those who surround us and illuminate us with their presence and with their life. To some the Lord has given them many years to be among us, and others have been with us a shorter time, but we all have to be grateful to God. And thus Evangelina provided the testimony of her faith in Jesus, a faith hardened by her experience and her pain. She shared what she had, and that was her way of providing relief and hope to the persons who were sad and sometimes without any hope at all. Evangelina was poor in the eyes of the world and rich in the eyes of God.

Evangelina's life story has driven me to think why Jesus resuscitated Lazarus. It makes no sense to think that he did so, considering that years later, Lazarus was going to die anyway. Lazarus had to travel the road from life to death twice, much like his loved ones had suffered their separation from him in two cases. There is another sense to that act of resurrection. In my opinion, what Jesus was doing was consoling the ones he found in extreme desperation. He felt compassion for them, and he acted in order to give them faith and hope. And he did so by resuscitating Lazarus but more still by allowing the glory of God to be manifested as he says, "This illness is not unto death; it is for the glory of God, so that the Son of God may be glorified by means of it" (John 11:4, RSV).

What is surprising from this narrative is Jesus's will to respond to the care needed by the sisters and friends of Lazarus because of his death. Moreover, this drives us to understand that the resurrection of Lazarus is not the only miracle narrated there. There is a second miracle, and it is the intimate conviction created in the heart of those who were present in fact, that the glory of God had manifested itself in front of them. On the one hand, a dead man had been resuscitated; on the other, they had witnessed the unequivocal manifestation that God carries out his promise of always being close to the one who is suffering. Jesus drew upon an extreme case, so that everyone who was present would have no doubts regarding the Lord's commitment to life and to the suffering of the persons who face the death of a loved one.

It is remarkable how in this narrative, Jesus preannounces his own resurrection and places it in the theological line of the manifestations of the glory of God. It is not by chance that in this scene we find the statement of Jesus, "I am the resurrection and the life; he who believes in me, though he die, yet shall he live" (John 11:25, RSV), and the awe-inspiring declaration of faith of Martha (v. 27), which is more profound and complex than Peter's (Matt. 16:16), but that is seldom remembered by us—and by "us" I am referring to theologians. Martha's declaration was stated in a context of resurrection, much like an affirmation that arose from within her and that included the declaration "the one coming into the world." We have coined the expression *Confessio Petri*, but we say nothing of Martha. I consider that Evangelina Rodríguez would identify more with Martha than with Peter, and for this reason, the church should speak also of a *Confessio Marthae* (a Latin expression that does not exist in Christian theology), because upon Peter's and Martha's confession the church was built.

There is a second aspect of Evangelina's life story that makes me ponder, and this is the fact that the tragedy of the death of her little one and the horrible circumstances that surrounded her were never removed from her life. She coexisted with the pain in her heart, and she was able to live and serve in her task of communicating the gospel. It is not often that theological discourse has comprehended the pain of the death of a loved one. Sometimes I have felt that our message is something like "Jesus will make you forget what happened and will provide aid" or "in due course and with the help of God you must look forward." Evangelina never thought Jesus was asking her to forget what had happened in her life, nor that she had to look forward as if she had no past. When we look with sensitive eyes at her life, we see that the death of her little one and the memory of those days served her to discover a reality in the souls of other people. That fact that she meditated and thought over in her heart is what provided an identity to her life and a meaning to her days.

The custom of the Wailing Women has existed for centuries in some countries and cultures (maybe also in Israel, cf. Jer. 9:20). These were women who were paid to cry at funerals and burials because there was a belief that a lot of crying would help the soul of the departed on his or her journey to heaven. I believe this custom never existed in Argentina, but for that matter the ministry of Evangelina was something wholly different. She did not cry but rather consoled the crying of others. And if she cried it was not because she wanted to ease the access to heaven of the deceased, but rather because she was moved and felt compassion for those who were suffering. In the same manner, Jesus cried (John 11:35) when he saw the crying of the sisters and of the friends.

The life of Evangelina Rodríguez illuminates that profound theological truth that the Spirit of God moves us to use what we are, even in our personal tragedies, in order to serve our neighbor and give testimony of the love of Christ.

Conclusion

All academic articles and talks are bound to have a conclusion. I teach this to my students. But I must confess that I do not feel comfortable looking for a conclusion for this chapter. I would like to leave with you the strength of those four women who found their identity, their profound identity, in the challenge of being faithful to the gospel. I have presented them as representatives of many others, and also of many men who inspired us and keep inspiring with their life stories. At the beginning, in the first narrative, I made a list of memorable biblical women: Shiphrah and Puah in Egypt; Naomi and her daughter-in-law Ruth; the cousins Elizabeth and Mary; Martha and Mary. I already mentioned that I wish to add to this list Sophia and Mary; today I also wish to add to them Regina and Evangelina. And I would like that each one of you add to this list those women and men who have been or still are an inspiration for your faith and your theology. They are those who in a silent manner pray every day, give testimony of their faith, try to be faithful to the gospel they have received, and so nourish the church of Christ in the world. We need them so they wake up our imagination and so they reveal new challenges for missionary work and for theological reflection.

In my book *Old Testament Theology* I state that the Old Testament is an unfinished work. Not because it needs a New Testament. The New Testament is also an open and unfinished book. The message of the Bible is unfinished because it proclaims what is yet to come, for the definitive redemption of all reality. In that hope we live, and while that does not yet occur, we give thanks because the Spirit calls for women and men, in the hardest of circumstances, to provide testimony of God's infinite love for the world.

Chapter Bibliography

Andiñach, Pablo. *The Book of Gratitudes: An Encounter between Life and Faith.* Eugene, OR: Wipf and Stock, 2016.

Jagessar, Michael N. "Early Methodism in the Caribbean: Through the Imaginary Optic of Gilbert's Slave Women—Another Reading." *Black Theology* 5, no. 2 (2007): 153–70.

Klapheck, Elisa. *Fräulein Rabbiner Jonas: The Story of the First Woman Rabbi.* San Francisco: Jossey-Bass, 2004.

A Deaconess Blueprint for the Revival of Global Methodism

Priscilla Pope-Levison

I'M GOING TO BEGIN THIS chapter by breaking a cardinal rule for historians cited by our colleague, Martin Wellings, in an article for a book ruminating on the future of the British Methodist church. Here's what Martin said: "Historians tend not to be builders of grand systems and purveyors of sweeping generalizations, much less predictors of the future in the light of the past."[1] Martin then proceeded to break this cardinal rule himself, so I am joining good company! I am not going to *predict* the future; rather, I will map a way forward for the revival of global Methodism in light of a movement from the past with remarkable promise and fortitude that, tragically, was never realized. I am speaking of the Methodist deaconess movement. So with a nod to my PhD training in practical theology, I will push the "So what?" question of the historical narrative to provide a glance at a grand system for the revival of global Methodism. The thesis to be advanced in this lecture is simple: the Methodist deaconess movement provided a blueprint with five core elements that—if put into practice with a twenty-first-century spin—have the potential to spark a revival in global Methodism. By "revival," I mean "an improvement in the condition or strength

1 Martin Wellings, "'A Time to Be Born and a Time to Die'? A Historian's Perspective on the Future of Methodism," in *Methodism and the Future: Facing the Challenge*, ed. Jane Craske and Clive Marsh (London: Cassell, 1999), 149.

of something." My thesis is simple. The putting it into practice will be the tough part.

A journalist in 1898 provided this synopsis of what a deaconess does on any given day:

> In the morning she will, perchance, visit a sick man, grumpy and ungrateful, recovering, it may be, from the results of a debauch. It is hers to speak comfortable words to him, to dress his wounds if he have any, and to pave the way for a reconciliation with his wife. . . . Perchance it is a widow she visits in the afternoon, accustomed to earn her scanty crusts as charwoman. Then it is as often as not a case of going down on her knees—not to pray, at least not just now, but to scrub the room out. Or, it may be, a weak mother needs fresh air. Then our Deaconess becomes nursemaid to the infant, and the ailing mother has a day in the country or a ride on a farm. To paper a room, nurse a fever case, make it up between lovers, conduct a service, fire a prayer-meeting, expound the Scriptures, advise in family crises—these are the items that make up a Deaconess' work. A bit of a judge, a bit of a lawyer, a skilled nurse, a preacher, and above all a lover of her kind—all this must a Deaconess be; and it is not easy to find such a combination.[2]

While nearly all Protestant denominations—from Lutheran to Baptist, Episcopal to Congregational—sponsored some iteration of the deaconess movement, its most vigorous success materialized within the Wesleyan family. The deaconess movement caught on in Methodism in the mid-1880s, particularly in Britain and the United States, and scores of Methodist women signed on for one or two years of a theological education combined with practical training before entering into full-time church work as teachers, nurses, evangelists, missionaries, house-to-house visitors, or Bible teachers. The deaconess movement hit its high mark around 1910. In American Methodism, the pertinent statistic in this regard was the peak enrollment of 256

2 "Much the Same in America," *Highways and Hedges: The Children's Advocate* 127 (July 1898): 164.

students at Lucy Rider Meyer's Chicago Training School.[3] From that high mark, enrollment eventually decreased to a trickle. The deaconess movement in Methodism continues today more than a century later, albeit as a shell of its former glory, with, for example, 161 active deaconesses in the UMC in the United States. Only in the Philippines does the deaconess movement continue to thrive, with approximately 440 active deaconesses.[4]

So what was a deaconess? Deaconess proponent and Methodist Episcopal Church bishop, James Thoburn, offered this description of a deaconess in 1890: "a Christian woman who is providentially disentangled from all other matters and can give all her time and talent to the Christian church. She offers herself to the church without any reservation. If she be given food and clothing and work, she will give all her energies in return. She does not stipulate in what direction she will work."[5] Although deaconesses were single women, they were not lifers who made an indissoluble vow, like Roman Catholic nuns, neither were they part-time volunteers who came and went one day a week while juggling family commitments. Deaconesses lived full-time among the people to whom they ministered. "We are in the heart of our work," wrote a deaconess in Salford, England. "The people we want to help live all around us. They pass our doors in their clattering 'wooden shoon,' at a quarter to six every morning; we hear their loud laughter, and alas!

---

3 Isabelle Horton, *High Adventure: Life of Lucy Rider Meyer* (New York: Garland Publishing, 1987), 315.

4 I am grateful to Cristina Mañabat and Sheila Binuya for this statistic. For more on deaconesses in the Philippines, see Liwliwa Robledo, "Gender, Religion and Social Change: A Study of Philippine Methodist Deaconesses, 1903–1978 (PhD diss., The Iliff School of Theology and University of Denver, 1996), and Amelita Grace G. Cajiuat and Liwliwa Tubayan Robledo, "The Impact of Deaconesses in the Life of the United Methodist Church in the Philippines," accessed February 21, 2022, https://www.unitedmethodistwomen.org/what-we-do/service-and-advocacy/deaconess-and-home-missioner-office/news-resources/cajiuatrobeldo.pdf.

5 James Thoburn, "Deaconesses and the Church," *The Message* 5, no. 9 (September 1890): 6.

sometimes their drunken cries late at night."[6] As such, the work of a deaconess never ended.

Plus, the work was grueling and often heartbreaking. Scenarios of human misery filled the pages of Elizabeth Ann Pitts's diary in 1900 during her London rounds shortly after she arrived at Mewburn House, the initial training institute for the Wesley Deaconess Order:

> The next was Mrs. Cooper, she seemed to be worn down with work, having 9 children, the baby only 7 weeks old, so I did not think it wise to hinder her from thronging duties, so after expressing my sympathy offered a few words in prayer, she appeared very thankful. . . . The next place was Mrs. Arrowsmith No 69, it is a sad poverty stricken home, her husband gets work now & then at the docks, the eldest child was kept in because she had not any boots to wear, the second child is suffering from ulcerated bowels, also Whooping Cough; the Mother with infant in arms looked weighed down with care.[7]

Not surprisingly, the strain on deaconesses showed up in illness or exhaustion so much so that Thomas Bowman Stephenson, founder of the Wesley Deaconess Order in England, was asked, "Why do so many of your Deaconesses break down in health?" He responded that such a question "reveals at once the fact that the querist is ignorant of the strain under which the worker, at any rate among the slum population, often lives."[8]

---

6 "Deaconess Work in Salford," *Highway and Hedges: The Children's Advocate* 86 (February 1895): 38.

7 Elizabeth Ann Pitts Diary, John Rylands Library. "The conditions under which they worked are hard to realize now. There was little or no national medical service, no maternity service, no pre-natal or child welfare clinics or district nurses. There was no financial aid from the State during sickness, unemployment or old age. The Sisters met a level of destitution which we do not know to-day." Wesley Deaconess Order pamphlet, n.d., 6, Wesley Historical Society, The Oxford Centre for Methodism and Church History.

8 "In Perils Oft. By a Wesley Deaconess," *Flying Leaves* 73 (February 1908): 201.

To compound the difficulties, Methodist deaconesses worked within an indifferent, even hostile Church that treated them like a third species, neither clergy nor laity. They were consecrated to the office of deaconess, yet what did the term *office* mean? What it meant in reality was that deaconesses were *not* clergy. They were not ordained as were male clergy, even though the consecration of a deaconess happened during a formal, ordination-type service. As did the clergyman's ordination, the deaconess consecration service took place in the church; both included prayers and hymns, both asked questions of the candidates, and both gave a charge to these servants of the Church to be faithful to their calling. Both involved clergy, even bishops, laying hands on the candidate with the trinitarian invocation. Yet the same ecclesial investiture consecrated a deaconess, while it ordained a clergyman.[9]

At the same time, being an officer of the Church meant that deaconesses were *not* laity either. Like pastors but unlike laity, women received a divine call to become a deaconess. No call, no deaconess. Like pastors but unlike laity, the deaconesses had to complete a course of study in theological education. In the American Methodist Church, for instance, the deaconess course of study nearly duplicated that for ministerial candidates; it included biblical studies, church history, logic, doctrine, ethics, psychology, biography, Christian education, and church government. The only courses assigned to clergy and not deaconesses were the preparation and delivery of sermons and church administration.[10]

---

9 For a lengthy discussion of whether deaconesses in the early church were ordained, see Henry Wheeler, *Deaconesses Ancient and Modern* (New York: Hunt & Eaton, 1889), 78–102. In subsequent chapters, he presented information on the deaconesses in Germany, England, and the United States. Curiously, he did not mention Moravian deaconesses, who *were* ordained. See Beverly Prior Smaby, "'Only Brothers Should Be Accepted into This Proposed Council': Restricting Women's Leadership in Moravian Bethlehem," in *Pietism in Germany and North America 1680–1820*, ed. Jonathan Strom, Hartmut Lehmann, James Van Horn Melton (Burlington, VT: Ashgate, 2009), 135.

10 Gerald McCulloh, *Ministerial Education in the American Methodist Movement* (Nashville: United Methodist Board of Higher Education and Ministry,

Nevertheless, deaconesses remained in limbo as to their church office; they were neither clergy nor laity. Fast forward seventy-five years. In a 1970 study of deaconesses in the United Methodist Church, a comment by a deaconess made clear that their limbo status remained in effect: "As a deaconess, a woman is no longer a full human being . . . she's accepted as a kind of maiden aunt, to be pitied, or step-daughter, to be looked after—but from her the church expects little."

So why look to the deaconess movement for a blueprint for the revival of global Methodism? This is a valid question, one I asked myself countless times after—in an unguarded moment of optimism—assigning myself this paper topic months ago. I have longed to change it, but there it was, and I could not turn back. And to be honest, I am glad I did not, because from the margins, the misunderstood, the alienated—rather than those in the center of power—have often come the ideas that show us a way forward to revival. Such was the deaconess movement. It occupied, for a time, a countercultural outpost on the margins that was increasingly less attended to by the institutional church as the church became more bourgeois and respectable. This is not to say that the deaconess movement was without its flaws and shortcomings. Not at all. They could be condescending to the poor, expecting them to pull themselves up by their own bootstraps if they only applied themselves. They were stuck in nineteenth-century revivalism, as if that approach was the only one for evangelism. There is more on that topic, but that is for another paper topic. For this chapter, we will consider five core elements of the deaconess movement that I believe can spark revival today in global Methodism.

1. Unite Knowledge and Vital Piety

> A great longing possessed me to know Christ as a living, bright reality. . . . Early and late I sought for this happy experience, wrestling and praying for hours. . . . There followed soul struggles, and it seemed that God had hidden His Face from me. For 18

1980), 12.

> months I scarcely smiled. [Then after reading Hannah Whitall Smith's bestselling book, *The Christian's Secret to a Happy Life*] . . . the mists cleared and the scales fell from my eyes. I saw that my efforts and soul chastening had been in vain, and that I had simply to surrender myself and my doubts to Christ.[11]

So wrote Sister Thirza Masters, who was raised, along with her thirteen siblings, in the Wesleyan Methodist Church in England.

Deaconesses experienced a definite, thorough conversion. Most were raised in Christian homes and in the Methodist Church, thus they were surrounded from birth in a Christian environment. Still, a moment happened when God became real to them in a new, intimately personal way. Deaconesses also experienced a definite call to serve God in full-time ministry. These calls were transformative and life changing. Louise Semple altered direction completely from pursuing her artistic talent to being consecrated a deaconess on December 2, 1895, due to God's call: "When I became convinced that the call was from the Lord, I could only say, 'Here am I, send me' and I never for a moment regretted the decision."[12] Similarly, Louise Golder, whose brother, Christian, advocated for deaconesses in the German Methodist Church in the United States, described her call with these words: "The more I prayed about it, the more my inner joy and impulse grew and was so strong that I felt, if I didn't obey the voice, I would be going against God's will."[13] As Sister Dora Stephenson of the Wesley Deaconess Order expressed it, the call for a deaconess acts as a "definite and prayerful covenant with God to do the work to which she believes He has called her."[14]

---

11 Thirza Masters, "Lives of Wesley Deaconesses. Sister Thirza Masters," *Flying Leaves* 23 (November 1903): 168.

12 *The Message and Deaconess Advocate* (January 1895): 10; quoted in Mary Agnes Dougherty, *My Calling to Fulfill: Deaconesses in the United Methodist Tradition* (New York: Women's Division, General Board of Global Ministries, 1997), 2.

13 Personal testimony of Louise Golder, consecrated 1893; quoted in Dougherty, *My Calling to Fulfill*, 2.

14 Sister Dora Stephenson, "What Is a Deaconess?" *Highways and Hedges: The Children's Advocate* 95 (December 1895): 219.

This profound Christian experience was then balanced by learning and training for the work. Once she answered the call, the would-be deaconess enrolled in a training school. Especially rigorous was the academic study of the Bible. At Lucy Rider Meyer's Chicago Training School, for at least an hour every morning, five days a week, deaconesses-in-training studied both the content and context of all sixty-six books of the Bible along with biblical history and geography of the ancient world; they even memorized maps and diagrams of principal cities and localities. They learned as well how to develop Bible lessons that included maps, charts, and simple drawings intended to reinforce the teachings. Such teaching tools proved invaluable as deaconesses taught the Bible in churches and industrial schools and as they visited, Bible in hand, in homes and tenements.

In the second year at the Chicago Training School, the required reading thickened academically, focusing on the life of Christ. The book assigned was Cunningham Geikie's *The Life and Words of Christ*, an encyclopedic tome referencing ancient authors like Josephus and Papius as well as leading contemporary biblical scholars from Johann Gottfried Eichorn and Ernest Renan to Constantin von Tischendorf. The corresponding bibliographic notes included Latin, Greek, and Hebrew citations. Geikie's book also introduced, albeit briefly, the basics of gospel criticism, particularly the dating of the fourth Gospel. Although biblical languages were not required at deaconess training schools as they were at theological seminaries, the Chicago Training School curriculum offered multiple elective courses in New Testament Greek that would give "the student a sufficient working knowledge of the principles of the Greek language to enable her to read the New Testament in the original."[15]

---

15 Isabelle Horton, *The Builders: A Story of Faith and Works* (Chicago: The Deaconess Advocate, 1910), 202. For instance, according to the 1895–96 Boston University School of Theology catalogue, the study of both Greek and Hebrew languages were required, not elective, courses. *Boston University School of Theology Quadrennial Report to the General Conference of the Methodist Episcopal Church* (Boston: Boston University School of Theology, 1896), 7.

Along with academic courses, the training school integrated practical work as the other major component of its curriculum. Particularly in the United States, training schools originated in high-density, urban locations such as Chicago, Boston, New York City, and St. Louis, where students had multiple choices in practical work. They worked in city missions, the jail, juvenile court, city hospitals, the workhouse, rescue missions, the old folks' home (now called nursing home), Travelers' Aid ministry to care for runaway children and unchaperoned girls, and settlement houses.[16] Even in the rural setting of Wesley Deaconess College in Ilkley, West Yorkshire, students visited in the community one afternoon a week on Wednesdays. "Shortly before one o'clock every Wednesday," wrote a student, "we wend our way, a blue-cloaked band, to the station. The afternoon is spent in Bradford, and the surrounding villages. Meetings are conducted, and sick people visited, thus affording a foretaste of the work awaiting us in the future."[17]

Knowledge and *vital piety*. Are these words alive today? In these same lands, loosely referred to as the West, where the deaconess movement once flourished, vital piety—as in conversion and consecration of one's life—is rarely mentioned in many Methodist contexts today. *If* such talk ever happens, it's potentially embarrassing. There's a pregnant silence when we look down at our feet and hope for someone else to say something in response. We've become thoroughly Bushnellian, as in Horace Bushnell, the Congregational pastor and theologian, who exercised a significant influence in this direction during the mid-nineteenth century. He criticized "emotional revivalists" for their insistence on the "radical breach-making character" of conversion

16 Similarly, at Chicago Training School, deaconesses spread out into the city to work in a wide variety of organizations and churches. "A pamphlet from the same period described how students served internships under pastors and relief agencies, visiting criminal courts and tenement houses, studying prostitution, alcoholism, and public health issues." Dana Robert, *American Women in Mission: A Social History of Their Thought and Practice* (Macon, GA: Mercer University Press, 1996), 156.

17 "A Student's View of College Life. By a Student," *Flying Leaves* 109 (May 1911): 73.

and advocated instead for an imperceptible growth into the Christian life, where "the child is to grow up a Christian, and never know himself as being otherwise."[18] Bushnell's perspective on conversion, recently described as "organic," relied on a steady, long-haul Christian influence at home and church rather than a speedy, spectacular one.[19] Mainline Protestant seminaries jumped on Bushnell's ideas and advanced a curriculum with religious education, replacing evangelism as "the new paradigm for ministry" for an educated clergy.[20] What appears now is that even religious education in the church also has been marginalized, so the question is, Where and when does conversation about conversion, consecration, or a call to ministry ever happen? Even to initiate these kinds of conversations, which were profoundly alive amid the deaconesses, could provide a spark toward revival in global Methodism.

2. Live Simply, Even Communally

> Deaconess work and the mode in which Deaconesses live is a protest against the utilitarian standard which pervades all our civilization. The poor appreciate it. It is a revelation to them that here are women who are working for the love of Christ, and who know something of the limitations of poverty as well as the people among whom they labor. "He became poor for our sakes." It is a voice in this modern age, saying to the multitude, there is

---

18 Martin Marty, *Protestantism in the United States: Righteous Empire* (Chicago: University of Chicago Press, 1986), 192. See Horace Bushnell, *Discourses on Christian Nurture* (Boston: Massachusetts Sabbath School Society, 1847). David I. Macleod, *Building Character in the American Boy: Boy Scouts, the YMCA, and Their Forerunners, 1870–1920* (Madison: University of Wisconsin Press, 1983), 23.

19 Catherine L. Albanese, "Horace Bushnell among the Metaphysicians," *Church History* 79, no. 3 (September 2010): 616.

20 Ann Taves, *Fits, Trances, and Visions: Experiencing Religion and Explaining Experience from Wesley to James* (Princeton, NJ: Princeton University Press, 1999), 343.

> something more precious than dollars and cents. There is a wealth of life more to be desired than silver and gold.[21]

Methodism in the late nineteenth century became increasingly middle class in outlook, architecture, and even in location. In 1877, a Chicago minister described its bourgeois ascent: "Methodism is in transition; moving up out of poverty into wealth; out of obscurity into notoriety; out of her plain garb into the latest fashions; out of the log-cabin into the white house; out of the old camp-grounds into the 'Ocean Groves' and the 'Lake Bluffs'; out of the plain old meeting house into the grand new church with organ and quartet-choir, and all with the ornamentation of a heavy mortgage."[22]

Deaconesses embodied—literally, as we shall see in a moment—the opposite. Detaching themselves from material goods, they stood against materialism by living and dressing simply. At the Chicago Training School, for instance, a group formed called the Do Without Band, and they looked constantly "for opportunities to *do without* for Jesus's sake."[23] What did deaconesses do without? First, they did without a salary. Living without an income silenced accusations that they worked for pay or that the deaconess movement cost the church money that was better spent elsewhere. "Money is . . . crystallized power," wrote Lucy Rider Meyer, "and God's children should hold it sacred for God's work, using only so much of it for their own comfort and adornment as will make them better workers for God."[24]

---

21 Addie G. Wardle, comp., *A Report on Deaconess Work* (Chicago: Methodist Deaconess Association, 1908), 11.

22 W. H. Burns, "Methodism in Transition," *Northwestern Christian Advocate,* August 22, 1877, 6. For a similar story in Great Britain, see Clive Field, "The Social Structure of English Methodism, Eighteenth to Twentieth Centuries," in *British Journal of Sociology* 28, no. 2 (June 1977): 199; Henry Rack, "Wesleyan Methodism 1849–1902," in *A History of the Methodist Church in Great Britain,* ed. Rupert Davies, A. Raymond George, and Gordon Rupp (London: Epworth Press, 1983), 3:127; Anthony Armstrong, *The Church of England, Methodists and Society, 1700–1850* (London: University of London Press, 1973), 207.

23 Horton, *The Builders,* 96.

24 Lucy Rider Meyer, *Deaconesses, Biblical, Early Church, European, American, With the Story of The Chicago Training School, For City, Home and Foreign*

They also did without a closet full, even a drawer full, of clothing. Consider the deaconess uniform. As with all clothing, it acted as a visible form of communication; like a sign, it provided information and orientation.[25] The deaconess uniform imparted the message to the church and to their critics that deaconesses undertook their work with intention and dedication enough to forego luxuries and frivolities. The uniform also communicated to the poor among whom they worked that the deaconesses chose to serve God among them in the simplest of ways. Meyer spoke forcefully about what it would be like for a poor woman "dressed in calico" to be visited by a woman wearing "even a plush cloak." Such a contrast in clothes precluded any possibility of honest sympathy between them due to the glaring wealth differences as represented by their respective clothing. "The rustle of a silk dress is worse than the rattle of musketry for driving poor people out from the reach of helpful Christian influences," Meyer decried. "But our serge dresses and plain bonnets show us willing to 'become all things to all *women*, that we may win some.'"[26]

Still more, deaconesses did without a home and family of their own. They viewed themselves as mothers of humanity and relinquished, as long as they were in the deaconess order, the role of wife and mother to their own children. Instead, they acquired a sisterhood, a company of like-minded women. Many deaconesses, especially in the United States, lived in a deaconess home. Not only was it more economical, but also the deaconess home provided a sacred place set apart from the world to which deaconesses returned after a long day of visiting in overcrowded tenements or nursing the infirmed. As a community, they gathered to eat, discuss the day's events, share each

Missions, and The Chicago Deaconess Home, 2nd ed. (Chicago: The Message Publishing Company, 1889), 236.

25 Alison Lurie writes, "Today, as semiotics becomes fashionable, sociologists tell us that fashion too is a language of signs, a nonverbal system of communication." Alison Lurie, *The Language of Clothes* (New York: Random House, 1981), 3. See also Nathan Joseph, *Uniforms and Nonuniforms: Communication through Clothing* (New York: Greenwood Press, 1986), 49.

26 Meyer, *Deaconesses*, 236.

other's burdens, worship together, and pray over the difficult situations they tended to throughout the day. In this home, deaconesses lived communally as family. For British Methodist deaconesses who lived more on their own, the annual weeklong convocation became the high point of the year when they met with those who understood their work as no one else did. They spoke in longing terms of the convocation as breathing new life into their work and giving them strength to return and resume the work.

The esprit de corps among deaconesses, whether in daily communal living or the annual convocation, enabled these women who had relinquished home and family, modern clothes and conveniences, to persevere in simplicity, economy, and purpose. They did not view themselves as separate individuals but as a sisterhood, even across national boundaries and different denominational communities. One illustration encapsulates this powerful, communal connection internationally: Sister Mina Fliedner, at the Kaiserswerth Motherhouse in Düsseldorf, Germany, was asked if she had a message of greetings for the Wesley Deaconess Order's Annual Convocation of 1904. " 'No,' she said. 'I think I can send them no message, as I do not know them well enough, but you may tell them that I love them all in the Lord Jesus, and that while their Convocation is meeting, I shall be praying for them night and day.' . . . Two days afterwards, Sister Mina was found in her room, dead, on her knees. She had passed away in the very act of prayer."[27]

All of this speaks so powerfully to global Methodism today, and the possibilities of connection are magnified exponentially with social media and our advanced communication tools. The simple yet profound act of praying for each other across national and international boundaries is a way to spark a revival in global Methodism. And what about doing without for Jesus's sake so that resources can be shared for God's work throughout global Methodism?

---

27 "A Pathetic Incident," *Flying Leaves* 32 (June 1904): 85.

3. Unify Evangelism and Humanitarianism

Sister Elise Searle, a deaconess who was elected by popular vote to the Board of Guardians in Norwich, engaged in political lobbying to make substantive changes to improve the food served to residents at the workhouse and to increase the supply of towels at the local hospital. "These details may seem very trivial to an outsider," Searle stated, "but they mean a great deal to the respectable poor, many of whom, through sickness and adversity, are forced to shelter their declining days in our workhouses."[28] Simultaneously, she engaged in evangelism with the people applying to the Board of Guardians for welfare aid. As recipients waited in line to submit their aid applications, Sister Searle would slip out of the board meeting and lead the people in a familiar hymn before talking to them about Jesus. In other words, she united evangelism and humanitarianism in order to reach people both physically and spiritually.

No matter the work, whether as nurse, teacher, daycare worker, class leader, Sunday school teacher, house-to-house visitor, or probation officer, the deaconess viewed it as an opportunity for evangelism. As Thomas Bowman Stephenson thundered, the Wesley Deaconess Order is "a 'soul-converting' agency. It must employ to the full all social influences and expedients, but in all, its object must be 'soul-winning.'"[29] From across the water, Lucy Rider Meyer responded as vociferously:

> Would you have everybody interested in the evangelistic work? Jesus would. A work for which God the Father spared not his own Son may well claim *the intensest energies of every one of us*, until it is done. But what my art, my literary pursuits, my society? May I not live for them? No, no, no! In a world full of souls with eternal life or death just before them—souls every one of whom has cost the heart's blood of a God to redeem—no one has a right to live for art, or for literature, or for science, or society, or wealth. . . .

28 Elise Searle, "Notes from Norwich," *Highways and Hedges: The Children's Advocate* (June 1895): 119.

29 William Bradfield, *The Life of the Reverend Thomas Bowman Stephenson, B.A., LL.D., D.D.* (London: Charles H. Kelly, 1913), 424.

> All these things God intends as means and means alone—not an end—not to live for. We may use them just as long as they . . . can be used directly in furthering God's work. . . . To amass money that one may simply have it—O foolish one. "This night shall thy soul be required of thee." It is to lie down, after all, in an empty coffin.[30]

The integration of evangelism and humanitarianism showed up in the service to bring British Methodist deaconesses into the order. A short statement read by the president of the conference listed various kinds of work that deaconesses might be called to undertake, including preaching, teaching, feeding, nursing, visiting, and rescuing. Then the president declared that "in all this you must be true evangelists of our Lord Jesus Christ translating your Gospel into the language of personal service, that it may be the better understood, not reckoning your ministry complete till those who you serve can say, Now we believe . . ."[31] In other words, service and evangelism—together—helped people see the gospel at work and believe it.

This holistic approach emerged across the deaconess movement in American Methodism. Mary Agnes Dougherty's dissertation, one of the first comprehensive studies done on the topic, tracks the career profiles of 509 graduates from the Chicago Training School. Using her statistics, the number of deaconess evangelists (eighty-eight) equaled the number of deaconess nurses (eighty-seven).[32] This parity in itself demonstrates the twofold commitment to evangelism and humanitarianism. In her interpretation of the data, Dougherty admits that deaconesses attended to the spiritual and physical simultaneously, so that in fact both evangelism and humanitarianism were requisite deaconess labors. She expressed the opinion that the attention to spiritual needs, often through evangelism, distinguished the deaconess movement from the

30 Lucy Rider Meyer, "Deaconesses and the Need," *The Message* 5 (1890): 9. Emphasis added.

31 "The Order of Service for the Ordination of Deaconesses" (London: Methodist Publishing House, n.d.), 12.

32 Mary Agnes Dougherty, "The Methodist Deaconess, 1885–1918: A Study in Religious Feminism" (PhD diss. University of California, Davis, 1979), 102.

settlement house movement, two movements that were otherwise very similar. Her statistics continue. The highest number in any category were deaconess visitors (381).[33] This statistic also demonstrates the intertwining of evangelism and humanitarianism because the deaconess visitor evangelized as she cooked a light meal for an invalid, swept the floor, or looked after a child while a mother rested. Meyer explained that the deaconess visitor rejoiced "in little children rescued, souls saved, and the 'sweetness and light' of the gospel penetrating homes and hearts."[34]

The bifurcation of evangelism and humanitarianism is alive and well today. In many Methodist contexts, the very word *evangelism*—the "e" word—raises hackles or at least discomfort. As a local church evangelism committee member commented, "The word *evangelism* kind of unnerves me and I think it unnerves a lot of people. . . . When you say 'evangelism,' people think Holy Roller."[35] The focus on humanitarianism to the neglect of evangelism comes up every time I teach an introduction to evangelism class. Again this spring, the hesitancy to evangelize showed up when a well-meaning, earnest student asked the question, "If the T-shirt I'm wearing when I helped with clean-up after Hurricane Harvey had my church's logo on it, was that evangelism? Did I have to say anything about Jesus or the gospel? Didn't the church's name speak for itself and identify me as a Christian engaged in hurricane relief work?"

According to Robert Wuthnow, an American sociologist of religion who conducted a comprehensive study of American churches in 2010, there are powerful "social pressures to emphasize service rather than evangelism."[36] Nevertheless, as a church leader in Wuthnow's study commented, "Evangelism is part of the Christian faith. It might be intrusive and it might step on the toes of some folks who don't think

33 Dougherty, "The Methodist Deaconess," 102.

34 Meyer, *Deaconesses*, 71.

35 Ronald J. Sider, Philip N. Olson, and Heidi Rolland Unruh, *Churches That Make a Difference: Reaching Your Community with Good News and Good Works* (Grand Rapids, MI: Baker, 2002), 64.

36 Robert Wuthnow, *Boundless Faith: The Global Outreach of American Churches* (Berkeley: University of California Press, 2009), 242.

it's right, but it's there and we have to recognize that it's there."[37] Certainly the deaconesses did, and for them, attending to evangelism and humanitarianism was a seamless venture.

4. Move Out beyond the Church Walls

> One great advantage of systematic woman's work, is that it can undertake pieces of work which are outside the ordinary sweep of the Church's activity. There are important classes of the community, which, by the hard demands of modern society, are practically excluded from anything like regular attendance at the House of God. Such are the police, the railway men, and the firemen. If the demands of the modern social system are to be met, such men must surrender much of the happy freedom of the Sabbath holiday. In such circumstances, how is their religious life and sympathy to be maintained?[38]

How indeed? Enter the deaconess who recognized the conundrum and managed it by offering a simple religious service so that these public servants had the opportunity to worship on a regular basis. As the deaconess described it, we "shall go to them, not wait for them to come; it shall suit the convenience of *their* work; not demand that it shall bend to ours; it shall provide for them religious services and influences which shall fit into the corners and crannies of *their* lives."[39]

For that reason, for firefighters who had to "man" the station to be ready in case of a fire, the deaconesses came to the station and held services there for them.

Here are other examples, initiated and staffed by deaconesses, that provided religious encounters outside the church walls and at times and places convenient to those being reached:

For female factory workers in Liverpool, a deaconess opened a dining room in the basement of the Liverpool Mission Hall, where on their

37 Wuthnow, *Boundless Faith*, 241–42.

38 *Highways and Hedges: The Children's Advocate* 129 (September 1898): 212.

39 *Highways and Hedges: The Children's Advocate* 129 (September 1898): 212.

lunch break they could eat and rest inside rather than out in the elements and make tea with the hot water provided. The deaconess joined them on occasion to sing with them and talk about Jesus.[40]

For ballerinas performing at the local theater, a deaconess arranged permission to meet with them in their dressing area, where she hosted a nice tea. After tea, she led them in singing hymns followed by a short talk. Being behind the scenes where the ballerinas spend so much of their time gave the deaconess a better understanding of their life and work.[41]

For children in Rotherhithe, one of the poorest areas in London, a deaconess was concerned about the children, so she launched "activities for them, including 'play' hours and guilds for both boys and girls where they could use books and games and see lantern shows." She also served more than 2,500 breakfasts to school-aged children who would otherwise go without breakfast to school.[42]

For young women—fifteen years of age and older—who labored in Nottingham warehouses and factories, the deaconess organized a weekly evening gathering intended simply to bring joy and light into lives filled during the workday with "long, grey, monotonous drudgery." She cleared the schoolroom of desks and chairs and filled it with lights, table games, music, and singing and sewing. She noticed that some of the girls looked pale from their factory work, so she started a Rambling Club and took them on countryside hikes every other week: "One gets to know and understand them better, for it gives the opportunity of a chat about their homes and factory life. . . . We are hoping this year to take a few excursions by train, and even hope for a glimpse of the sea, many of them not having yet seen it."[43]

---

40 "Some Wesley Deaconesses and Their Work," *Flying Leaves* 98 (May 1910): 77.

41 "A Letter from Leeds," *Flying Leaves* 70 (November 1907): 154.

42 Dorothy E. Graham, *Saved to Serve: The Story of the Wesley Deaconess Order, 1890–1978* (Werrington, UK: Methodist Publishing House, 2002), 37.

43 Lena Harbord, "Girls' Clubs," *Highways and Hedges: The Children's Advocate* 121 (January 1898): 19–20.

For people waiting in line to apply for relief aid, as I mentioned earlier, Sister Elise Searle slipped out of the Board of Guardians' meeting to lead the applicants in hymns like "Jesu, lover of my soul" or "Safe in the arms of Jesus": "Between the hymns I have a little homely talk with them, about the Jesus to whom we have been singing, and it is delightful to see some of the sin-hardened faces relax, and a new light dawn in the dim eyes, as we speak and sing of the love of our Savior."[44]

For construction workers far from home while building a London hospital, a deaconess held a dinner-hour service: "For nearly two years, they have held a simple meeting—talking to the men, singing to them, praying with them."[45]

For young women working in a large woolen mill in Bradford, the deaconess came at dinner time with hymn sheets to hold a brief service. Some sixty to seventy girls sat on improvised seats to sing, hear a short talk, and pray until the bell rang. Then, "the machinery starts; the girls take their places at the looms, and all is clatter and noise."[46]

For travelers in a busy railway station, "from seven each morning till late in the evening, she [a deaconess] is here to lead the blind, to help the lame, to advise the wandering, to comfort the sick, to protect girls and women, and to speak, as opportunity offers, a word for Jesus."[47]

Today these outreach ministries might be labeled "fresh expressions." Since the 2004 Mission Shaped Church report from a working group of the Church of England's Mission and Public Affairs Council, a growing movement of practitioners and pioneers have formed Fresh Expressions of Church in the United Kingdom, across Europe, and in North America. These ministries revolve around the belief "that God is already at work in the world. Fresh Expressions reimagine how the

---

44 Elise Searle, "A Unique Congregation," *Highways and Hedges: The Children's Advocate* 91 (July 1895): 136.

45 "A Dinner-Hour Service," *Highways and Hedges: The Children's Advocate* 131 (November 1898): 260.

46 "The White-Striped Veil," *Flying Leaves* 54 (May 1906): 71.

47 "The Mission Field at Home and Abroad: Notanda," *Highways and Hedges: The Children's Advocate* 118 (October 1897): 232.

Body of Christ can live and work in diverse and changing contexts."[48] This was what deaconesses engaged in more than a century earlier. Deaconesses were acute observers of those who were not currently making it to church for whatever reason, and in response, they moved beyond the church walls to set up sacred places for people to worship in a courthouse waiting room, a fire station, or a railway station. At the same time, however, not so fresh were the services put on by the deaconesses because they were revivalism repeated ad nauseam, relying solely on gospel hymns followed by an evangelistic talk. Nonetheless, they were there among the poor and working class, making visible the church beyond its walls.

5. Share Knowledge and Experience across a Global Network

The badge of the Wesley Deaconess Order encapsulates this final core element, the generous and free sharing of knowledge and experience, what today we might call *intellectual property*. On the reverse side of the badge were three words—"For Jesus's sake"; this was the motto of Lucy Rider Meyer's Chicago Training School. In these words, the American Methodist deaconess movement was represented on the badge. Also, in the dove, the deaconess work at Kaiserswerth near Düsseldorf, Germany, was represented on the badge.[49] Three different deaconess communities, three different nations, two different languages, two different ecclesial traditions, and all on one small badge. Truly, the quintessential representation of sharing knowledge and experience across a global network.

In 1836, a quiet revival of the ancient female diaconate of the early church began when Pastor Theodore Fleidner opened Kaiserswerth, a deaconess Motherhouse with a wide-ranging outreach to meet the community's needs. Kaiserswerth became the model and inspiration for

---

48 Fresh Expressions, "What Is a Fresh Expression?," September 10, 2018, http://freshexpressions.org.uk/about/what-is-a-fresh-expression/.

49 "True," *Flying Leaves* 33 (July–August 1904): 102.

many around the world. Florence Nightingale came to Kaiserswerth in 1850 to learn nursing. Many American Methodist deaconess proponents, including Bishop Matthew Simpson, Jane Bancroft Robinson, Bishop James Thoburn, and Lucy Meyer Rider, spent time at Kaiserswerth. Even more enamored with Kaiserswerth was Thomas Bowman Stephenson, who emulated it in myriad ways as he set up the Wesley Deaconess Order.

The influence and sharing of knowledge and experience crisscrossed the continents in an easy and generous exchange without any concern for plagiarism or extended footnotes to cite sources. This was not an issue; any idea, writing, or document was freely exchanged. Here are some examples:

- The service for the recognition of deaconesses used by the Wesley Deaconess Order was taken, with some modifications, from that used at Kaiserswerth.[50]
- *Flying Leaves*, the title of the Wesley Deaconess Order monthly journal, was the English translation of the Kaiserswerth journal, *Fliegende Blätter*.[51]
- British and American Methodist deaconesses followed the daily Bible reading plan set up by Kaiserswerth. That meant that in 1906 "twelve hundred Deaconesses at Kaiserswerth, the Methodist Episcopal Deaconesses of America, and the Wesley Deaconess Order, with many Associates and friends,

50 "A Recognition Service," *Highways and Hedges: The Children's Advocate, The Organ of the Children's Home* 57 (September 1892): 178.

51 Bradfield, *The Life*, 407. In turn, Theodore Fleidner, founder of Kaiserswerth, copied the title from Emmanuel Wichern of Rauhe Haus, who, along with his mother, "gave to the world the first example of the 'Family System' in its redemptive power. The leaves flew far and wide, and, lodging here and there and yonder, gave this germinant thought to other minds, and, in a word, revolutionized the world's ideas as to the method of training the children of want and woe. If our modest 'Leaves' can fly as far and far, and can do for our Deaconess work what its German cousin has done for salvation work amongst the children, it will have justified and adorned its title." "Why the Title, *Flying Leaves*?," *Flying Leaves* 3 (January 1902): 5.

are all united in such a spirit of faith and prayer and meditation as will be produced when we daily tread together the same sacred path of Bible Reading."[52]

- Deaconess periodicals freely published articles from each other without concern for copyright or plagiarism. Stephenson issued this statement in acknowledgment of this free exchange: "We are glad that Mrs. Meyer feels free to reproduce in its pages, occasional paragraphs from *Highways and Hedges*; and we are still more glad to know that we are welcome to use anything from *The Message* which may be useful and opportune for our purpose."[53]

Deaconesses recognized that "we're all in this deaconess thing together so let's do all we can to make each other better." Feel free to use our consecration service and adapt it for your context. Feel free to use whatever articles we've written that you think might help secure support and enthusiasm for the movement. Feel free to come stay in our deaconess home when you're in town. And all of this sharing was before the telephone, email, internet, cell phone, Twitter, and Instagram. They communicated between continents regularly and openly so that the work of God through deaconesses everywhere would be strengthened and encouraged. Again, imagine such a spirit of sharing knowledge and experience characterizing the global network of Methodism.

These, then, are five core elements we garner from the Methodist deaconess movement of the nineteenth and twentieth centuries:

Unite knowledge and vital piety
Live simply, even communally
Unify evangelism and humanitarianism
Move out beyond the church walls

52 "Our Bible Reading Table for 1906," *Flying Leaves* 50 (January 1906): 14.

53 "Our American Sisters," *Highways and Hedges: The Children's Advocate, The Organ of the Children's Home* 60 (December 1892): 234.

Share knowledge and experience across a global network

These elements supply a much-needed blueprint toward a revival in global Methodism today.

Chapter Bibliography

Primary Sources

Burns, W. H. "Methodism in Transition," *Northwestern Christian Advocate* (August 22, 1877): 6.

"Deaconess Work in Salford." *Highways and Hedges: The Children's Advocate, The Organ of the Children's Home* 86 (February 1895): 38.

"A Dinner-Hour Service." *Highways and Hedges: The Children's Advocate, The Organ of the Children's Home* 131 (November 1898): 260.

Harbord, Lena. "Girls' Clubs." *Highways and Hedges: The Children's Advocate, The Organ of the Children's Home* 121 (January 1898): 19–20.

"A Letter from Leeds." *Flying Leaves* 70 (November 1907): 154.

Masters, Thirza. "Lives of Wesley Deaconesses. Sister Thirza Masters." *Flying Leaves* 25 (November 1903): 168–69.

Meyer, Lucy Rider. *Deaconesses, Biblical, Early Church, European, American, with the Story of the Chicago Training School, for City, Home and Foreign Missions, and the Chicago Deaconess Home.* 2nd ed. Chicago: The Message Publishing Company, 1889.

———. "Deaconesses and the Need." *The Message* 5 (1890): 9.

"The Mission Field at Home and Abroad: Notanda." *Highways and Hedges: The Children's Advocate, The Organ of the Children's Home* 118 (October 1897): 232.

"Much the Same in America." *Highways and Hedges: The Children's Advocate, The Organ of the Children's Home* 127 (July 1898): 164.

"The Order of Service for the Ordination of Deaconesses." London: Methodist Publishing House, n.d.

"Our American Sisters." *Highways and Hedges: The Children's Advocate, The Organ of the Children's Home* 60 (December 1892): 234.

"Our Bible Reading Table for 1906." *Flying Leaves* 50 (January 1906): 14.

"A Pathetic Incident." *Flying Leaves* 32 (June 1904): 85.

"In Perils Oft. By a Wesley Deaconess." *Flying Leaves* 73 (February 1908): 201–2.

Pitts, Elizabeth Ann. Diary. John Rylands Library.

"A Recognition Service." *Highways and Hedges: The Children's Advocate, The Organ of the Children's Home* 57 (September 1892): 178.

Searle, Elise. "Notes from Norwich." *Highways and Hedges: The Children's Advocate, The Organ of the Children's Home* (June 1895): 118–19.

———. "A Unique Congregation." *Highways and Hedges: The Children's Advocate, The Organ of the Children's Home* 91 (July 1895): 136.

"Some Wesley Deaconesses and Their Work." *Flying Leaves* 98 (May 1910): 77.

Stephenson, Dora. "What Is a Deaconess?" *Highways and Hedges: The Children's Advocate, The Organ of the Children's Home* 95 (December 1895): 219–20.

"A Student's View of College Life. By a Student." *Flying Leaves* 109 (May 1911): 72–73.

Thoburn, James. "Deaconesses and the Church." *The Message* 5, no. 9 (September 1890): 6–8.

"True." *Flying Leaves* 33 (July–August 1904): 102.

Wardle, Addie G., comp. *A Report on Deaconess Work.* Chicago: Methodist Deaconess Association, 1908.

Wheeler, Henry. *Deaconesses Ancient and Modern*. New York: Hunt & Eaton, 1889.

"The White-Striped Veil." *Flying Leaves* 54 (May 1906): 71.

Secondary Sources

Albanese, Catherine L. "Horace Bushnell among the Metaphysicians." *Church History* 79, no. 3 (September 2010): 614–53.

Armstrong, Anthony. *The Church of England, Methodists and Society, 1700–1850.* London: University of London Press, 1973.

Bradfield, William. *The Life of the Reverend Thomas Bowman Stephenson, B.A., LL.D., D.D.* London: Charles H. Kelly, 1913.

Bushnell, Horace. *Discourses on Christian Nurture.* Boston: Massachusetts Sabbath School Society, 1847.

Cajiuat, Amelita Grace G., and Liwliwa Tubayan Robledo. "The Impact of Deaconesses in the Life of the United Methodist Church in the Philippines." https://www.unitedmethodistwomen.org/what-we-do/service-and-advocacy/deaconess-and-home-missioner-office/news-resources/cajiuat robeldo.pdf.

Dougherty, Mary Agnes. "The Methodist Deaconess, 1885–1918: A Study in Religious Feminism." PhD diss., University of California, Davis, 1979.

Field, Clive. "The Social Structure of English Methodism, Eighteenth to Twentieth Centuries." *British Journal of Sociology* 28, no. 2 (June 1977): 199–225.

Fresh Expressions. "What Is a Fresh Expression?" September 10, 2018. http://freshexpressions.org.uk/about/what-is-a-fresh-expression/.

Graham, Dorothy E. *Saved to Serve: The Story of the Wesley Deaconess Order, 1890–1978*. Werrington, UK: Methodist Publishing House, 2002.

Horton, Isabelle. *The Builders: A Story of Faith and Works.* Chicago: The Deaconess Advocate, 1910.

———. *High Adventure: Life of Lucy Rider Meyer.* New York: Garland Publishing, 1987.

Joseph, Nathan. *Uniforms and Nonuniforms: Communication through Clothing.* New York: Greenwood Press, 1986.

Lurie, Alison. *The Language of Clothes.* New York: Random House, 1981.

Macleod, David I. *Building Character in the American Boy: Boy Scouts, the YMCA, and Their Forerunners, 1870–1920.* Madison: University of Wisconsin Press, 1983.

Marty, Martin. *Protestantism in the United States: Righteous Empire.* Chicago: University of Chicago Press, 1986.

McCulloh, Gerald. *Ministerial Education in the American Methodist Movement.* Nashville: United Methodist Board of Higher Education and Ministry, 1980.

Rack, Henry. "Wesleyan Methodism 1849–1902." In *A History of the Methodist Church in Great Britain*, edited by Rupert Davies, A. Raymond George, and Gordon Rupp, 119–66. London: Epworth Press, 1983.

Robert, Dana. *American Women in Mission: A Social History of Their Thought and Practice.* Macon, GA: Mercer University Press, 1996.

Robledo, Liwliwa. "Gender, Religion and Social Change: A Study of Philippine Methodist Deaconesses, 1903–1978." PhD diss., The Iliff School of Theology and University of Denver, 1996.

Sider, Ronald J., Philip N. Olson, and Heidi Rolland Unruh, *Churches That Make a Difference: Reaching Your Community with Good News and Good Works.* Grand Rapids, MI: Baker, 2002.

Smaby, Beverly Prior. "'Only Brothers Should Be Accepted into This Proposed Council': Restricting Women's Leadership in Moravian Bethlehem." In *Pietism in Germany and North America 1680–1820*, edited by Jonathan Strom, Hartmut Lehmann, James Van Horn Melton, 133–62. Burlington, VT: Ashgate, 2009.

Taves, Ann. *Fits, Trances, and Visions: Experiencing Religion and Explaining Experience from Wesley to James.* Princeton, NJ: Princeton University University Press, 1999.

Wellings, Martin. "'A Time to Be Born and a Time to Die'? A Historian's Perspective on the Future of Methodism." In *Methodism and the Future: Facing the Challenge,* edited by Jane Craske and Clive Marsh, 148–56. London: Cassell, 1999.

Wuthnow, Robert. *Boundless Faith: The Global Outreach of American Churches.* Berkeley: University of California Press, 2009.

Rethinking Gospel, Mission, and Church in Contemporary Sri Lanka

Albert W. Jebanesan

THE PRIMARY PURPOSE OF THIS chapter is to identify the principal opportunities and challenges for global Methodism in presenting the gospel of Jesus Christ. In the very composition of this chapter, one certain but double-edged implication became clear: global Methodism presents Christians with a rare opportunity to think afresh about how we steward the gospel in light of complex global realities as well as how we conduct ourselves as members of a genuine global faith. One warning confronting all who consider this rethinking is the troubling consequence of not taking appropriate advantage of this opportunity. If we take seriously the theme of the 2018 Oxford Institute—"Thy Grace Restore, Thy Work Revive"—such rethinking of mission is unavoidable. To understand this concept, in the following pages, we focus on Sri Lanka as an example. Roman Catholic Christianity came to Sri Lanka in 1505 with the Portuguese. Today about two million people call themselves Christians because of Roman Catholic and Protestant missions.

The Christian faith stands on the command of Jesus: "Go therefore and make disciples of all nations" (Matt. 28:19, RSV). Those who have heard and known the good tidings are to call others to share in it. From this simple and direct beginning in the words of Jesus, Christians have evolved a rich complex of religious ideas and institutions under the name of mission and evangelism. But the very mention of the word *evangelism* nowadays inevitably stirs deep emotions. Whether people are passionately in favor of it or vaguely uneasy about it, evangelism is an issue important to the church.

The word suggests many images. An older generation in Sri Lanka may remember the tent meetings organized by the Tent Mission in villages, with its impassioned preaching and enthusiastic singing. Others may recall revival services held on open-air stages or in chapels or rural churches where the gospel was proclaimed to rescue people from immorality and eternal damnation.[1]

In the popular mind, however, evangelism, at least as it has been practiced in recent times, has caused considerable ambiguity. Criticism of evangelists has come from those not only outside the church but also within. While all churches are officially committed to fulfilling Christ's Great Commission, many have deep reservations about some of the techniques being used today. When Christian missionaries—the Portuguese, Dutch, and British—invaded the island of Sri Lanka in the sixteenth, seventeenth, and eighteenth centuries using aggressive mission campaigns, this generated a backlash that still, today, poisons Buddhist–Christian or Hindu–Christian relationships in Sri Lanka. Christians spreading the gospel, Buddhists and Hindus making attempts to revive their religions using the education received through the missionary schools, will throw light on this crucial encounter.

The hate campaign started against Christians by the Buddhists and Hindus might illuminate the methodologies adopted by the Christian missions. On Monday, December 29, 2003, dozens of Buddhist monks protested against "unethical conversions" by Christians and demanded anti-conversion laws be enacted immediately.[2] One hundred Buddhist monks of the Jathika Sangha Sammelanaya (National

1 Anna B. Taft, *The Tent Mission* (New York: Department of Church and Country Life, The Board of Home Missions of the Presbyterian Church in the U.S.A., n.d.), https://ia600503.us.archive.org/26/items/tentmission03taft/tentmission03taft.pdf.

2 "Buddhist Monks Demand Anti-Conversion Bill in Sri Lanka," Zee News, December 29, 2003, https://zeenews.india.com/news/south-asia/buddhist-monks-demand-anticonversion-bill-in-sri-lanka_139032.html.

Sanga Council) commenced a hunger strike "unto death" opposite the Ministry of Buddhist Affairs (Buddha Sasana) building, urging the government and President Chandrika Kumaratunga to bring in laws to curb "unethical conversions."[3] Various events, demonstrations, and, at times, attacks led by Buddhist monks overpowering police, vandalizing church properties, and assaulting Christian workers also have taken place in different parts of Sri Lanka.[4] On December 26, 2013, an incident occurred against a Methodist church construction as a monument at Buttala to mark the bicentenary of the Methodist Church Sri Lanka. The construction began after obtaining the necessary approvals but was stopped by a group of more than two hundred people after a demonstration, in spite of the intervention of the divisional secretary and police.

Defining Mission

Twice in the last century, the Church of England has attempted to formulate the nature and scope of evangelism. A commission appointed by the archbishops of Canterbury and York offered the well-known definition of evangelism: "To evangelize is so to present Christ Jesus in the power of the Holy Spirit, that men shall come to put their trust in God

3 "The anxiety that Sri Lankan Buddhists feel about the question of conversion cannot be divorced from the political domination they experienced for five centuries under the colonial powers. The oppressions that the Buddhist monks, temples, and communities had to undergo as well as the aggressive evangelistic methods used to convert people during that period are well documented. Colonial governments that originally disdained the missionary movement later supported the missionaries, when they discovered that conversion to Christianity also shifted the political allegiances of many in favor of the colonial government, or that at least subdued the potential for political agitation." Shanta Premawardhana, ed., "Introduction," in *Religious Conversion: Religion Scholars Thinking Together* (West Sussex, UK: John Wiley & Sons Limited, 2015), 1.

4 "Monks Attack Church in Sri Lanka," *Christian Today*, December 12, 2012, http://www.christiantoday.com/article/monks.attack.church.in.sri.lanka/31232.htm.

through him, to accept him as their Saviour, and serve him as their king in the fellowship of his Church."[5] This definition contains the classical New Testament elements of evangelism. The focus is on calling all people to faith in Jesus Christ. The call is given in the power of the Holy Spirit. In other words, we are able to offer up our best efforts in preaching, teaching, counseling, visiting, praying, and organizing for evangelism, but it is still the work of the Holy Spirit that finally convinces people and brings them to faith. Faith in Christ involves a new personal relationship of trust in God, which brings eternal life. From this relationship to God flows service to Christ. To be a disciple of Jesus is to serve God in every part of the created order because Christ rules over all. This faith and service link us in fellowship with other believers in the life of the church, where faith is strengthened and moral commitment guided.

The commission's definition of evangelism states the task in classical Christian terms. Its use of the language of the New Testament, however, raises the question of whether it can be translated into modern terms. Any theology of evangelism deals with two matters. On the one hand, there is the question of faithfulness to God's saving work in Christ. On the other hand, there is the question, no less important, of the world to which this saving word is addressed. The message must be expressed in a language people can understand. As we seek to witness to our neighbor, we are aware that the neighbor speaks the language of his or her culture and religion, not Christian religious language. Effective evangelism requires careful thinking about how the Christian faith may be interpreted for our contemporaries.

The task of bringing the good news of Jesus Christ as Savior and Lord is no longer simply the renewing and encouraging of a faith already present. What is needed is a new way of expressing the good news of God's grace in Jesus Christ. Perhaps the best way to get at this

---

5 Bishop of Rochester (Christopher Chavasse) et al., *Towards the Conversion of England: A Plan Dedicated to the Memory of Bishop William Temple, Being the Report of a Commission on Evangelism Appointed by the Archbishops of Canterbury and York* (London: Press and Publications Board of the Church Assembly, 1945), 156.

reformulation is to start with a basic question: What are people really asked to accept when they are urged to have faith in Jesus Christ?

The Great Commission

Many Christians in Sri Lanka possess, in addition to the Bible and prayer book or devotional text, a book on the adventures of missionaries. These books tell of those heroes and heroines of the faith who, in obedience to Christ's Great Commission to make disciples of all people (Matt. 28:19), had gone to distant and dangerous places with the message of salvation. The stories of David Livingstone, adventuring in a trackless wilderness to oppose slave traders, made fascinating fare for faith and imagination. Missionaries were pictured, being confronted by lions, or praying unaware to stealthy intruders of murderous intent. The life of a missionary seemed to be one adventure after another, with little mention of dreary months of trekking, learning languages, or overcoming the ravages of disease. Missionaries always seemed to be delivered by direct divine intervention or, failing this, they died peacefully, with blessings on their lips.

The vigor of missionary outreach that promises salvation to those lost in pagan religions and autocratic societies has continued among mainline Methodists, Anglicans, and other Protestants, as well as Roman Catholics. Faithful missionaries still serve in distant and difficult places, but the media of the mission organizations no longer supply us with pious adventure stories. Mission organizations have even changed their names to suit modern thinking.[6] Now we may purchase books on interreligious dialogue and anthropological study. Christians of the United Kingdom who send missionaries to "heathens" no longer find tales of grateful natives receiving the gospel interesting. Instead,

6 For example, what was formerly called the United Society for the Propagation of the Gospel (USPG) now goes by the new name United Society, to be known as "Us." "Anglican Mission Agency USPG Announces Plans to Change Its Name," Anglican Communion News Service, June 26, 2012, https://www.anglicannews.org/news/2012/06/anglican-mission-agency-uspg-announces-plans-to-change-its-name.aspx.

Christian missions are faced with sharp questions about the injustices caused by multinational corporations. We see the need to draw from the creative insights of traditional religions. What has happened to the Christian mission? Have we lost our commitment so that we no longer share Christ enthusiastically with others? Or has the Christian mission entered a new phase in response to God's leading? To answer these questions we need to look at what Christian missions have accomplished already. We also need to find what it means to express faith in Christ in a culture different from our own. What does faith in Jesus Christ as Savior and Lord mean for those whose lives are guided by ethnic memories and spiritual visions so different from our own Christian culture? What form does Christian discipleship take in modern Africa, Asia, Latin America, or the Middle East? To deal with these questions, we need to develop a theology of mission. The first step in learning to do a mission theology is to go back and look at what impelled the modern missionary movement as it traveled from Europe and North America into the rest of the world.

The Missionary Movement

The missionary movement grew out of the evangelical renewal of the churches that swept through Europe and North America in the seventeenth and eighteenth centuries. The Lutherans of Germany and Scandinavia, the puritans, nonconformists, and Methodists in England and later in the United States, the Moravians, Baptists, and a host of spiritualistic groups were being renewed by a fresh vision of the converting power of a personal relationship with Jesus Christ. The vitality of their newfound faith at home was not to be limited to their own communities. This was also the age of exploration, colonization, and imperialism. Europe and the United States were expanding their influence and culture into the rest of the world. Trade brought not only exotic goods, spices and silk, china dishes and tea, gold and gunpowder, but tales of exotic peoples. Western Christians were becoming aware in a dramatic way of the peoples of Asia, Africa, Latin America, and the Middle East. Non-Western countries were people who had no notion of Christ, church, or the message of salvation. The inhabitants of these distant lands were now perceived as ripe for conversion and ready to hear the gospel of Jesus Christ. The reports of merchant traders and military adventurers told of people in slavery who were bound by superstitious religions and barbarous cults. The missionary movement started to bring to these people the freeing power of Jesus Christ. These missionaries believed that the gospel not only delivered people from eternal damnation, but transformed their lives and opened the way to modern education, medicine, agriculture, and commerce.

William Harvard, a pioneer Methodist missionary to Sri Lanka, wrote a book called *A Narrative of the Establishment and Progress of Mission to Ceylon and India* (1823). The title itself expresses his main idea. Harvard argued that people had the freedom to accept Christ. But to make good on this offer of salvation, carefully planned means of witness were to be used so that the message could be heard by those who were ignorant of it. The learning of native languages, the translation of the Bible, the study of the cultural background of non-Christian peoples, and the teaching of natives to be pastors were the means by which Harvard and the missionaries brought about the conversion of non-Christian populations. They were inventive in their approach to preaching and not only saw to it that the gospel was heard but also lived in the places where they settled. Harvard did not believe the missionary worked alone. The Holy Spirit also worked in and through those who had made their commitment to Christ. Their own commitment was vital. Another Methodist missionary, Thomas Squance, preached his first Methodist sermon at the Dutch Church in Galle on Sunday, July 3, 1814, based on 2 Corinthians 10:14 (KJV): "We are come as far as to you also in preaching the gospel of Christ." The non-Christians would be converted and the kingdom of Christ spread across the world. Here was a dynamic, democratic theology, launched with the vigorous confidence of the Western world.

What missionaries saw in Sri Lanka as technological backwardness, injustice, superstition, fear, and chaos were proof to them of the folly of the religions of the natives. The missionaries of Europe and North America were convinced that they brought not only a superior religion, but the superior culture that grew out of it. Christianity and Western civilization were closely linked. Mission was a matter not simply of preaching, but of sharing the full resources of an advanced civilization. When modern farming had replaced inefficient traditional ways, modern medicine had brought the healing that native medicine could not, and vigorous trading societies had made slavery unprofitable, the full impact of Christianity would be felt. Jesus Christ eventually would be Lord of all. The missionaries came with not only Bible in hand, but also plows, printing presses, medicine chests, and schoolbooks. The vision was one of great vigor and confidence. It reflected a vital religious faith and an expansive culture confident of its own rightness. There was for these missionaries only one way to God. There was also only one way for humankind to move into the future—the way of modern Western civilization.

Colonization

Deep and pervasive changes have come into mission theology in the twentieth century. Church leaders no longer look to the mission theology of the eighteenth and nineteenth centuries as a norm to which they must adhere. Rather, they see it as the beginning of Christian missions in the age of colonialism. With the emergence of new nations of the developing world, new theologies are needed to deal with the challenges and opportunities of today. Mission theology has been challenged at two points. It has been challenged in those situations in which its vision of triumph has not been fulfilled, and paradoxically, it also has been most deeply challenged at those places in which the church has been established and experienced its greatest growth.

If you look at the Sri Lankan context, Christianity is still a small fraction of the Sri Lankan population (8 percent). All Christian actions take place in a non-Christian world and are intimately interwoven with the actions and collaboration of peoples of other faiths and ideologies. Christians have to interact with non-Christians in all places of work and study to survive. The Christians cannot filter, as it were, only what they find morally good by the standards of a hypothetical Christian ethics, religiously true by the standards of Christian dogma. They cannot ignore the rest, and they must offer their most cordial indiscriminate collaboration to whatever is good, true, and beautiful in the cultures where the community of the Christian faithful have to live. The transition from missionary compound to immersion in the world is not easy and is often painful, but it is an irreversible process. Christians cannot refuse collaboration with others in nation-building on the grounds that the optimal conditions for collaboration are not visible there or that the peoples of other faiths are unable or unwilling to agree with them.[7]

The historical fact is that Christianity has not won a large-scale acceptance in Asia with the exception of the Philippines.[8] With this fact in view, Aloysius Pieris argues that when Christianity came to Asia, it created a Christ-against-religions theology.[9] Mission in the Sri Lankan context, then, emerges from a different perspective and angle. It adds fresh and refreshing reflections to the traditional Christian theologies and at the same time initiates new praxis to work among the human communities of Sri Lanka, saturated as they are with religiosity. This is again an important factor to do mission among people of Sri Lanka and by Sri Lankans. The Christian theology of incarnation also must become incarnate in the Asian cultural and economic flesh of the Asian masses. This theology will be done in the context of non-Christian experience and will gravitate between the two poles of the social reality today and the normative message received from the past.

Some Observations

The Limits of Mission

The vision of a Christian triumph over all the religions of the world has not been fulfilled. Neither the twentieth nor the twenty-first century

7 Raimundo Panikkar, "Common Grounds for Christian–Non-Christian Collaboration," in *Religion and Society*, ed. R. W. Taylor (Bangalore: The Christian Institute for the Study of Religion and Society, 1982), 27–28.

8 Aloysius Pieris, *An Asian Theology of Liberation* (Edinburgh: T&T Clark, 1988), 59.

9 Pieris, *An Asian Theology of Liberation*, 60.

have become "The Christian Century" as was earnestly expected. Christians make up about 30 percent of the world, according to the most optimistic estimates. As Christianity grows rapidly in Africa, it is shrinking in its old centers of strength, North America, Europe, and Russia. Hinduism, Buddhism, and Islam have not vanished from the earth; instead, they have experienced renewal and growth. The ancient religions of China have diminished, not to be replaced by Christianity, but by Marxism. The nations of Africa and Asia have returned to their ancient spiritual resources for guidance. Hindu, Buddhist, and Sufi teachers now journey to the West to offer new religious resources to dispirited secularists.

The world at the beginning of the twenty-first century is religiously plural and shows every sign of remaining that way. If the claim for the universal lordship of Christ is to be more than an assertion, it must be reinterpreted in relation to the continuing existence and vitality of non-Christian religions. Is it possible to believe that God, the creator and sustainer of the whole world, is graciously disposed toward less than a third of his children because they were born into a culture affording them a chance of responding to the word?

From Mission to Church

The hopes of the missionary pioneers of the nineteenth century for the spread of the church have largely been fulfilled. Christianity is found throughout the world. In some places, its existence is marginal; in others, it has vigor and expansive power. In the year 2000, there were more Christians in Africa than on any other continent. Christianity has claimed the minds and hearts of millions of Koreans and Indonesians. Christian leaders, notably the late Bishop Desmond Tutu, shaped the anti-apartheid struggle in South Africa. The churches of Latin America struggle for liberation in response to the freeing power of Jesus. Intellectual leaders, writers, and artists in Japan and India ponder the meaning of Jesus for them and their culture.

This transition from foreign mission to Indigenous church reflects more than administrative reorganization. It reflects deep theological change. The modern missionary movement has fulfilled its vision in which Christianity has become expressed through the culture of the people to which it has gone. Here is where the transition from mission to church has taken place. It is the transition from Christianity as a foreign religion brought by outsiders to being a religion rooted in its own time and place and led by its own people. That Christianity is capable of such transition is what makes mission to non-Christians possible. The name given to the process of transition is *Indigenization* or *contextualization*. It is the process by which Christian faith becomes incarnate in another culture and shares its values, visions, and symbols yet does not lose its own identity. It is the process by which Christian faith is lived in a new and different context of life from that of the missionaries who brought it. To understand the theology of Indigenization, we need to go back and look at the way in which missionaries brought Christianity to the non-Western world.

Christianity and Culture

Christian missionaries took a faith that was closely tied to Western civilization beyond the bounds of Europe and the Americas. Students in mission schools built by missionaries were more likely to be reading Shakespeare or studying the history of Washington and Lincoln than learning the traditions and history of Sri Lankans. Sri Lankan societies in the colonial world were weakened by colonial economies that tied them to the mills and factories of the West. Home gardens and small farms were submerged into great tea, coffee, rubber, and cocoa plantations. English, the language of the mission school, became the language of the new elite. Tribal burial practices, naming ceremonies, marriage rites, and harvest festivals were rejected by missionaries as dangerous pagan customs. Hymns were sung in native languages, although the hymn tunes were from English or American hymnbooks. The Sri Lankan cultural music and musical instruments were kept outside the church because of their association with the religious rituals of the unconverted. Inside, organs wheezed out hymns and music of the Western world or the revival songs of Charles Wesley, according to the taste of the missionaries.

To use the distinction between theologies that look at the bright side or the shadow side of human nature, we might say the modern missionary movement tended to see the bright side of Western civilization and the shadow side of the civilizations of Sri Lanka. With such a vision, Christianity made little progress in becoming part of the new context of life to which it had been taken. Christianity lived in little islands of Western civilization created in other lands. It needed a radical contextualization. The church needed to be planted firmly on Sri Lankan soil and allowed to draw nourishment from its native ground. When Christianity is Indigenized, it is born afresh as part of that time and place without losing its own genius.

As daring as this seemed at the time and as sharply rebutted as it was by conservatives, Indigenization remained largely an intellectual matter stage-managed by Americans and Europeans. With the end of colonialism after World War II, Indigenization, or as it is more frequently called today, contextualization, has entered a new phase. The new theologies of contextualization see it as a process involving the whole church, not something Western intellectuals can do for others. Contextualizing the Christian faith must be done from within a culture by those who belong to it.

The churches of Asia, including the independent churches, are drawing freely on the music and ecstatic worship of Asian traditions in place of the staid liturgies of their missionary past. Can Christians use the burial rites, naming ceremonies, or wedding customs of their communities? Did Christian missionaries bring God to Asia? Or was God there already? The key affirmation of Asian theologians in contextualizing Christian faith is that Jesus came not to abolish but to fulfill what had come before him (Matt. 5:17). To be a Christian means building on the strengths of one's culture while transforming its weaknesses.

In Asia, C. S. Song has used Chinese and Polynesian folktales to interpret the gospel.[10] The Japanese theologian Kosuke Koyama[11] has

---

10 See C. S. Song, *Tell Us Our Names: Story Theology from an Asian Perspective* (Eugene, OR: Wipf and Stock, 2005).

11 See Kosuke Koyama, *Mount Fuji and Mount Sinai: A Critique of Idols* (Maryknoll, NY: Orbis Books, 1985).

developed a critical theology by his meditation on Mount Fuji and Mount Sinai: a critique of idols. And in Latin America, Christianity is being contextualized afresh from within the struggle for social, economic, and political liberation. A new generation of theologians has plunged more deeply into the religious culture of India to discover what Raimundo Panikkar called "the unknown Christ of Hinduism."[12] In Korea, Christians are fashioning a new theology based on the tense sociopolitical situation in which these people have lived so long. Kim Yong Bock works with a Minjung theology,[13] articulating the gospel in light of the Korean experience of unjustified suffering and the resolve to establish an ideal realm in redemption. It is a theology drawing on the deepest memories of folk culture and existential concerns for the present day.

No one of these theologies is complete, nor have the churches given considered judgment to them all. They are theologies in process. But the key is the shift in consciousness they represent. The churches of developing nations are not waiting to take over ready-made theology from the West. They are fashioning a theology out of the resources that their own cultures and experiences have given them.

It is not possible for Christians, the contextual theologians argue, to divide the world into realms of light and darkness. As they insist, "The light shines in the darkness, and the darkness has not overcome it" (John 1:5, RSV). As the presence of God becomes real in any place, the elements of its culture that have the power of deepening and enlarging human life become evident. Wherever compassion is present, truth is known and love is at work. They are there as God's gift to be accepted and rejoiced in by Christians, even when they bear names given them by other religions and cultures.

The old images used to describe religious change do not fit the present realities. We have been used to thinking of mission in terms of crusades or campaigns that would end up with a conquest of lands

12 See Raimundo Panikkar, *The Unknown Christ of Hinduism: Towards an Ecumenical Christophany* (Maryknoll, NY: Orbis Books, 1981).

13 Wikiwand, s.v., "Minjung Theology," accessed January 19, 2021, http://www.wikiwand.com/en/Minjung_theology.

and the replacement of one religion by another. What is happening can better be described as a process of transformation. The proclamation of the gospel in word and deed is a transforming power that encounters the spiritual vision, ethical values, and community life of the people to which it comes. The power of God's love appropriates from each culture the means of expressing the new being in Christ. In this process, the culture is transformed but not destroyed. The negative elements of the culture are rejected; the creative elements are given new life.

"The deeds of boldness" of the Methodist missionaries of the past live on. Today they take different forms. The process of contextualization is a difficult and demanding one. It requires spiritual, emotional, and intellectual courage to claim unfamiliar ideas and customs for the proclamation of the gospel. Yet if the risks of contextualization are not taken, Christianity increasingly will become a ghetto religion of the Western world. Making the biblical message meaningful in terms that the people can understand, facilitating critical reflection on the message of Scripture in the particular cultural context, and helping the people internalize the message will continue to make Methodism relevant to people within a particular culture. As Raimundo Panikkar observed, Jesus did not come to found the one holy catholic and apostolic sect.[14] The goal of contextualization is not comfort but clarity. The church of Jesus Christ is by its nature in and for the world. It is not a sectarian enclave but a light. What the theologians and peoples of the churches of developing nations are doing is finding how that light is entering their own time and place.

Chapter Bibliography

"Anglican Mission Agency USPG Announces Plans to Change Its Name." Anglican Communion News Service, June 26, 2012. https://www.anglicannews.org/news/2012/06/anglican-mission-agency-uspg-announces-plans-to-change-its-name.aspx.

14 Panikkar, *The Unknown Christ of Hinduism*, Introduction.

"Buddhist Monks Demand Anti-Conversion Bill in Sri Lanka." Zee News, December 29, 2003. https://zeenews.india.com/news/south-asia/buddhist-monks-demand-anticonversion-bill-in-sri-lanka_139032.html.

Chavasse, Christopher, et al. *Towards the Conversion of England: A Plan Dedicated to the Memory of Bishop William Temple, Being the Report of a Commission on Evangelism Appointed by the Archbishops of Canterbury and York* London: Press and Publications Board of the Church Assembly, 1945.

Koyama, Kosuke. *Mount Fuji and Mount Sinai: A Critique of Idols.* Maryknoll, NY: Orbis Books, 1985.

"Monks Attack Church in Sri Lanka." *Christian Today*, December 12, 2012. http://www.christiantoday.com/article/monks.attack.church.in.sri.lanka/31232.htm.

Panikkar, Raimundo. "Common Grounds for Christian–Non-Christian Collaboration." In *Religion and Society*, edited by R. W. Taylor, 5:26–36. Bangalore: The Christian Institute for the Study of Religion and Society, 1982.

———. *The Unknown Christ of Hinduism: Towards an Ecumenical Christophany.* Maryknoll, NY: Orbis Books, 1981.

Pieris, Aloysius. *An Asian Theology of Liberation.* Edinburgh: T&T Clark, 1988.

Song, C. S. *Tell Us Our Names: Story Theology from an Asian Perspective.* Eugene, OR: Wipf and Stock, 2005.

Taft, Anna B. *The Tent Mission.* New York: Department of Church and Country Life, The Board of Home Missions of the Presbyterian Church in the U.S.A., n.d. https://ia600503.us.archive.org/26/items/tentmission03taft/tentmission03taft.pdf.

Wikiwand, s.v. "Minjung Theology." http://www.wikiwand.com/en/Minjung_theology.

Immigration, Religion, and the Working Class: Toni Morrison's Disremembering and the Politics of a New Minority

Nichole R. Phillips

Introduction

History *and* memory as well as history *as* memory function to recount the minoritized status of working-class whites in Barking and Dagenham, East London and in Youngstown, Ohio. Both groups represent what political scientist Justin Gest terms the *new* minorities of the United Kingdom and United States. History *and* memory as well as history *as* memory additionally relate the experiences of an ethnocultural group conventionally known to hold minority-status, working-class Black Americans and their youth. What distinguishes history *and* memory from history *as* memory—both forms of remembering—is selective forgetting. Selective forgetting poses the following questions based on the power of framing: What is included in retelling group history? What details are excluded? Are there aspects of a group's history that are essential to the group's self-image?

In terms of selective forgetting, particular features of social history are overlooked or selected by group members based on the relevance and significance to group identity and self-image. For these three groups, history *and* memory as well as history *as* memory are rehearsed social narratives of displacement and, for one of the three, also a narrative about Toni Morrison's concept of disremembering—or tragedy. Each group's history *and* memory will be contextualized and explored.

Though different social processes, remembering and forgetting are two sides of the same coin.[1] And so, selective forgetting in this context raises the question of the minoritization of white working classes. In other words, to what extent can the term *minority* be applied to white people and (rooted in social disadvantage)?

I argue that the tension between history *and* memory, evidenced by selective forgetting, communicates the plight of all three groups that have been exposed to drastic and macrostructural social changes and transformations, which leaves them struggling to fit into wider British and American social, economic, and political systems. Subsequently, I must ask, What is the role of religion or the church born of Methodism in reacting to these groups, many of whom are denominational members? What is an appropriate religious response to their respective plights? Each group warrants a church response. However, in light of potentially "closed borders" (the Brexit decision) and "building walls" (Trumpism), what becomes important is the question of whose minoritized status (e.g., working-class whites, working-class Blacks, undocumented immigrants, refugees, migrants, or a sundry of other displaced persons) and *to whom* will the church recognize and respond?

Cultural Memory: A Place to Call Home

A trans-/inter-/multidisciplinary field, cultural memory studies (CMS) is dedicated to studying the relationship between culture and memory. Social and cultural contexts shape memory. The interplay is described as a dialogue between the past and present. Memory is *not* observable; it is a capacity. Remembering, however, is a process observable in specific sociocultural contexts that assists our understanding of the nature and function of memory.[2] Three conceptual frameworks drive CMS: (1) lived experiences, (2) the selectivity and identity-related nature of

1 Astrid Erll, *Memory in Culture*, trans. Sara B. Young (New York: Palgrave Macmillan, 2011), 8.

2 Erll, *Memory in Culture*, 8.

group memory, and (3) the cultural transmission of memory through tradition.[3]

Social groups that experience trauma exit the historical moment with fragile collective memories, described as "having holes in them."[4] After such experiences, cultural memory is what remains.[5] Group members revisit social traditions and exchange shared versions of the past in order to create cultural meaning in the present. That lays the foundation for a collective future. Collective memories assist group members in (1) renegotiating group identity through the process of intentional remembering, which allows group members to focus on themselves and to reconstruct their social identities; (2) intentionally remembering a socially shared past through commemorations, celebrations, festivals, religious holidays, and intergenerational networks of communication; and (3) facilitating healing and repair to reconcile families and communities to the concept of "home."[6]

Individuals who experience displacement, forced migration, and expulsion, as well as members of a community exiled from native lands who afterwards spend an uncertain existence in refugee camps, anticipate and yearn for geographic spaces and places to call "home." Jewish feminist scholar Julia Epstein speaks to this by declaring, "It is the concept of home that is torn from victims of genocide and [social

---

3 Erll, *Memory in Culture*, 13–18.

4 Erll, *Memory in Culture*, 110.

5 Dan Stone, "Genocide and Memory," in *The Oxford Handbook of Genocide Studies*, ed. Donald Bloxham and A. Kirk Moses (Oxford: Oxford University Press, 2013), 102.

6 Julia Epstein, "Remember to Forget: The Problem of Traumatic Cultural Memory," in *Shaping Losses: Cultural Memory and the Holocaust*, ed. Julia Epstein and Lori Hope Lefkowitz (Urbana and Chicago: University of Illinois Press, 2001), 186–206. Julia Epstein writes about the influence of the community in shaping the individual self and consequently individual and social identities. Memory is a crucial aspect of self-development that occurs in relationship to "other selves in community" (194). When social selves experience a rupture of community because of a social threat, the interpretation of "home" is disrupted. Epstein further explains, "Under these conditions, acts of remembering replace the mental geography of place and of home" (194).

trauma]. . . . [These violations] slice through the continuity of selfhood in a collective way. . . . Under catastrophic historical circumstances, memory becomes a homeland."[7] Forms of cultural remembering are then captured by the "mediality of memory"—books, monuments, statues, museums, television, radio, visual art, music, and other media that serve collective interests through the group's interactions with a wider world.

History corresponds to cultural memory in two ways. History *and* memory suggests independent and distinguishable processes that mutually affect each other. Memory is the raw material of history based in a belief that the past happened in particular ways. Memory supplies oral, written, mental material to historians who objectively shape such material and conceptions into truth. In turn, history informs memory by involving individuals and societies that shape and produce collective memories through the dialectical experience of remembering and forgetting.[8] History *as* memory, on the other hand, is history-as-it-is-remembered or, said another way, history-as-cultural-remembering. History-as-cultural-remembering is interested in the "cultural practices of memory" or the "historical situatedness of memory cultures," meaning groups strongly influence selection and interpretation of past events.[9]

I will address how history *and* memory is more so a historical project by supplying cultural histories of the groups and how history *as* memory is more a memorial project making selective forgetting a critical concept. Examples of how the groups operationalize history *as* memory will also be shared. I contend that both history *and* memory and history *as* memory contribute to reinforcing the minoritized status of three groups—working-class whites in East London and Youngstown and working-class Blacks and Black youth in America who are heavily involved with Black Lives Matter demonstrations.

I argue there is a tension and, at times, a disconnect between what is written in the historical record about the global, social, and

7 Epstein, "Remember to Forget," 194.

8 Erll, *Memory in Culture*, 41.

9 Erll, *Memory in Culture*, 45.

economic changes these groups experience as opposed to how these groups *remember, respond to*, and *interpret* these changes. This disconnect between history and memory also works as a bridge to reinforce working-class marginality and social displacement, especially that of working-class whites.[10] Although working-class whites are marginalized, questions remain about their minoritized status. How is "minoritization" defined? Is it by marginalization due to socioeconomic status and social displacement, by race, or by both? If the church born of Methodism is to address the border control and immigration problems challenging the United Kingdom and the United States, the church must first recognize minority status and marginalized populations and then decide to which groups and how it will respond.

History *and* Memory in East London

A brief history *and* memory of the East London cities of Barking and Dagenham, as written by Harvard- and London School of Economics–trained scholar Justin Gest, begins this section. Ethnographic research produced material from interviews of fifty-five people, including fifteen elites, during a three-month cultural immersion meant to capture the mindset, actions, and attitudes of the people. Gest declares: "The story of Barking and Dagenham gets told countless times, every day of every week, in every house and meeting place in the borough. From nan to her grandson, from mum to her daughter, from a barmaid to her regular, from one man smoking cigarettes in front of a betting shop to the passerby. Each time it is told, it changes ever so slightly."[11]

This history is written and also recorded as a proud oral history that continues to be circulated among the residents of the borough. That is Gest's claim. Barking and Dagenham emerged from a promise made by Prime Minister David Lloyd George to servicemen returning home from World War I. George developed a public housing complex

10 Justin Gest, *The New Minority: White Working Class Politics in an Age of Immigration and Inequality* (Oxford: Oxford University Press, 2016), 39, 74.

11 Gest, *The New Minority*, 39.

in 1920 to reward these servicemen with "homes fit for heroes."[12] On farmland east of the Barking town center, twenty-seven thousand cottages were constructed from 1921 to 1932. Designed to exceed working-class expectations, these cottages connected and featured indoor lavatories, fitted baths, electric furnishings, telephone lines, and front and back gardens.[13]

The first set of tenants, however, were impoverished, but with the arrival of May & Baker's chemical plant, which had relocated to Dagenham, the Barking Power House electric station established in Creekmouth, and Ford Motor Company's enormous factory on Dagenham's riverfront, thousands of transplants were attracted to the borough. During and after World War II, these employers provided plentifully and supplied dependable jobs to a growing labor market. In fact, Ford Motor Company's expansion in Dagenham produced a workforce of forty thousand employees at its peak in 1953 and three thousand cars daily on four million square feet of land. Housing development followed an exploding Dagenham population, which increased from nine thousand to ninety thousand between 1921 and 1931, adding to the combined populations of Dagenham and Barking and increasing another 50 percent before 1951.

Economic opportunity initially drew working-class white men and women from what Gest describes as a "congested and tumultuous" East End of London.[14] Wanting less competition and distraction, a simpler life, and greater independence, these women and men also migrated to Dagenham and Barking for the benefits of personal transformation. However, with Britain experiencing social transformation because of the spread of imperialism and the growth of industry, the East End was also becoming populated with Eastern European Jewish immigrants and South Asians fleeing the politics and poverty of a contentious Indian subcontinent. Another reason these East Enders found the borough attractive was because it became a "refuge for London's white

---

12 Gest, *The New Minority*, 41.

13 Gest, *The New Minority*, 41.

14 Gest, *The New Minority*, 42.

working class," who were employed in a coterie of industries by the 1960s, and where community life became a haven for the good life.[15]

However, by the mid-1970s, the Ford Motor Company in Dagenham faced increasing competition from the European car market, which led to the company restructuring its European operations and which signaled the eventual end of car production. The company dropped from more than 28,000 employees in 1975 to 7,300 in 2000 and finally stopped its vehicle assembly line in 2002. What happened at the Ford factory was indicative of the massive downsizing that would occur across industries because of market declines. Along with the shift to a postindustrial economy came "weakened unions, liberalized labor laws, and the move of industrial jobs abroad."[16] A more global and technological economy and extensive service sector had little use for Barking's and Dagenham's tradesmen.

As of today, manufacturing is considerably smaller and continuing to decline in Barking and Dagenham, where the major businesses are in logistics and transport. Furthermore, the borough could not insulate itself from the global economy and demographic shifts foreshadowed by the 1960s restructurings and transformations. A new generation of residents moved into Barking and Dagenham when working-class whites, whose jobs were eliminated, sold their homes and left the borough. Many of the new residents are immigrants who took advantage of the lower mortgages and rental homes in the east that were a fraction of the prices in London. They are a combination of highly skilled professionals who comprise Britain's diverse middle class as well as unskilled laborers who seek work in the service and construction sectors. Many are also refugees who are seeking to better their quality of life. Nevertheless, these drastic economic changes have precipitated social and macrostructural shifts that give Gest reason to identify Barking and Dagenham in East London as a "post-traumatic" city. Such cities he describes as "exurbs and urban communities that lost signature industries in the mid-to-late twentieth century and never really recovered."[17]

---

15 Gest, *The New Minority*, 42.

16 Gest, *The New Minority*, 9, 43.

17 Gest, *The New Minority*, 7.

History *as* Memory in East London

History retold is history *as* memory or history-as-cultural-remembering. Instead of retelling history-as-it-is-culturally-remembered, I offer vignettes of cultural memories for how residents of Barking and Dagenham *remember*, *interpret*, and *reacted to* global transformations. I will conclude with some thoughts about the ways in which these working-class whites have been marginalized.

East London eventually succumbed to massive cultural revolutions. These cultural changes are those from which generations of white working-class East Enders were fleeing and attempting to find shelter. People of immigrant origins did not simply complement the white working class; rather, by moving into empty spaces left by those who had moved out, these newcomers were perceived as supplanting East Enders' former neighbors, friends, colleagues, unionists, and drinking partners. The smells of foreign and exotic dishes emanated throughout hallways and buildings. Residents heard dialects, nontraditional English, and foreign languages in public buses. Grocers imported products from the newcomers' home countries to meet the demands of these immigrant groups. Neighborhood pubs closed and empty commercial spaces were turned into Muslim mosques and other types of religious sanctuaries. Gest observes, "Though Barking and Dagenham's remaining working class white people have been witnessing these changes for 30 years, they are still revising their narratives of them, reinterpreting their meaning and, in so doing, reimagining their past."[18]

How societies remember is the substance of social memories. Social memories communicate the experience of social and cultural groups and express their collective memories, while solidifying group identities. Following are three anecdotes from Barking and Dagenham residents and local officials representing history-as-cultural-remembering and the collectives' social memories over thirty years.[19]

---

18 Gest, *The New Minority*, 44.

19 Gest, *The New Minority*, 206. Gest supplied pseudonyms for the names of residents, local officials, and political and community leaders in order to facilitate free speech and to prevent repercussions locally after his book's

Lou and Maggie Griffiths are an older couple who live in a rented home in the old part of Dagenham. As they reimagine the past, they loudly proclaim:

> The borough was full of East Enders. People were very friendly. It was easy to settle in. People had come in after wartime, and the neighbors were good. *There was a sense of community, more so than there is now.* Since about 2004 or 2005, there was change in the borough that came with the influx of other cultures. Goresbrook Ward was previously 5% foreign; now 50% or 60% of the ward is foreign. *It is a massive change that happened too fast for people to cope with.* There's a heavy Muslim population. Africans have flooded in. They don't seem to mix with the existing community. *There's no infrastructure to deal with it, so everything got fragmented. We live in a multicultural society and I think that's good.* But when it happened so quickly, *the existing community feels threatened.* In the 1960s when the West Indians came in, no one was taken over and they mixed in. But the way we've been flooded, it inspires the animosity of right-wing groups. It's a matter of adapting, but some of these people don't speak English or make any attempt to fit in.[20]

Further, there was a time when local pubs were scattered throughout Barking and Dagenham; however, a majority of them have now closed. Pubs attract residents and regulars who connect with each other like an extended family. With the closings, locals are having to find new institutions for social engagement, and although that has increased social mixing and afforded new interactions, pub clientele are left without a place to call home. Eighteen-year-old Terry Hammonds, whom Gest encountered at one of the area's remaining and largest pubs, the Barking Dog, proves this argument by revising the past in sharing the following sentiments: "People come to the pub to have a rest from the outside. This is where they have their time together. They're just looking for a

publication. The only public officials exempted from pseudonymity were Barking MP Margaret Hodge and Youngstown mayor John McNally.

20 Gest, *The New Minority*, 46 (emphasis added).

beverage and a chat with other Englishmen. They can't get that outside. Here you can play darts, watch sports, and talk."[21]

In 2007, the Barking and Dagenham's borough council administered a survey asking several hundred [white] residents: "What can we do to make Barking and Dagenham better?"[22] The most prevalent answer that council administrators received was: "Make it like it used to be 50 years ago."[23] Working-class whites could have conceived of neither such radical changes nor their disorienting capacity, changes that nevertheless remain markers for future social progress.

Vincent Dogan is thirty-eight years old, was raised in Hackney, and was born to a Turkish Cypriot Muslim who married an Englishwoman. His father was naturalized as a British citizen before his death a few years ago. Dogan is a member of the British National Party, a splinter group from the far-right National Front party. The BNP's political platform is the immediate return of immigrants to their countries of origin and preferential treatment for indigenous [meaning white] British citizens. Dogan joined the BNP at seventeen years old after suffering a brutal mugging by Black teenagers. Here he reinterprets the past, stating:

> When I arrived in 2004, [Dagenham] was a sight for sore eyes. There weren't as many ethnics living here as in Hackney then. *The first thing I noticed when I came out of Dagenham Heathway Station was how white it was.* And I told people here, "You've got a nasty surprise coming your way." I saw it as a political opportunity. The white demographics were vastly in favor of the BNP. If you're not part of the [Liberal Democrat, Labour, or Conservative Parties'] trick, you're not mainstream. They all agree on everything, except for the minutiae of tax. They all want to stay in Europe, allow migration, and destroy British industry. We've lost our identity.[24]

---

21 Gest, *The New Minority*, 49.

22 Gest, *The New Minority*, 52.

23 Gest, *The New Minority*, 52.

24 Gest, *The New Minority*, 66 (emphasis added).

In *The Broken Covenant*, the late American sociologist Robert N. Bellah acknowledges, "One man's 'cultural pluralism' can then become another man's 'nativism' with all the classic elements of violence and repression that that entails."[25] What cannot be dismissed from all three history-as-cultural-remembering anecdotes is the implied nativism of respondents. How these white working-class East Enders remember, interpret, and react to their present is *by selectively forgetting* many aspects of their history.

Respecting population statistics, the 2011 census reported: "50% of the Barking and Dagenham borough is white British, 22% is of African or Afro-Caribbean origins, 16% South Asian origins, and 8% of Eastern European origins."[26] Notwithstanding these demographics, the more turbulent the macrostructural and global changes, the more inviting the past becomes through shared collective memories.

Although these social memories are conveyed from the perspective of nativity and its entitlements, history and memory point out the challenges facing these working-class white East Londoners in this new age. Both history and memory account for labor and economic shifts that have precipitated social, political, and economic displacement made evident through the decline in manufacturing jobs, disintegration of social and cultural networks, and loss of social and political identities. Therefore, a case can be made that these white working-class nativists are marginalized, having been pushed from the center of British life to its periphery.

History *and* Memory in Youngstown (Steel Capital, USA)

A brief history *and* memory of Youngstown, Ohio, part of the Rust Belt region of the United States, is shared here. As previously stated, Justin Gest examines the actions, attitudes, and mindset of this subpopulation

25 Robert N. Bellah, *The Broken Covenant: American Civil Religion in Time of Trial*, 2nd ed. (Chicago: University of Chicago Press, 1992), 109–10.

26 Gest's 2011 census findings were reported by the Office for National Statistics, UK, 2012, 47, https://www.ons.gov.uk/.

by way of ethnographic research. He fully immersed himself in the region and culture for three months and interviewed seventy-five people, twenty of whom were elites.[27] Elites were comprised of local community leaders and active citizens, executives and managers within the steel mill industry, city heads invested in local politics, and town members as participants in governmental affairs.

Locals profess that Youngstown was the steel capital of the world. The steel industry began in 1844 when a trace of black coal was found on David Tod's Brier Hill estate.[28] With this discovery came the establishment of a thirty-mile-long stretch of steel mills along the Mahoning River. Throughout the late 1800s and early 1900s, three major plants were created: the Youngstown Sheet and Tube Company of Campbell and Brier Hill; the Ohio Works of the United States Steel Corporation, west of Youngstown; and the Republic Steel Corporation, located in the downtown area. Steel production stimulated rapid population growth, which was also attributed to the arrival of European immigrants from the Levant (then known as the Eastern Mediterranean, now known as the historical region of Syria) and other parts of Europe. By 1930s, almost half of the residents owned their homes, and by the 1940s, the population reached 170,000.[29]

Steel workers and steelmaking came to symbolize and denote goodness, productivity, and power—three qualities that defined the spirit of Youngstown.[30] It was a town known for industry. Yet Youngstown's foundations are paradoxical. For more than a century, an oligarchy of families organized and structured workers' social lives and labor. Unions developed to protest unfair labor practices, wages, and working conditions. Nonetheless, ethnic segregation and discrimination simmered and threatened to disrupt worker protest movements. As Gest explains, housing and jobs were based on a social hierarchy with "white Protestants at the top, followed by the mix of Central and Eastern Europeans, the Jews, the Irish and Italians, and at the very bottom,

27 Gest, *The New Minority*, 75.
28 Gest, *The New Minority*, 76.
29 Gest, *The New Minority*, 76.
30 Gest, *The New Minority*, 76.

African Americans."[31] Laborers were exclusively represented as white and Protestant, giving rise to the Ku Klux Klan in the 1920s.

The group gained a foothold in local politics as they contested the arrival and growing influence of immigrant groups. To counteract this, organized crime syndicates developed. Italian, Sicilian, Neapolitan crime families, and other immigrant groups would comprise the Mafia. It cared for immigrant families during economic downturns and ensured immigrant access to jobs. An alternative police force, as Gest describes it, "the mob was . . . 'providing a measure of fairness' in a seemingly unjust, prejudiced and conflictive environment."[32]

The Mafia continued to grow from the 1960s to 1980s, becoming a powerful organization that infiltrated local politics and the business sector. For many working-class whites, "mafia days were golden days" in Youngstown.[33] However, death, destruction, and corruption followed backroom dealings with the mob. Despite that, their influence came to a halt in the late 1970s and early 1980s when Youngstown's steel industry buckled. On "Black Monday," September 19, 1977, Youngstown Sheet and Tube closed its Campbell Works mill.[34] The closings of the other two major steel mills followed in close proximity.

Afterwards, deindustrialization triggered the loss of fifty thousand jobs in steel and related industries over the course of the next six years. The working class lost $1.3 billion dollars in manufacturing wages and endured bankruptcies and home foreclosures as a result of these huge job losses. Youngstown was up against a changing and highly technological economy, and the white working class experienced the brunt with companies moving jobs offshore to reduce the cost of overhead in order to compete globally.

Such staggering unemployment sent the city into a tailspin, resulting in the mass exodus of more than two-thirds of its population. By the 2010 census, Youngstown counted sixty-seven thousand residents, down from its peak of 170,000. The city experienced a threefold

31 Gest, *The New Minority*, 77.

32 Gest, *The New Minority*, 77

33 Gest, *The New Minority*, 77–79.

34 Gest, *The New Minority*, 79.

increase in domestic violence, child and alcohol abuse, drug trafficking, divorce, and suicide.[35] In the shadow of a weakened economy and the flight of a primarily white working class, Blacks and Latinos remained and have ascended from their low positions to an almost majority demographic.[36] Similar to East London, Youngstown, Ohio, is a "post-traumatic" city.[37]

History *as* Memory in Youngstown (Steel Capital, USA)

In this section, history retold or history *as* memory is expressed as contested, social memories of a Youngstown white working class. History-as-culturally-remembered is not aligned with the written and recorded history. Like the historical record, residents remember, interpret, and react to massive cultural reformulations in a way that points out their feelings of social deprivation as well as political and economic marginalization. In the following two vignettes, history-as-cultural-remembering is shared by white working-class community members. Ralph Mickelson, a retired steelworker, asserts: "*We were better off under organized crime.* All the streets were plowed, there was no nonsense. Now cops have their hands tied behind their backs and a patch over one eye. At least back then, the trouble they created was among themselves. Now we're all suffering."[38]

Similarly reminiscing, Hank Thompson, an industrial painter, declares:

> [Former Congressman] Jimmy Traficant cared. He was always right. Jimmy had his finger in bad things, but he was the man. He got caught, but they all do it. So you take him out and put in another guy who's stealing instead. *When the mobs were running things—the Strollos, the Predos, the Carabbias—you didn't see all*

35 Gest, *The New Minority*, 79.

36 Gest, *The New Minority*, 81.

37 Gest, *The New Minority*, 7.

38 Gest, *The New Minority*, 83 (emphasis added).

> *these drug houses, car jackings, shootings, and murders.* If you crossed them, yeah, they'd knock you off. But you probably deserved it. And they always paid in cash. It was better back then.[39]

Mickelson reinterprets the past, and Thompson reimagines the past. Paradoxically, Gil McMahon, a retiree, explains:

> White working class people don't know who to be frustrated with—the city, the state, the feds. It's just awfully hard to find a job. *Nobody cares about the white working class. We just try to hang on and do what you can for yourself.* It's just that before the mills [shut], we were working and the guys there would walk home together and felt cohesive as a group. The only remnant left of that is the bars, and most of them have closed down. That's where the neighborhoods came together. They'd start with a stiff one at 7:00 am and tell everyone what they were going to do that day.[40]

Likewise, Mo Kerrigan, an unemployed sixty-five-year-old, claims:

> *There's the NAACP, the Muslim Brotherhood—the white guy?* All he has is his little church. *White people don't have the strength or support to accomplish anything.* All the wealthy [white] people haven't done me any favors; I would have had to do something for them first. And all the black folks look at me and literally say, *"What do you want honkey?" I was born here, and they say, "Get out. This is our hood." I'm the cannon fodder.*[41]

McMahon and Kerrigan revise the past.

All four men engage in selective forgetting in constructing collective memories of the past. What is most significant about them recounting history *as* memory is *not* the misalignment of their stories with historical record, but their feelings of dispossession. Thompson's and Mickelson's nostalgia around the "better times" experienced by Youngstown's white working class when the mob was on the scene is more about them

39 Gest, *The New Minority*, 83 (emphasis added).

40 Gest, *The New Minority*, 101 (emphasis added).

41 Gest, *The New Minority*, 101 (emphasis added).

articulating their hopes for the reinvestment and restructuring of what is now a "post-traumatic" city. Youngstown was once thriving even in the midst of conflicts that arose between the oligarchies, unions, and the Mafia running the city and who were in charge and in control of residents' labor and community actions and activities.

McMahon and Kerrigan react to what they perceive as turbulent times and tumultuous change by saying, "The white guy? Nobody cares about the white working class." For them, America is a failing meritocracy because even wealthy whites do not do them any favors. Moreover, white working-class social capital is diminishing, which is proven by the men's enfeebled social networks. Both the East London and Youngstown case studies are critical to reconsidering the tension between history *and* memory. The selective forgetting of residents in East London and Youngstown is proven by McMahon and Kerrigan's final point: working-class whites and especially those in "post-traumatic" cities are being socially displaced and therefore feeling like marginalized minorities.

Multidirectional Memory, Minority Status, and Marginalization

Theorist Michael Rothberg proposes the concept of multidirectional memory. Multidirectional memory shows how one discourse of memory can enable other discourses of memory.[42] Rather than understanding memory as competitive, Rothberg conceives of it as "multidirectional, as subject to ongoing negotiation, cross-referencing and borrowing."[43] He and other scholars think about the "multidirectionality of memory"[44] as enabling diverse victim groups to be witnesses to another group's mistreatment.

Appealing to multidirectional memory suggests that the plight of a Black American working class and youth, though distinct, is similar

42 Michael Rothberg, *Multicultural Memory: Remembering the Holocaust in the Age of Decolonization* (Redwood City, CA: Stanford University Press, 2009), 6.

43 Rothberg, *Multicultural Memory*, 3.

44 Rothberg, *Multicultural Memory*, 6, 15.

to the residents of East London and Youngstown. History *and* memory as well as history *as* memory are rehearsed social narratives of displacement, but for African Americans, history-as-cultural-remembering is also a narrative about Toni Morrison's concept of disremembering—or tragedy—in the midst of unsettling social, political, and economic turbulence intensifying, what is traditionally identified as both a marginalized and minority group status.

History *and* Memory in 1960s America and the "Black Problem"

To begin, in order to recount history *and* memory, we will consider the tradition of African American social protest by using the example of the Rev. Dr. Martin Luther King Jr. in the fifty-year anniversary (2018) of his assassination. He was an exemplary 1960s civil rights figure, thought leader,[45] and proponent for American democracy. King was keenly aware of an agony of deprivation[46] stymieing American progress and advancement of peoples around the globe. In the late 1960s, this "agony of deprivation" triggered Northern Black rioting and threatened America's poor, prompting King and the Southern Christian Leadership Conference (SCLC) to organize the 1968 Poor People's Campaign for economic justice. Agonies of deprivation heralded King's final statement about issues that were critical to him.

The Trumpet of Conscience, a social commentary on national and global issues that were pertinent to him, was King's final volume of

45 The likes of public intellectuals, cultural critics, and public theologians are presently referred to as thought leaders. In the late 1800s, Henry Ward Beecher was identified as one of America's earliest thought leaders. Such people wield influence and authority over the collective. Regarding Black America, thought leaders are informed by and shape the social, political, cultural, and moral thoughts of Black America. Thought leaders supply social commentary about and constructive criticism of American society and moral discourse on the meaning of Blackness in America.

46 Martin Luther King Jr., *The Trumpet of Conscience* (New York: HarperCollins, 1987), 6.

essays written prior to his death in 1968. In it, he critiques American race relations and questions the morality of war and society's indifference to poverty. The repression of Blacks amounted to a trumpet of conscience that King recognized for "developing a sense of black consciousness and peoplehood [that] does not require that we scorn the white race as a whole. It is not the race per se that we fight but the policies and ideology that leaders of that race have formulated to perpetuate oppression."[47] Anglo-Americans as a race were not the problem; instead, harmful social policies limiting the progress and prosperity of peoples of color were problematic, especially for Blacks, since these policies were being instituted by a white majority and ruling class.

Between 1955 and 1965, the social and political conditions of Black Americans had only barely and superficially improved. Blacks had received the right to vote, legal segregation of interstate bus travel and public restrooms was dismantled, educational advancement and access to jobs were on the horizon, albeit nominally. Black Southerners were the primary beneficiaries of these legislative advancements. However, tokenism was to blame for the broader Black public's slow progression. Inequality continued to reign supreme across America, typifying a racialized Black social experience.

During that period, Northern Blacks quickly became intolerant of and outraged by the lasting inequity, reinforced by high levels of poverty, low employment and job security, unequal education, housing discrimination, and the creation of Black ghettoes. Implicated in these poor social conditions were public and legislative policies that were added to white lawmakers' refusal to accept or promote radical structural change.[48] Oppressive living conditions precipitated Black rebellion in Northern inner cities. Blacks were blamed for the destruction of their communities, lawlessness, and disrupting social order. Pinpointing their unruly behavior as the catalyst for this destruction quickly resulted in them being identified as menaces to American society.

Instead of accusing an unyielding white power structure that maintained harsh policies, Blacks who were being subjected to a

---

47 King, *The Trumpet of Conscience*, 9.

48 King, *The Trumpet of Conscience*, 7–9.

partial, unfair, and violent American sociopolitical system anchored by unshakable ideologies were then held responsible for frustrations that boiled over and into revolt. Their mid- to late-1960s revolt harkened back to W. E. B. Du Bois's 1903 question, "How does it feel to be a problem?"[49] Despite social and political gains, Blacks were still viewed as "problem people."[50] King evaluated the Northern situation, comparing it to other parts of the country. Trenchant social beliefs, policies, and racist structures would endure and continue to stifle Blacks for many years to come.

History *as* Memory and the Racial Politics of Disremembering

History-as-cultural-remembering in the African American experience began in the early part of the twenty-first century and was reignited in the second half of 2014 with the death of Michael Brown and the videotaped chokehold of Eric Garner, both of which sparked nationwide demonstrations because of the failure of each selected grand jury to indict the white officers involved in the deaths. Social media users were instrumental in popularizing Garner's final words—"I can't breathe." This refrain has since shaped the collective and social memories of Black people around Black victims of overpolicing, from the 1980s to the present. For participants in the Black Lives Matter social movement, "I can't breathe" is a popular refrain cried aloud to express their dissatisfaction with the excessive use of force by police in their encounters with underrepresented ethnic and racial groups, particularly young Black American men and women.

"I can't breathe" encapsulates much of what it means to be Black in America today, especially for the masses of working-class Blacks and the economically poor. "I can't breathe" embraces the plight of diverse subpopulations of people in society and abroad, suffocating from social

49 W. E. B. Du Bois, *The Souls of Black Folk* (New York: Signet of Penguin Group, 1995), 7.

50 Cornel West, *Race Matters*, 2nd ed. (New York: Vintage, 2001), 4–5.

inequity and injustice. These memorial protests bear witness to victims of state violence. Renowned professor, writer, political activist, and Holocaust survivor Elie Wiesel talked about "remembering" as a process "not meant to enshrine a memorial but to point to and affect present action."[51]

Out of this history *as* memory, a tradition and practice of remembering, is born the current social activism of millennial and other post–civil rights generations. These youthful intergenerational groups empathize with the current pain and suffering of disenfranchised Black Americans, disenfranchisement caused by and resulting from unjust social, political, and economic conditions reified by structural racism. Similar to the Black youth of King's day, the political protests of marginalized young Blacks denote rebellion against a system unknowledgeable about and indifferent to their plight of economic deprivation, unemployment and underemployment, discrimination, undereducation, and police violence fueled by racism and eventually replicating generational social death.

With respect to social death,[52] the rate at which young Black men and women are being incarcerated and are dying at the hands of law enforcement officials who use excessive force as a form of social control is disproportionate to their population numbers. Further, social death comes as a consequence of them being dismissed and devalued;

---

51 Flora A. Keshegian, *Redeeming Memories: A Theology of Healing and Transformation* (Nashville: Abingdon Press, 2000), 25.

52 Orlando Patterson, *Slavery and Social Death: A Comparative Study* (Cambridge, MA: Harvard University Press, 1985). Patterson introduced this term in his groundbreaking 1980s text, a study of sixty-six societies that practiced slavery. Social death is part of the institutionalization process of enslavement. Patterson describes the internal and external dynamics of slavery, stressing the violent domination of the enslaver over the captive involving recruitment and including incorporation into the new society. To be incorporated into the new society would entail numerous losses including the loss of social bonds and family ties, erasure of former identity, and separation of persons possessing a previous heritage. All of these losses would contribute to their impotence and powerlessness. These social factors contribute to natally alienated and socially dead peoples, even though they are native to a particular land.

though born on American soil, they are nevertheless natally alienated,[53] stripped of an identity that should brim with promise yet offers limited future possibilities and little hope because of active and aggressive forms of systemic violence that are inescapable. Revolts led by Black youth in places like Ferguson, Missouri; Baltimore, Maryland; and Chicago, Illinois, have resulted in the destruction of businesses and properties in their own communities. And, like the Blacks described by King in the 1960s, they are implicated as both cause and effect of their own suffering, thus deflecting attention from the real source—an intransigent racialized social and political system rendering them invisible and, for that reason, invaluable.

Demonstrators who become eyewitnesses to their pain are *remembering* (reconstructing a traumatic past) and responding to the social ferment by agitating for wide-ranging social changes through die-ins, rallies, marches, Twitterverse, and Facebook. Accordingly, the memorial protests of young Black activists come to represent history *as* memory since they bear witness to past distress and to traumatic wounds. Theologian Shelly Rambo argues that trauma[54] is the "wound" that remains after a life-altering encounter with death.[55]

---

53 Patterson, *Slavery and Social Death.*

54 Shelly Rambo, *Spirit and Trauma: A Theology of Remaining* (Louisville, KY: Westminster John Knox Press, 2010), 4.

55 Judith Lewis Herman, *Trauma and Recovery: The Aftermath of Violence—From Domestic Abuse to Political Terror* (New York: Basic Books, 1997), 37, 45. Herman explains that trauma disrupts normal psychological development because it overwhelms the integrated systems people have in place to respond to danger and threat with a degree of care, control, and connection. Trauma causes persons to self-fragment; a consequence is maladaptation to everyday life. The symptomology of traumatized people emerges in the aftermath of the psychological trauma. Two of the symptoms I will describe are intrusion and constriction. Long after the violence or other trauma has passed, survivors are unable to forget the event because the traumatic moment repeatedly intrudes into their daily course of waking and sleeping life. Intrusions spontaneously break into memory as flashbacks and nightmares, making memory abnormal. Constriction is a close opposite to intrusion. During the traumatic moment, the traumatized person, feeling helpless and powerless, might dissociate—that is, separate the painful event from the rest of consciousness. A

Although the encounter might not result in literal death, the effect is a fundamentally different view of life—a shattered perspective, inextricably linking life and death, making room for the possibility of future suffering.[56] Eyewitnesses are themselves traumatized persons and/or those left behind who re-member and listen for memorial protests and cries of survival from open wounds.[57] They testify to what survives—what remains—after the trauma; ergo, cultural remembrances are what remains after the wound.

Toni Morrison's concept of "disremembering"[58] can be applied here because it expresses "a post-calamity language required to decipher the language of the scars left by collective, [social] trauma."[59] With her concept, she takes up the paradox of traumatic cultural remembering articulated by the character Sethe in *Beloved.* The scars on the formerly enslaved Sethe's back are a physical reminder of the violence perpetrated on her body and its long-lasting aftereffects. The scars prevent her from "forgetting" even though forgetting the traumatic moment of merciless and ferocious slavery lashings is necessary to her-story/history if she is to ever move toward true liberation.

Subsequently, disremembering is somaticized memory; the body registers collective trauma and remembers.[60] Disremembering (i.e., remembering forgetfully) remembers the trauma and gives witnesses

---

post-traumatic stress characteristic, constriction emerges as a numbing and emotional response that can cause "forgetfulness" of the painful event, thus manifesting as a form of amnesia.

56 Herman, *Trauma and Recovery*, 4.

57 Rambo, *Spirit and Trauma*, 4, 15, 22.

58 Epstein, "Remember to Forget," in *Shaping Losses*. In this essay, Epstein interrogates the maxim "never forget" by examining the dialectic that inheres traumatic cultural memory: remembering and forgetting. She explains the double bind of traumatic memory as expressed in the essay, "Instructions for Crossing the Border": "You are not allowed to remember. . . . You are not allowed to forget" (186). She introduces Toni Morrison's concept, disremembering, as an imperfect yet plausible resolution to the double bind of traumatic cultural memory (197).

59 Epstein, "Remember to Forget," 198.

60 Babette Rothschild, *The Body Remembers: Psychophysiology of Trauma and Trauma Treatment* (New York: W.W. Norton, 2000), xv.

the opportunity to mourn and to process the meaning of the scars. For Black Lives Matter protesters, the scars left behind are dead Black bodies that bear witness to the unconscionable acts of law enforcement authorities whose violence toward these bodies also marks the community. The scars call forth history-as-cultural-remembering, where Black bodies that have been historically subjected to race-based state violence (i.e., huntings, lynchings, attack dogs) are openly remembered.

Disremembering charges the American public to selectively forget (the social trauma) in order to focus on the victims. Dead Black bodies that remain in the aftermath of overpolicing are a way for Black Lives Matter activists to disremember the victims in the absence of words, by ironically "reinstating [the dead] as embodied selves because the [eyewitnesses] remember [victims] disremembering."[61] Protesters ultimately set the atmosphere for public and social memories by grieving the numerous losses and by disremembering and speaking life into a crowded void, the names of once-embodied selves, selves whose dead bodies initiated the modern Black Lives Matter and Say Her Name racial justice and social movements,[62] some of which are the names of disremembered Black bodies:

2012: Trayvon Martin (Sanford, Florida)
2014: Tamir Rice (Cleveland, Ohio)
2014: Akai Gurley (Brooklyn, New York)
2014: Ramarley Graham (Bronx, New York)
2014: Renisha McBride (Dearborn Heights, Michigan)
2014: Michael Brown (Ferguson, Missouri)
2014: Eric Garner (New York, New York)
2014: Yvette Smith (Bastrop, Texas)
2014: Jordan Baker (Houston, Texas)

---

61 Epstein, *Shaping Losses*, 197.

62 Homa Khaleeli, "#SayHerName: Why Kimberlé Crenshaw Is Fighting for Forgotten Women," *The Guardian*, May 20, 2016, http://www.theguardian.com/lifeandstyle/2016/may/30/sayhername-why-kimberle-crenshaw-is-fighting-for-forgotten-women.

2014: Laquan McDonald (Chicago, Illinois)
2015: Sandra Bland (Dallas, Texas)
2015: Freddie Gray (Baltimore, Maryland)
2016: Alton Sterling (Baton Rouge, Louisiana)
2016: Philando Castile (St. Paul, Minnesota)
2017: Terence Crutcher (Tulsa, Oklahoma)
2018: Jemel Roberson (Oak Lawn, Illinois)
2019: Eric Logan (South Bend, Indiana)
2019: Brandon Webber (Memphis, Tennessee)
2019: Botham Jean (Dallas, Texas)
2019: Atatiana Jefferson (Fort Worth, Texas)
2020: Ahmaud Arbery (Brunswick, Georgia)
2020: Breonna Taylor (Louisville, Kentucky)
2020: George Floyd (Minneapolis, Minnesota)

Disremembering is a form of history-as-cultural-remembering that reinterprets, revises, and reimagines the past. It remembers (commemorates) and *re-members* Black dehumanization. By virtue of selectively forgetting the trauma of death, it simultaneously selectively remembers the gift of life. Yet, disremembering ironically cements Black American marginalization and minority status.

This returns us to the question of minoritization: What constitutes minority status? Socioeconomics; histories of disempowerment; geographic locale; demographics; racial, ethnic, and cultural discrimination; or race?[63]

Answers to these pressing questions about minoritization point to a combination of social and cultural factors that contribute to identifying minority status. Yet, I continue to raise them to consider the marginalizations of white working-class residents of East London and Youngstown who are members of "post-traumatic" cities as well as America's working-class Blacks and Black youth. Nevertheless, the following queries do remain: How shall global Methodism address mainstay issues in today's turbulent social, economic, and political climate? Does the Church have an active role in addressing justice issues?

63 Gest, *The New Minority*, 31.

Which social and cultural groups' postindustrial economic, political, and social trauma will be recognized? In what ways will the Methodist Church respond to dispossessed and marginalized groups, some of whom are identified as working-class whites, Blacks, immigrants, migrants, and youth? What is the Church's stance on nationalism and globalism—diametrically opposed and contentious concepts defining, influencing, and shaping our present world?

Chapter Bibliography

Bellah, Robert N. *The Broken Covenant: American Civil Religion in Time of Trial*, 2nd edition. Chicago: University of Chicago Press, 1992.

Du Bois, W. E. B. *The Souls of Black Folk.* New York: Signet of Penguin Group, 1995.

Epstein, Julia. "Remember to Forget: The Problem of Traumatic Cultural Memory." In *Shaping Losses: Cultural Memory and the Holocaust*, edited by Julia Epstein and Lori Hope Lefkowitz, 186–204. Urbana and Chicago: University of Illinois Press, 2001.

Erll, Astrid. *Memory in Culture.* Translated by Sara B. Young. New York: Palgrave Macmillan, 2011.

Gest, Justin. *The New Minority: White Working Class Politics in an Age of Immigration and Inequality.* Oxford: Oxford University Press, 2016.

Herman, Judith Lewis. *Trauma and Recovery: The Aftermath of Violence—From Domestic Abuse to Political Terror.* New York: Basic Books, 1997.

Keshegian, Flora A. *Redeeming Memories: A Theology of Healing and Transformation.* Nashville: Abingdon Press, 2000.

Khaleeli, Homa. "#SayHerName: Why Kimberlé Crenshaw Is Fighting for Forgotten Women." *The Guardian,* May 20, 2016. http://www.theguardian.com/lifeandstyle/2016/may/30/sayhername-why-kimberle-crenshaw-is-fighting-for-forgotten-women.

King, Martin Luther, Jr. *The Trumpet of Conscience.* New York: HarperCollins, 1987.

Patterson, Orlando. *Slavery and Social Death: A Comparative Study.* Cambridge, MA: Harvard University Press, 1985.

Rambo, Shelly. *Spirit and Trauma: A Theology of Remaining.* Louisville, KY: Westminster John Knox Press, 2010.

Rothberg, Michael. *Multicultural Memory: Remembering the Holocaust in the Age of Decolonization.* Redwood City, CA: Stanford University Press, 2009.

Rothschild, Babette. *The Body Remembers: Psychophysiology of Trauma and Trauma Treatment.* New York: W.W. Norton, 2000.

Stone, Dan. "Genocide and Memory." In *The Oxford Handbook of Genocide Studies*, edited by Donald Bloxham and A. Kirk Moses, 102–19. Oxford: Oxford University Press, 2013.

West, Cornel. *Race Matters.* 2nd ed. New York: Vintage, 2001.

Revival and Staying Alive: Spiritual Respiration in John Wesley's Theology

Sarah Heaner Lancaster

"THY GRACE RESTORE, THY WORK REVIVE." These words, used as the title of the theme for this Oxford Institute, come from a hymn written for a preacher by Charles Wesley.[1] The hymn recounts the preacher's desire and prayer to be as zealous now as in the beginning of ministry to bring people to God.

My father was a Methodist preacher in the Southwest Texas conference (which has since become the Rio Texas conference). He mostly served small-town communities in Texas, and every place to which we itinerated he invited an evangelist to come to preach a weeklong revival. Perhaps he arranged these revivals because he, like the preacher that Charles Wesley wrote about, needed them himself, but as a child I came to expect those revivals and I loved them. They meant exciting and joyful music and special activities for children, and my father would get up very early to make doughnuts for the services held on weekday mornings before school and work.

The first revival I remember was when I was six or seven years old. It was the usual practice to end each service with an altar call,

1 Charles Wesley, *Hymns and Sacred Poems*, vol. 1 (Bristol: Farley, 1749), 300–301, #189. See the website of the Center for Studies in the Wesleyan Tradition, Duke Divinity School, accessed January 22, 2021, https://divinity.duke.edu/sites/divinity.duke.edu/files/documents/cswt/45_Hymns_and_Sacred_Poems_%281749%29_Vol_1.pdf.

inviting people to give their lives to Christ and to join the church. I remember this revival because one night as the invitation was given, I felt called to go forward. Because I was so young, my father was surprised to see me walk up, but he treated me as he would any adult, and he received me into membership in the church. (I should say this was before The United Methodist Church worked out the understanding it now has of "baptized member" as distinct from "professing member.") He did insist as I got older that I go through the confirmation lessons with him, but that night I publicly responded to Christ and joined the church at an early age.

I begin with this personal story because I want to explore the theme of this Institute from the point of view of a child of the church who never left the church but nevertheless benefited from the opportunities to be revived. I will draw from my experiences but not to suggest the same pattern for everyone. Rather, I am trying to use my autobiography only insofar as it opens avenues for me to think through a theological problem. I would add that my viewpoint is inevitably shaped by United Methodist theology, and there may be some differences in theological understandings in other churches represented here. I hope, though, that the questions I am thinking about may be thought-provoking even across those differences. I should also say that in my childhood, revivals usually used language of being born again, which accounts for some of the associations I make in this chapter.

I have puzzled for some time over the internal tension in the theology we have inherited from John Wesley between the practice of acknowledging through infant baptism that God is at work to regenerate us from the beginning of our lives and yet calling people to repentance and new birth as adults. When our lives start with grace, how do we get to the point of needing such "conversion"? Can we maintain a life with God that does not die so thoroughly that it requires dramatic revival to bring it back to life? I cannot say to what extent Wesley was himself aware of or concerned about this tension, but regardless of his own self-consciousness of the problem, he was reflecting theologically in the context of a movement. As Methodism has changed from society to church, though, it needs theology for a church, including theology for the infant baptism that Wesley gave to us through the materials he himself sent to the newly forming church in North America. Because this region is where I am located, this is the situation I presume for this chapter.

Although Wesley called already-baptized people to new birth, both the Sunday Service and the article "Of Baptism" in the Articles of Religion of the Methodist Episcopal Church link infant baptism to regeneration.[2] We have and use both theological approaches—baptizing infants and calling the baptized to be born again—without always making clear the connection between them.[3] Even if Wesley himself did not work out this tension, our churches have to. As a movement, Methodism sought to spread scriptural holiness across a land that already had churches, calling people to be better Christians within those churches. As churches now, we must continue this mission in a way that is in keeping with our own churchly character. This churchly character includes offering baptism. The tension in Wesley's theology between the practice of infant baptism and calling the baptized to new birth needs to be worked out. If we think of revival only as the need to be born again, then we are simply taking over theology of a movement without taking into account what it means to be church. It would seem odd, for instance, to simply expect that every baptism, which we understand sacramentally to be an act of God, will necessarily fail and require yet another birth. Failure is, of course, possible and even likely as I will go on to show, but to simply expect it undermines confidence

---

2 *John Wesley's Sunday Service of the Methodists in North America, with an Introduction by James F. White* (Nashville: Quarterly Review United Methodist Publishing House, 1984), 140. *The Book of Discipline of the United Methodist Church 2016* (Nashville: The United Methodist Publishing House, 2016), ¶103.

3 This tension with regard to baptism is especially apparent in ecumenical dialogue. See section III, "Baptism and New Life," in *Encountering Christ the Saviour: Church and Sacraments* (Lake Junaluska, NC: The World Methodist Council, 2011), http://worldmethodistcouncil.org/wp-content/uploads/2014/10/Encountering-Christ-the-Saviour-Church-and-Sacraments.pdf.

in the work of God's unfailing grace that baptism signifies.[4] I hope to expand the meaning of revival so that it is not restricted to bringing dead Christians back to life. I want to show how infant baptism can make sense within the theology of salvation we have received from Wesley, and I will use Wesley's image of spiritual respiration to help work through this problem.

In this chapter, I will first explore Wesley's own understanding of spiritual respiration and new birth and then examine why sustaining spiritual respiration is important. Next I will explore some ways that Wesley's reflection on spiritual respiration for a movement may need to be adjusted or expanded to serve churches that baptize infants. Finally, even though there is much to learn directly from Wesley, I will suggest two ways that our own reflection and practice regarding revival and spiritual respiration need to go beyond his own.

Spiritual Respiration and New Birth

Wesley uses the image of spiritual respiration in connection with the idea of being born again, specifically in two sermons, "The Great Privilege of Those That Are Born of God" and "The New Birth." The revivals I knew about in my childhood often called people to be born again. Wesley speaks of new birth as necessary because of the condition into which we are born as humans. As he understood it, although human beings were created in the image of God, this image was marred by the fall. He is careful to distinguish new birth (the work of God *in* us) from justification (the work of God *for* us). New birth, as the work of God *in* us, is the way God renews our fallen nature and restores us to the moral image of God.[5] New birth brings a real change, taking away

---

4 *By Water and the Spirit*, the United Methodist statement on baptism, identifies God's gift of unfailing grace as the defining difference between a sacrament and dedication (30). Gayle Carlton Felton, *By Water and the Spirit* (Nashville: Discipleship Resources, 1998), https://gbod-assets.s3.amazonaws.com/drint/resources/english/bywaterandthespirit.pdf.

5 John Wesley, Sermon 19, "The Great Privilege of Those That Are Born of God," §preface 2, in *Sermons*, ed. Albert C. Outler, in *Works* 1:431–32.

the power of sin so that we might become holy in love as God intended us to be.[6] As he describes new birth, Wesley makes use of a comparison with physical birth to convey what happens to us. Before physical birth, we have organs—his examples are eyes, ears, lungs—but they do not function as they are made to do because they are closed off from light, sound, and air. Upon being born, though, those organs are released from confinement in the womb to function properly—seeing, hearing, breathing. Wesley uses these bodily functions to explain what happens in the soul. With new birth, our spiritual senses are released from the power of sin to be able to discern and relate to God in a wholly different way.[7]

Like our physical senses, our renewed spiritual senses function to allow us to see and hear God as we could not before. Like our physical lungs, our reborn soul is able to "breathe" God differently. Although physically an unborn child has been sustained by oxygen even in the womb as the mother's body mediates access by delivering oxygen through the placenta, at birth the lungs directly fill with the air needed to sustain life. Similarly, although God's grace has always been around us and has always been inviting us into relationship, with new birth we may deeply take it in and respond.[8] Wesley describes this respiration in the sermon "The New Birth" as God's breathing grace into us and our breathing back prayer and praise.[9]

This change in the ability to breathe with God is the change that happens in new birth. The spiritual senses or abilities that God gave to us in creation had been closed off by sin, but with new birth they are enabled to function as they were made to do. It is a change from a nonfunctioning spirit (breath) to a functioning one. Wesley thinks of this change as bringing the soul to life.[10]

Sermon 45, "The New Birth," §preface 1, §I.1, in *Works* 2:187–88.

6 Wesley, Sermon 45, "New Birth," §I.1, in *Works* 2:188. Sermon 19, "Great Privilege," §preface 2, in *Works* 1:431–32.

7 Wesley, Sermon 19, "Great Privilege," §I.2–10, in *Works* 1:432–35.

8 Wesley, Sermon 19, "Great Privilege," §I.8, in *Works* 1:434–35.

9 Wesley, Sermon 45, "New Birth," §II.4, in *Works* 2:192–93.

10 Wesley, Sermon 45, "New Birth," §II.4, in *Works* 2:192–93.

Wesley calls the change that comes about with new birth a great change; he could even call it a total change because we go from being spiritually dead to being spiritually alive.[11] The idea of a total change refers to the vast difference between death and life, not the total completion of the work of God in us. New birth is the entry to sanctification, not the whole of it.[12] The functioning of these spiritual abilities allows us to keep breathing to stay alive in Christ, but we still need to grow. As Wesley says in the sermon "The Great Privilege of Those Born of God," "And by this new kind of spiritual respiration, spiritual life is not only sustained but increased day by day, together with spiritual strength and motion and sensation; all the senses of the soul being now awake, and capable of 'discerning' spiritual 'good and evil.'"[13] And in "The New Birth" he says, "As by a kind of spiritual respiration, the life of God in the soul is sustained: and the child of God grows up, till he comes to 'the full measure of the stature of Christ.'"[14] In the context of Methodist revival, this new birth was distinct from but usually occurring with justification, the powerful experience of knowing oneself to be a pardoned and beloved child of God.

Because in the theology of the Church of England new birth was also associated with baptism, Wesley distinguishes between the sign act and the reality it represents in order to distinguish the sign act in the church from what his movement called people to. The outward sign of water is not identical to the inward renewal that God works in us, but the sign points to what God is doing. With the use of this distinction, Wesley recognizes that the sign and the thing signified do not always go together. He makes this point with reference to what happens in what he calls "riper years," not in infancy.[15] He did not refute the Church of England's position that infants are born again at the time of baptism, but the distinction helps to identify and explain two possibilities. First, some who are baptized in their riper years show no evidence of having

11 Wesley, Sermon 45, "New Birth," §II.4–5, in *Works* 2:192–94.

12 Wesley, Sermon 45, "New Birth," §IV.3, in *Works* 2:198.

13 Wesley, Sermon 19, "Great Privilege," §I.8, in *Works* 1:434–35.

14 Wesley, Sermon 45, "New Birth," §II.4, in *Works* 2:192–93.

15 Wesley, Sermon 45, "New Birth," §IV.2, in *Works* 2:197–98.

been inwardly changed at all. They are washed by water, but their spirits are not renewed. Second, because new birth is only the entrance to sanctification, not the whole of it, it is possible to conceive of how God's work in us is progressive. No matter what our age, we have to grow in holiness the way a child grows into an adult. So even when the inward change does accompany the outward sign, God still continues to work in us to bring us to greater holiness.

The second possibility is especially important for thinking about spiritual respiration. In order to grow, we have to keep breathing. The ability and necessity to take air into one's lungs after physical birth is like the ability and necessity to take God into one's soul after spiritual birth. With air and with God, a human life can flourish. Without breathing air, a person eventually will die physically; without breathing God, a person eventually will die spiritually. Spiritual respiration is the kind of intimate fellowship with God that is needed not only daily, but moment by moment. When God is as close as one's own breath, spiritual growth is sustained. When that relationship is neglected, spiritual growth is threatened.

In "The Great Privilege of Those That Are Born of God," Wesley recounts how a small failure to keep firmly attached to God through prayer and through attention to the way God's grace is working in one's life can lead to a sliding away from God, even to the point of committing a grievous outward sin.[16] He names David, Barnabas, and Peter as examples of those who underwent this slide, but David becomes the premiere example. The first step in sliding away from God is negative inward sin, that is, not stirring up the gift of God within you. Think about this step as not breathing God in spiritual respiration—that is, not taking in grace and returning prayer and praise. This failure leads to the second step, positive inward sin—that is, inclining toward some evil desire or temper. When we do not breathe God, we lean away from God and toward something else. What follows from allowing oneself to be drawn in the wrong direction is loss of faith in God. Wesley describes faith as recumbency, a resting or leaning on God, which is obviously weakened when you start resting or leaning on something

16 Wesley, Sermon 19, "Great Privilege," §II.7, in *Works* 1:438–39.

else.[17] Once that happens, we become capable of committing outward sin, that is, voluntarily breaking a known law of God, such as David did with Bathsheba.[18]

In the way that Wesley outlines what he calls the "progress from grace to sin," we begin to see how natural birth and spiritual birth are different.[19] They both mark the beginning of a certain kind of "breathing," but its continuation in each case is quite different. While human beings have control of physical breathing to some extent, involuntary processes assure that we get the oxygen we need even when we are not thinking about it. Such is not the case with spiritual respiration. No involuntary, automatic system takes over to provide for our spiritual lives when we neglect them. It is, of course, possible to develop good spiritual habits that sustain us in times of trouble without conscious thought, but such habits are formed precisely because we have not neglected spiritual respiration in ordinary times. The great change that takes place with new birth allows the possibility of a qualitatively different kind of relationship with God, whom we now know as close to us as our own breath, but it does not guarantee growth in that relationship. As Wesley makes clear, new birth marks the beginning, not the entirety, of sanctification. Depending on new birth without constantly attending to the relationship it makes possible is a serious mistake that leads to the kind of complacency that Wesley encountered everywhere around him (and is all too common still). Those who did become complacent were "dead" Christians; that is, they had stopped breathing God and so had lost the very life that had been made available to them through their baptisms.

What Wesley saw in his time was the clear presence of dead Christians all around. Even if many, according to Anglican theology, had been born again through God's work in infant baptism with the possibility of breathing God, they may never have willingly taken their first spiritual breath or they had held their breath long enough to fall as David did back into sin. At a gathering such as this one, we do not all

17 Wesley, Sermon 1, "Salvation by Faith," §I.5, in *Works* 1:121.

18 Wesley, Sermon 19, "Great Privilege," §II.1–7, in *Works* 1:438–39.

19 Wesley, Sermon 19, "Great Privilege," §II.9, in *Works* 1:440.

share the assumption that Wesley had of at least nominal Christianity in the culture around us, but as churches we all face the problem of how to keep baptized Christians breathing God.

Sustaining Revived Lives

To address the problem that he saw in his time and place, Wesley began a movement; he organized societies that were intended to draw people together in the pursuit of holiness. These societies were not churches, but rather were focused opportunities for growth. Since Wesley's own time, Methodists around the world have become churches. Because churches can be prone to institutional staleness and lethargy, many of us today long for the energy and discipline of that early movement. Even as we try to recover that heritage, though, we must also reckon theologically with our current status as churches. This means that the theology Wesley developed for a movement may need to be expanded to account for more than he himself needed to do. I want to use his notion of spiritual respiration to talk not only about revival as resuscitation from death, but also about the means to sustain breathing—a constant turning from death to life that constitutes the ongoing growth of Christians to fulfill the claim God has made on their lives through baptism. Wesley himself desired that the Methodist movement would sustain breathing for those who had been born again by an experience of God's love that had brought them back from death, so I will start with his own understanding of what was possible and necessary after new birth. Why and how do we sustain spiritual respiration once it has started?

As for why, I want to explore how spiritual respiration is vulnerable after we have been born into the air that is God. Wesley understood that being born again came with the privilege of not committing sin, but he also recognized that this privilege could be lost. In his sermon "The Great Privilege," Wesley reflects on the slide from grace to sin in the context of a question the Bible itself presents. He notes that 1 John 3:9 asserts that whosoever is born of God does not commit sin, but he also notes that Paul's account in Galatians (2:12–14) about Peter's hypocrisy in Antioch with regard to eating with Gentiles indicates that even such a holy person as Peter did commit sin. Wesley's answer is to say that the possibility of sin depends on whether a reborn person "keeps" him- or herself in faith.[20] This language of "keeping" oneself is found throughout Wesley's writings, and it suggests the kind of ongoing process of spiritual respiration I have just described. In other words, the way to prevent sliding into sin is to keep breathing God. If you continue to stir up God's gift in prayer and praise, you will find all the grace and power you need to avoid the steps of sliding into sin.

In *A Plain Account of Christian Perfection*, Wesley connects this idea of "keeping" yourself to having a "single eye," a phrase he bases on Matthew 6:22–23.[21] To review the slide from grace to sin that I covered earlier, if you neglect spiritual respiration, you take the first step away from grace and toward sin. (Wesley calls this first step "negative inward sin," a failure to stir up God's gift.) After taking that first step, it is very easy to take the second step, "positive inward sin"—which he explains as inclining toward something other than God. If you fail to breathe God, you will not be empowered to avoid further sliding. He describes the further slide into positive inward sin as "giving way to some evil desire or temper."[22] So "keeping" yourself with a "single eye" is constantly keeping yourself focused on the life God gives instead of turning toward death.

The single eye has particular reference to our desires because Wesley uses the metaphor of the eye to talk about the intention of the soul.[23] The nature of new birth is that it renews the image of God in us so that we can gain the mind of Christ.[24] When we have the mind of Christ, we intend what Christ intends. Sanctification is holiness understood

---

20 Wesley, Sermon 19, "The Great Privilege," §II.7, in *Works* 1:438–39.

21 Wesley, *A Plain Account of Christian Perfection*, ed. and annotated by Randy L. Maddox and Paul W. Chilcote (Kansas City, MO: Beacon Hill Press, 2015), 141. See question 36, his fifth advice.

22 Wesley, Sermon 19, "The Great Privilege," §II.7, in *Works* 1:438–39.

23 Wesley, Sermon 125, "On a Single Eye" §preface 2, in *Works* 4:121. "And what the eye is to the body, the intention is to the soul."

24 Wesley, Sermon 45, "The New Birth," §II.5, in *Works* 2:193–94.

as the "whole mind which was in Jesus Christ."[25] As we grow, we will gain more and more of the mind of Christ, but in the time of growing, we also will still struggle with the distractions that are around us that may cause us to take our minds and eyes off of God. The importance of "keeping oneself" is crucial for maintaining a single eye—keeping the intention of the soul focused on God in the same way our physical eyes focus on what is in front of us.

In this struggle to avoid distraction that would lead us away from God, three desires are paramount in Wesley's thinking. He takes these categories from 1 John 2:16, and he lists and explains these desires in a number of places in his works. In "The Unity of the Divine Being," Wesley names three "rivals of God," that is, three categories of things that serve as idols to draw us away from worshiping the one, true God, and these three rivals correspond to the three sinful desires he talks about. The rivals are first "objects of sense," the things that please our bodily senses. Second, "objects of the imagination" are the things that please our fancy. In other words, they satisfy a mental state rather than a physical one. We want them not because they make the body feel good, but rather because they make us feel good internally. Wesley often mentions in this category novelty because it includes things that give you the pleasure you feel when you wear the latest fashion or have the newest gadget. Finally, he names the pride of life, a phrase taken directly and translated literally from 1 John 2:16. Wesley uses this phrase to talk about things that give us status in life, such as honor and wealth.[26] These three idols produce in us three desires. Objects of sense awaken desire of the flesh. Objects of the imagination awaken desire of the eye. The pride of life awakens desire of praise.

When we fail to breathe in grace and breathe out prayer and praise, we are more prone to the attraction of these idols, so we lean on them instead of leaning on God. The organization of the Methodist movement from the beginning showed great concern about helping Methodists "keep" themselves with a single eye. As early as 1738, Wesley drew up "The Rules of the Band Societies," stating the explicit intention "to

25 Wesley, Sermon 45, "The New Birth," §III.1, in *Works* 2:194.

26 Wesley, Sermon 120, "The Unity of the Divine Being," §12, in *Works* 4:65.

speak, each of us in order, freely and plainly the true state of our souls, with the faults we have committed in thought, word, or deed, and the temptations we have felt since our last meeting."[27] To be admitted to the band, individuals had to answer questions about their willingness to hear what others had to say about their faults. They were further expected to be open about their own self-understanding, and at each meeting, they were asked the following questions:

1. What known sins have you committed since our last meeting?
2. What temptations have you met with?
3. How were you delivered?
4. What have you thought, said, or done, of which you doubt whether it be sin or not?
5. Have you nothing you desire to keep secret?[28]

These questions serve the purpose of thorough self-examination so that any slide from grace could be caught and corrected.

Wesley found it useful to organize members of the movement according to their struggles. As membership grew, he saw the need "to separate the precious from the vile," a need that led him to issue tickets as "commendatory letters" for participation.[29] He also began to organize separate groups for believers and penitents who had fallen into sin because of his observation that the prayers and exhortations that would profit one group did not profit the other.[30] Eventually, he also organized a select group of those who were committed to "press after perfection."[31] So the Methodist movement was designed not only to

27 Wesley, "The Rules of the Band Societies," in *The Methodist Societies: History, Nature, and Design*, ed. Rupert E. Davies, in *Works* 9:77.

28 Wesley, "The Rules of the Band Societies," in *Works* 9:78.

29 Wesley, "A Plain Account of the People Called Methodists," §IV.1–3, in *Works* 9:265.

30 Wesley, "A Plain Account of the People Called Methodists," §VII.1, in *Works* 9:268–69.

31 Wesley, "A Plain Account of the People Called Methodists," §VIII.2, in *Works* 9:269.

bring members to being born again, but also to help members "keep" themselves so they could grow in holiness.

The design of the movement matched the problem Wesley saw in his time and place. He observed that many people around him had been baptized but neglected their baptism. Many people needed spiritual resuscitation after they had let their spiritual lives die from lack of breathing God. His words could be harsh, as they are at the end of "The New Birth." There he addresses an objection raised about his method that it is uncharitable to call the baptized to be born again. This objection arises because the theology of the Church of England tied new birth to baptism. It seemed unnecessary and presumptuous to call Christians already born again by baptism to be born yet again. The call to be born yet again could seem to call into question the work of God in their baptism. Wesley is firm in his response that even the baptized need to be born again. His answer makes sense in light of spiritual respiration. Every Christian needs the experience of a living relationship with God to be able to live lives of true holiness. Baptism offers that possibility, but it does not guarantee it. Even though God's work of offering new life through baptism opens us to spiritual respiration, keeping ourselves by breathing God is not automatic. Through baptism we become part of the church as the community with resources to keep ourselves in the way of salvation, but all too often, we neglect those resources and stop breathing God. Wesley's call to the baptized to be born again does not question God's work in the sign, but rather it targets our failed response to what God has done.

Spiritual Respiration in a Church That Baptizes Children

In "The New Birth," Wesley addresses two different situations of baptized Christians who need to be born again. First were baptized persons who engaged in open sin. Second were baptized persons who avoided open sin and even participated fully in the church, but they did not know the relationship with God that spiritual respiration is intended to keep alive. In the case of open sin, Wesley saw an outright denial of baptism that results in spiritual death. In the second case, of those who think they are saved by their decent lives and church participation, Wesley saw that these outwardly holy practices are not the same as real inward holiness.[32] Those in this second group have mistaken the means for the end; that is, merely performing the practices given to us to strengthen living relationship with God is not itself the living relationship. They may not have denied their baptisms outright, but they have surely stifled the work of God by an attitude that keeps them from breathing deeply enough—their actions have not been true expressions of praise and thanksgiving in response to grace. I think with this second group Wesley may be making a distinction similar to the one he makes for baptism between the sign and the thing signified. Generally, decent lives are not the same as holy lives. There is a reality that is not to be confused with the outward action. Wesley is clear in this sermon that whether baptized or not, people in these situations must be born again; that is, they must be brought into the light and air of God where their spiritual senses can function as they should.

Because the focus of the movement was for people of riper years, Wesley's model for new birth is described in terms experienced by people of riper years. When he writes about the witness of the spirit, he argues that one can know that the witness of one's own spirit is genuine because of the great change from darkness to light. Without such a change, the feeling of being a child of God might be nothing more than presumption, that is, trusting in one's own perceived decency and innocence rather than trusting in God. Wesley was himself suspicious of anyone who claimed to have always been a Christian.[33] Not only was this great change an internal test, it could also be a test for the effectiveness of preaching. In "A Caution Against Bigotry," Wesley argues that no one who is casting out devils should be forbidden from preaching, and proof of casting out devils lies in "a gross, open sinner" breaking off from sin and living a Christian life as a result of the preaching.[34]

---

32 Wesley, Sermon 45, "The New Birth," §IV.4, in *Works* 2:199–201.

33 Wesley, Sermon 10, "The Witness of the Spirit (I)," §II.5, in *Works* 1:279.

34 Wesley, Sermon 38, "A Caution Against Bigotry," §III.3, in *Works* 2:73.

Even though he used this great change as a marker of new birth, Wesley did not only look to some past experience of change, but also to present marks of humble joy and fruits of the spirit as ways to distinguish presumption from the genuine work of God.[35] Even in "The New Birth," where he is so suspicious of what the baptized may claim, he could qualify his call to the baptized to be born again by saying, "if you have not already experienced this inward work of God."[36] His most pointed assessment for the need for new birth was to ask, "What are you now?"[37] One of Wesley's great concerns was for people to be fully Christian. His distinction between almost and altogether Christians is familiar, and he spoke often about real, or true, or genuine religion as opposed to religion that falls short of what he knew Christianity to offer. He knew it was important to know what brought life and what did not. As an internal test, the question "What are you now?" is exactly right for assessing one's own response to God. One way that churches now need to regain the energy and discipline of a movement is to call people to this self-examination, not simply to assume that because the church offers means of grace then people are making effective use of them. If the church wants people to be real Christians, it must hold up the possibility of fullness of life in Christ to them and call them to respond.

We should also acknowledge, though, how potentially harmful it can be to distinguish real Christians from those who are not. Setting litmus tests for who is in and who is out has been all too common and divisive in the history of Christian faith. Because self-examination in the Methodist tradition includes conversation with others including feedback about faults, to some degree external assessment about one's authentic effort to be holy can and should have an important place. But any external feedback is in service of self-examination, and it must allow that God may work differently according to our circumstance, personality, and more. We need to find a way to be serious about calling people to be fully Christian, which includes calling them

35 Wesley, Sermon 10, "The Witness of the Spirit (I)," §II.6, in *Works* 1:279–80.

36 Wesley, Sermon 45, "The New Birth," §IV.4, in *Works* 2:199–201.

37 Wesley, Sermon 18, "The Marks of the New Birth," §IV.2, in *Works* 1:2.

away from false presumption without being ourselves presumptuous to think that we know more than we can know about what God is doing in their lives.

Wesley's total commitment to calling even baptized Christians to new birth makes a lot of sense considering he was responsible for a movement to provide disciplined conversation and spiritual practices to help people begin or maintain spiritual respiration to keep a single eye on God so they could be holy and happy. The attempt to draw the baptized into this movement was not necessarily a challenge to the theology of baptism in the Church of England. Wesley did not have to question the theology of the Church regarding new birth in baptism to see all around him the need to call people to more than what they had taken their baptisms to mean. Wesley's lifelong reluctance to break with the Church of England as well as his retention of infant baptism in the Articles of Religion and Sunday Service he sent to the newly forming church in North America certainly indicates that even though he could distinguish between the sign and the thing signified, he did not deny the understanding that God was at work in the sign when it came at the beginning of life.[38] As we have become churches in dialogue with other churches, Methodists have had to acknowledge Wesley's ambivalence about the sign as well as his apparent acceptance of what the sign signifies, namely, the work of God to regenerate human lives. The World Methodist Council document titled *Encountering Christ the Saviour: Church and Sacraments* states, "This text does describe regeneration as the true effect of Baptism, while recognizing the pastoral reality which might mean that this effect is not immediate or even inevitable with regard to personal conversion and transformation of life."[39] Because sanctification takes time and spiritual respiration is not involuntary, new birth at any time of life is vulnerable to our neglect, so there is need for practices to cultivate spiritual respiration. In our time, when Methodists have churches that offer the opportunity to

38 I have said more on this point in "Baptism and Justification: A Methodist Understanding," *Ecclesiology* 4, no. 3 (2008): 1–19.

39 *Encountering Christ the Saviour: Church and Sacrament*, chap. 2, §III, Baptism and New Life, ¶53.

begin breathing God from birth, we should pay attention to sustaining breathing to prevent the spiritual neglect that leads to spiritual death. The means for doing so are present in our tradition as movement. But as churches, we need to think of revival as calling from death to life, not only in a dramatic spiritual crisis but also as keeping souls alive through sustained breathing of the grace we need—a kind of constant conversion from death to life.

I think that in my own life the specific practice called revivals worked in that way. As a six-year-old, surely I disobeyed my parents at times and I did not always have the best temper, but I was hardly what Wesley would call a "gross, open sinner"[40] when I walked forward during the altar call. Nor do I think at that age I presumed I was saved by my church-going. As best as I can remember and interpret my former self, I really did have some sense of wanting a deeper relationship with Jesus Christ. Perhaps the position of baptized children raised in the community of faith has some relation to the way people of riper years who are justified and born again continue to struggle with sin after justification. The comparison is not perfect, I know, largely because of the developmental stages children are still going through to reach adulthood. But what I mean is that the work of God had begun in my life with baptism, and the opportunity to respond to God in that moment of the altar call helped strengthen in me the work of God that had already started in my baptism. The preaching and worship event we called *revival* was not spiritual resuscitation at that point in my life. Rather, it was a boost like going to an oxygen bar. I use this analogy with a great deal of caution. I have never been to an oxygen bar (i.e., a place where you can breathe a higher concentration of oxygen than is available in the normal atmosphere), and there is no scientific confirmation of the health benefits of doing so. I am only trying to suggest the difference between reviving a person who has suffocated and enhancing an already-breathing person. Is it so strange to imagine that churches that offer new life to infants in baptism might be able to help them sustain that life? Notwithstanding Wesley's own conviction that he had sinned away the washing of his baptism by about the age

40 Wesley, Sermon 38, "A Caution Against Bigotry," §III.3, in *Works* 2:73.

of ten, it would be very odd to imagine that God's work to sanctify human life using the church that God has established for that purpose necessarily fails for everyone.[41] Although we do well to call people to serious self-examination, we do not need to take it as a general rule that no one could remain on the path to sanctification after baptism had opened the way to new life. But we do need to think generally that all the baptized need to be called constantly to deeper breathing in their life with God.

We do well to take seriously that Wesley identifies two kinds of repentance along the Scripture way of salvation. The first is the repentance "antecedent" to justification, and the other is repentance "consequent upon" justification.[42] When Wesley made this distinction, he meant that antecedent repentance was repentance before being justified, for instance, the situation of people of riper years who had lost the justification they had received in baptism and needed to be justified again. Consequent repentance indicated the ongoing repentance of the justified until they were fully sanctified. We may find the idea of consequent repentance to be useful to help us think about how to revive baptized Christians, even children. In "The Repentance of Believers," Wesley describes the repentance consequent upon justification as a "kind of self-knowledge—the knowing ourselves to be sinners, yea, guilty, helpless sinners, even though we know we are children of God."[43] Until it pleases God to perfect us in this life in love, this is our situation.[44] So it will be the situation for most of us throughout our lives. As Wesley reminds us, after justification sin remains, although it does not reign.[45] What we need in the period when we grow in sanctification is spiritual respiration, breathing in God's grace and breathing

41 Wesley reflects on this in his journal entry for May 24, 1738. See *Journals and Diaries*, ed. W. Reginald Ward and Richard P. Heitzenrater, in *Works* 18:242–43.

42 Wesley, Sermon 43, "The Scripture Way of Salvation," §III.6, in *Works* 2:164–65.

43 Wesley, Sermon 14, "The Repentance of Believers," §I.1, in *Works* 1:336.

44 Wesley, Sermon 14, "The Repentance of Believers," §I.20, in *Works* 1:346–47.

45 Wesley, Sermon 43, "The Scripture Way of Salvation," §III.6, in *Works* 2:164–65.

out prayer and praise to remind us of our constant need for grace not only to pardon the sin that remains, but also to empower us to resist it. Although Wesley gained this insight as he reflected on a movement primarily of people of riper years, churches that baptize children can make good use of this insight. Claimed by God and regenerated in baptism, children as well as adults need to continue to grow in faith as recumbency on God's grace. All the baptized in the church need to learn from the church how to sustain spiritual respiration. Because it is the church's job to nurture response to the gift of baptism, the church should want to enable people to say that they have always been Christian. I do take Wesley's suspicion of that claim seriously, but I think it should be used primarily to point the church to the continual need for repentance as self-knowledge rather than ruling out the possibility of growing over a lifetime in Christ. We should always be asking, "What am I now?," and we should be mindful of the ways we can and do get distracted by idols and begin to slide from our trust in God.

If we develop in this direction the idea of spiritual respiration that Wesley describes, we may be able to see how someone who has always understood him- or herself to be a Christian and a child of God needs to be revived nonetheless, that is, brought regularly to experiences of God that amplify our spiritual respiration and continue to turn us from death to life. Wesley's question "What are you now?" is ever relevant, and his suspicion of complacency of baptized Christians is justified. What we need to do differently than he did is to approach this problem as churches so we think of revival as our responsibility to call people to make use of the means of grace that we offer and call them to honest self-examination about their spiritual respiration. I am suggesting that when the sign and the thing signified go together in baptism, as Wesley says they ordinarily do (especially for infants), baptism opens up a possibility of spiritual respiration that needs to be tended, and we remain vulnerable to letting our breathing lapse.[46] This vulnerability remains through every stage of life, although I imagine

46 Wesley states the privileges of being born again "are ordinarily annexed to baptism" in Sermon 18, "The Marks of the New Birth," §preface, 1, in *Works* 1:417.

that we are especially vulnerable during the early time of life when we are still developing physically, mentally, and emotionally. Wesley's own experience, which he described as sinning away the washing of his baptism, is no doubt shared by many people. The objects of sense, objects of imagination, and pride of life might have especially strong power to draw us away from God when our personality and character are still being formed. But that also means that the means of grace given to and used by the church may be especially effective in forming us to lean on God.

As a movement, Methodism found its place and its effectiveness in calling people to lived experience of new birth and then provided means for them to sustain and grow their life with God. We are not simply a movement anymore, and we need to take seriously what it means to be church. As a church we have the same aim—to call people to lived experience of God and provide them with the means for such experience—but now among those means for Methodists to use is the sacrament of baptism in which God offers new life. In this new circumstance as church, we make a claim about the work of God in baptism from the beginning of life. It is our job, then, to make it possible for people to say they have always been Christian, not simply because of baptism, but because they have made good use of the means of grace that the church offers to keep breathing God. But we should also be ready to call back to life all those who have neglected their baptisms to the point of suffocation. We have reason as a church to learn from the way Wesley organized the movement not to wait until respiration fails to call people to deep breathing in God.

Some Further Thoughts

The self-examination practiced among early Methodists is critical for maintaining the breathing we need in order to lean on God as we should. If we do not engage this practice, the churches that came from Methodism will be in constant need of reform and revival from death. So this revival is very important, but churches also have to think about more than the internal lives of individuals when we think about how

Methodists need to be revived from death to life. There are other kinds of death-dealing we need to be aware of. I will mention two, although no doubt others could be mentioned.

First, spiritual respiration as Wesley described it is highly focused on personal salvation. Those of you who do not know well the history of the Oxford Institute may not realize that an entire Institute was devoted in 1977 to sanctification and liberation, precisely to expand Methodist theology beyond personal salvation to the wider scope of sin in oppression, where the stakes for the oppressed are often life and death. Some of the resources from that Institute are available on the Oxford Institute website archives. The need to address lived oppression, especially through systems, is something we need to keep exploring as Methodists. As we think about the slide into sin, we must reflect not only on internal desires and tempers as Wesley identified them, but also on how the systems we live in shape what we desire, as well as how our desires draw us into participation in sinful systems and not just individual sins.

Second, spiritual respiration is motivated by an eschatological vision of human life with God, to have the image of God restored in us. I would also note that the Oxford Institute explored a Methodist understanding of God's eschatological vision in a previous meeting. At least some of the presentations for the theme "The New Creation" at the eleventh Institute held in 2002 reminded us that God's vision for the world includes more than human life. As we contemplate the way spiritual respiration keeps us from starting the slide into sin, we would do well to consider the way that our desires not only draw us away from God, but also lead us into appetites of consumption that affect God's creation. Breathing out thanks to God must include care for the world that God has given us so that we show our gratitude for this gift.

When we ask Wesley's question "What are you now?" I urge us to consider these more expansive ways that sin exerts its death-dealing in our lives so that our spiritual respiration can empower us to live for God in more ways than the earliest Methodists, and even Wesley, may have sought.

Chapter Bibliography

Lancaster, Sarah Heaner. "Baptism and Justification: A Methodist Understanding." *Ecclesiology* 4, no. 3 (2008): 1–19.

The United Methodist Church. *The Book of Discipline of the United Methodist Church 2016*. Nashville: The United Methodist Publishing House, 2016.

Wesley, Charles. *Hymns and Sacred Poems*. Vol. 1. Bristol, UK: Farley, 1749.

Wesley, John. *John Wesley's Sunday Service of the Methodists in North America*. Edited by James F. White. Nashville: Quarterly Review United Methodist Publishing House, 1984

———. *Journals and Diaries*. Edited by W. Reginald Ward and Richard P. Heitzenrater. Vol. 18 of *The Bicentennial Edition of the Works of John Wesley*. Nashville: Abingdon Press, 1988.

———. *A Plain Account of Christian Perfection*. Edited and annotated by Randy L. Maddox and Paul W. Chilcote. Kansas City, MO: Beacon Hill Press, 2015.

———. *The Methodist Societies: History, Nature, and Design*. Edited by Rupert E. Davies. Vol. 9 of *The Bicentennial Edition of the Works of John Wesley*. Nashville: Abingdon Press, 1989.

———. *Sermons*. Edited by Albert C. Outler. Vols. 1–4 of *The Bicentennial Edition of the Works of John Wesley*. Nashville: Abingdon Press, 1984–1987.

Documents

Encountering Christ the Saviour: Church and Sacraments. Lake Junaluska, NC: The World Methodist Council, 2011. http://worldmethodistcouncil.org/wp-content/uploads/2014/10/Encountering-Christ-the-Saviour-Church-and-Sacraments.pdf.

Felton, Gayle Carlton. *By Water and the Spirit*. Nashville: Discipleship Resources, 1998. https://gbod-assets.s3.amazonaws.com/drint/resources/english/bywaterandthespirit.pdf.

Connexionalism in Flux

In the British Methodist Context

Nicola V. Price-Tebbutt

THE METHODIST CHURCH IN BRITAIN has been considering, or reconsidering, connexionalism these past few years, and last year the Conference adopted a report called *The Gift of Connexionalism in the 21st Century*, which reaffirmed that the connexional principle is fundamental to how Methodists understand church and a way of being Christian.[1]

The reconsideration of connexionalism came about because there were various challenges as to how connexionalism was being understood, expressed, and embodied. The report did not deny that connexionalism in British Methodism is imperfectly expressed and is misunderstood (and not always understood at all), and it was explicit about the kinds of challenges it faced in a twenty-first-century context (and these challenges are continuing); yet the 2017 Conference overwhelmingly and positively affirmed the centrality of connexionalism; indeed the title changed during the process from *Issues of Connexionalism in the 21st*

1 The Methodist Conference, 2017, *The Gift of Connexionalism in the 21st Century*, §4, https://www.methodist.org.uk/downloads/conf-2017-37-The-Gift-of-Connexionalism-in-the-21st-Century.pdf. By adopting a report the Conference endorses its recommendations or conclusions but not (without so stating) any reasons given for them (SO 131[17d]). The report was also commended for study and reflection throughout the Connexion.

Century to *The Gift of Connexionalism in the 21st Century*, reflecting connexionalism's value in the British Methodist Church.

The work of reflection on connexionalism continues: the report was commended for study and reflection, and the Methodist people were encouraged to work through issues and aspects of connexionalism in their own contexts. But I do wonder how much that has been taken up. My question highlights a further challenge: corporately, the Methodist Church in Britain affirms connexionalism as a gift, but in circuits and local churches I wonder how many have engaged with the report, wrestled with the questions, or sought to understand what connexionalism is and reflected on how to embody that understanding in practice and action.

I therefore want to say something briefly about the Methodist Church in Britain's understanding of connexionalism, drawing attention to ways in which that understanding has changed or developed over time, and then name some of the contemporary challenges before identifying five tensions, or dynamics, that have both helped to shape our understanding of connexionalism and may illuminate aspects of the continuing challenges, indicating areas that perhaps need further attention.

How Connexionalism Is Understood and Embodied in the Methodist Church in Britain

The Gift of Connexionalism in the 21st Century reaffirms that "for Methodists connexionalism is . . . a way of being Christian."[2] It builds on the understanding of connexionalism expressed in our significant Statement about the nature of the Church, which identifies that one of the distinctive emphases of Methodist ecclesiology is "an emphasis on 'relatedness' as essential to the concept of 'church', finding expression in 'the connexional principle.'"[3] The Methodist Church in Britain thus understands that the connexional principle enshrines "a vital truth about the nature

---

2 The Methodist Conference, *The Gift of Connexionalism*, §4.

3 A Conference Statement is adopted by the Conference under particular Standing Orders after a two-year consultation process with the Methodist people. Statements set out the Methodist Church in Britain's position. For the

of the Church" and "witnesses to a mutuality and interdependence which derive from the participation of all Christians through Christ in the very life of God."[4] It is a reflection of New Testament teaching and practice (e.g., the Church as the body of Christ with every organ or limb having its own distinctive function and being part of a living whole) and is the Methodist expression of that koinonia, or communion, that is at the heart of Christianity.[5] So, the Statement continues, "the Methodist sense of 'belonging', at its best, derives from a consciousness that all Christians are related at all levels of the Church to each other."[6]

The connexional principle has been intrinsic to Methodism since its origins, and it is expressed through our structures of fellowship and governance, through the way in which we consult and make decisions and how we exercise oversight. The recent review, however, noted that the way in which it is expressed and embodied has changed and developed over time; it has "shaped, and been lived out in, the faith, practice and assumptions of generations of Methodist people."[7]

The Methodist connexion came into being because John Wesley saw a need for more systematic spiritual guidance and mutual fellowship among his converts. In the eighteenth century the word *connexion* was used in other areas of life (among politicians, for example, as well as in religious bodies) and referred both to those who were connected to some person or group and to the relationship itself. "Connexion" came to be applied to individuals, societies, and preachers who were "in connexion" with John Wesley (and through him with each other) and to the emerging Methodist movement, a movement that

---

nature of the Church see The Methodist Conference, 1999, *Called to Love and Praise,* especially §4.6 and §4.7.1.

4 The Methodist Conference, 1999, *Called to Love and Praise*, §4.6.1.

5 *Called to Love and Praise* discusses *koinonia* in §3.1, ¶7–9. Note especially ¶3.1.8: "*koinonia*, then, denotes both what Christians share and also that sharing is at the heart of Christian faith." For a full review of the use of the term ecumenically, see Thomas F. Best and Günther Gassmann, eds., *On the Way to Fuller Koinonia: The Official Report of the Fifth World Conference on Faith and Order* (Geneva: WCC Publications, 1994).

6 The Methodist Conference, *Called to Love and Praise*, §4.6.4.

7 The Methodist Conference, *The Gift of Connexionalism*, §1.

was motivated by the three convictions that Christ had died for all, that all were called to holy love, and that there was no such thing as solitary religion. There is no doubt that while he lived it was John Wesley who held together those who became known as Methodists, but he did make provision for a corporate body to succeed to his authority as he sought to establish the Legal Conference of one hundred preachers (the Legal Hundred), and supreme authority today continues to be vested in the Conference, although it is now a more representative body of lay and ordained and those who represent specific areas of the Church's life. Today the foundational rules of the Methodist Church in Britain, as expressed in the Deed of Union and the Standing Orders based on them, both inform and are informed by the connexional principle, and it continues to underpin our structures. Local Churches are grouped into Circuits (which now vary in size from one-church Circuits to large Circuits). The Circuit is understood as "the primary unit in which Local Churches express and experience their interconnexion in the Body of Christ, for purposes of mission, mutual encouragement and help," and it is in the Circuit "that presbyters, deacons and probationers are stationed and local preachers are trained and admitted and exercise their calling."[8] They are then grouped into Districts, which make up the Connexion, and there is a Connexional Team who support Local Churches, Circuits, and Districts, and carry out work on behalf of the Conference.[9] The Conference remains the supreme authority, and ministers and members agree to abide by its discipline. In practice, though, the question continues of how well-known decisions of the Conference are and how well they are acted upon.

Challenges to Connexionalism

As I mentioned in my introduction, five years ago the Methodist Conference directed the Faith and Order Committee to reexamine

8 *The Constitutional Practice and Discipline of the Methodist Church*, 2017, Standing Order 500.

9 *The Constitutional Practice and Discipline of the Methodist Church*, Standing Order 302.

connexionalism in the face of a host of challenges and issues that could be understood to call it into question. The idea that connexionalism "no longer worked" was not uncommon (and when that phrase was used it seemed to mean different things to different people), and there was a sense that British Methodism was becoming, or had become, more congregational, with many people having little sense of the Circuit (let alone the wider Connexion). The issues raised included pressures on the discipline of stationing (whereby ministers are annually appointed—or sent—to a circuit by the Conference) and a questioning of the level of commitment to ministerial itinerancy (there continues to be the expectation that ministers are available to be deployed anywhere in the Connexion according to need, and therefore most appointments are normally for only an initial five years). The report noted "the difficulties of sustaining circuit structures with a shrinking volunteer base, the implications for denominational loyalties of stronger local ecumenical relationships, [and] the consequences of increasing organisational diversity and theological, ethical and liturgical pluralism in Methodism."[10] Furthermore, "The perception has grown that an independent, local and properly ecumenical Christian identity has come to matter far more to many Methodists than a connected and connexional denominational identity. It is feared, moreover, that grassroots Methodism sees 'the Connexion' as something other than itself: the Conference, the Connexional Team, 'headquarters'—a separate entity disconnected from Local Church and Circuit."[11]

And yet, it was found that "for Methodists connexionalism is not an abstract principle or a piece of historical baggage, but a way of being Christian. The overall conclusions . . . were that connexionalism is still fundamental to how Methodists understand the Church."[12] Most who responded to the consultation that had taken place expressed a personal sense of belonging to Methodism and found this important, although expressed and experienced in different ways. The report also pointed to a prophetic and apologetic aspect of connexionalism. Written when the

10 The Methodist Conference, *The Gift of Connexionalism*, §2.

11 The Methodist Conference, *The Gift of Connexionalism*, §2.

12 The Methodist Conference, *The Gift of Connexionalism*, §4.

United Kingdom had not long ago voted to leave the European Union and when there were increased incidents of hate crimes reported—when, as the report says, "Many are wrestling with social and political questions in relation to issues of human identity and belonging; seeking to work out how we live together as members of diverse communities with sometimes competing needs, values and priorities"—it was noted that the Methodist Church in Britain had an opportunity to reflect on what its own patterns of relating reveal "about the nature of relationships rooted, through Jesus, in the love of God."[13] It was stated that "connexionalism challenges us to a broader understanding of belonging, inviting us to see our experience of being church as reaching beyond those whom we meet week by week, to other Methodisms elsewhere, offering the opportunity of increased connection with other people and the world. Such connection deepens our experience of God and enriches our witness."[14] The 2017 Conference adopted *The Gift of Connexionalism* report overwhelmingly.

Inherent Dynamics in the British Methodist Understanding and Expression of Connexionalism

Reflecting on our understanding of connexionalism, on the challenges it continues to face, and on how it has developed over time, there were five tensions, or dynamics (because none are an "either-or" but a "both-and"), that I want to highlight, which help to illuminate how and why connexionalism has developed in this way and why such challenges continue, as well as indicate where further work (both practical and theological) could be needed.

1. Ecclesiological Principle or Means of Structuring

It is significant that the earlier 1937 British Methodist Conference Statement on the *Nature of the Church* did not refer to connexionalism, although it was considered fundamental to practice. While this

13 The Methodist Conference, *The Gift of Connexionalism*, §8.

14 The Methodist Conference, *The Gift of Connexionalism*, §8.

was rectified in the 1999 Statement, it is only relatively recently that the theological and ecclesiological convictions underpinning it were more clearly and corporately articulated, and it can be argued that even now our understanding of connexionalism could bear more theological depth. Many of our ecumenical partners, for example, see much value in the connexional principle, but it remains questionable as to how far we are yet able to adequately and robustly distinguish understandings of connexionalism from understandings of communion.

The development of the connexional structure of Methodism during John Wesley's lifetime was a response to need: there was no particular plan (and, unlike today, no concerns about a need to "grow" the church); the Connexion just grew. After Wesley's death, the emphasis was greater on the Connexion as a system of mutual support through which the societies and the preachers related to each other, and an emphasis (or expectation) of the Connexion being a means of receiving (and sometimes giving) support continues to be prevalent, although it is now often understood as pragmatic (through sharing or giving financial or other resources) more than anything else. For Wesley, connexionalism was a pastoral and practical way of ordering for mission, and he did not intend to establish a new church. Today, connexionalism is used to refer both to an ecclesiological principle and to the structures through which the Methodist Church in Britain expresses this understanding, but which one is being spoken of at any one time is not always clear. The most recent reflection revealed that while the ecclesiological principle continues to be affirmed, the structures and methods of expression are more frequently referred to as "broken."

2. Theological Ideal or Pragmatic Ordering

The distinction between ecclesiological principle and structures leads me to the dynamic between the theological ideal and the pragmatic ordering, the gap between the theory and the practice. The Conference did not hesitate to reaffirm the connexional principle; indeed, it adopted a report overwhelmingly that, as I mentioned, indicated that it had the potential to witness to the life-giving nature of relationships rooted, through Jesus, in the love of God. Yet the challenge of realizing that potential should not be underestimated: such witness can only happen if we are able to embody something of our understanding. It is acknowledged that relationships can be very, very, very hard and profoundly challenging, "sustained . . . through time, attention and commitment."[15] We might well affirm the connexional principle and celebrate its contribution to our theology, but how well do we try to live it out? How much of our time, attention, and commitment do we give to embodying the principle in our practice, our decision-making, our prayers, our ways of relating, our priorities? If one wanted to, one could possibly trace the development of the connexional principle from a pragmatic ordering to encourage spiritual growth to a theological ideal that we are unable to live up to, but I hope that is not the case.

3. Individual Growth and Corporate Witness (Being in Relationship)

The dynamic between the individual and the corporate, the community, is key, and the extent to which the boundaries of one need to be expanded or contained in order to allow the flourishing of the other is a constant question and movement and dynamic. Within it are, inevitably, questions about personal and corporate identity; about self-esteem and self-awareness (both individually and corporately); about generosity, appropriate self-denial, and an ability to truly live together with contradictory convictions (a subject that the Methodist Church in Britain continues to wrestle with). The 1999 Statement acknowledges that connexionalism relates closely to the overall balance between discipline and joy that is at the heart of Christian discipleship, individual and corporate. The system imposes restraints on the individual, the Local Church, and indeed other parts of the Church, such as the Circuit or District, in the interests of the common good and the overall mission. At the same time, it is productive of great joy and enrichment. Ideally, as the Church grows in maturity and love, the structures should be seen as embodiments of mutual love and support. Whether this is in fact the case is obviously a matter of sometimes heated debate!

15 The Methodist Conference, *The Gift of Connexionalism*, §11.

It is also worth noting that Methodist church life began from a movement structured to encourage growth in holiness in all its members, but many of the ways in which this was encouraged have faded (e.g., the class meeting). Today it has been emphasized that we are structured for mission, which is commonly understood as enabling a sharing of resources of money, property, and people in the places where they are most needed. In our 1999 Statement about the Church we say that as "the natural corollary of connexionalism, Local Churches, Circuits and Districts exercise the greatest possible degree of autonomy. This is necessary if they are to express their own cultural identity and to respond to local calls of mission and service in an appropriate way."[16] We have recognized that "their dependence on the larger whole is also necessary for their own continuing vitality and well-being. Such local autonomy may also need to be limited from time to time in the light of the needs of the whole Church,"[17] but some of the recent work has highlighted continuing questions about whether our structures enable us to make decisions together about where resources are most needed, about what the specific missional priorities are, and about whether individuals are truly encouraged and enabled to participate in decision-making as part of a wider community. Questions also arise about whether individuals have the time, commitment, and inclination to undertake the hard work of doing so.

Connexionalism is experienced in a way of life that assumes that all contribute to and receive from the life and mission of the whole Church. British Methodists are known for their meetings. People may joke about Methodist meetings, find them tedious, time-consuming, and frustrating, but consulting, conferring together, coming to shared decisions, and seeking other views *can* be tedious, time-consuming, and sometimes frustrating—and it profoundly reflects our connexional understanding! The purpose of gathering together in meetings is perhaps not always understood or appreciated, particularly if they are viewed as a means of making effective decisions rather than as part of a process of conferring about our response to God's call in order

16 The Methodist Conference, *Called to Love and Praise*, §4.6.2.

17 The Methodist Conference, *Called to Love and Praise*, §4.6.2.

to discern how together we best share in God's mission. At its best, the dynamic in connexionalism between individual and corporate growth and witness works to enable the flourishing of both, but it can quickly become a costly tension between individual, or local, and the wider community of Methodists, be it Circuit, District, or the whole Connexion.

4. "All Are Welcome" and Methodist Identity (Belonging . . .)

John Wesley once wrote, "I have only one thing in view, to keep all the Methodists in Great Britain one connected people."[18] Former secretary of the Conference and past president Brian Beck, reflecting on connexionalism, describes how, in the twentieth century, "traditional tight spiritual discipline has given way to broader and more varied understandings of spirituality, and a greater openness to all comers."[19] Whereas once societies, and their members, were expected to adhere to a clear discipline at the risk of ceasing to be "in connexion" with Mr. Wesley, it is not uncommon today for churches to be reluctant to remove those they have not seen for several years from membership. There is perhaps a greater expectation that the Local Church is a place of hospitality and welcome for all (reflecting something of the love and grace of God), and therefore common discipline, theological diversity, and other boundaries have expanded in various ways. There is more variety in how those who wish to call themselves Methodist express their belonging, and membership is no longer the defining factor. Patterns of relating and belonging are challenged by various communities such as Fresh Expressions of church, local ecumenical partnerships, and the cultural- or language-specific fellowship groups. The Methodist Church in Britain is undoubtedly richer for such diversity and difference, and it faces the challenges of where the boundaries of its identity lie. Our connexionalism enables us to hold in relationship

18 Wesley to friends in Trowbridge (March 3, 1790) in *The Letters of John Wesley*, vol. 8, *July 24, 1787, to February 24, 1791*, ed. John Telford (London: Epworth Press 1931), 205.

19 Brian Beck, "Reflections on Connexionalism," in *Methodist Heritage and Identity*, Routledge Methodist Studies (Oxford: Routledge, 2017), 48.

a rich diversity of people and of expressions of Local Church (and it allows for more diversity than is often understood), yet there is also a perceived weakening of those things that are held in common and questions about what it means to be Methodist today; the dynamic between living with diversity and expressing a common identity is profoundly challenging.

5. Shared Oversight and the Visionary Leader (Issues of Power)

I could not reflect on tensions or dynamics without mentioning power, perhaps most clearly seen in the dynamic between our understanding that oversight is shared (and this is an understanding deeply embedded in British Methodist DNA) and the ambivalent relationship we have with personal power and authority: at times seeking and bemoaning the lack of visionary leaders and at other times refusing to give too much power to any one individual (e.g., each time the question of extending the presidency or vice-presidency beyond one year has come up, the Conference has not agreed to that). The tension between individual authority and power and corporate authority can be seen in the development of Methodism. John Wesley saw the Connexion as linked personally to and through himself (especially the preachers), and in the *Minutes of 1766* he explains the power he has: "It is a power of admitting into and excluding from the Societies under my care; of choosing and removing Stewards; of receiving or not receiving Helpers; of appointing them when, where and how to help me; and of desiring any of them to meet me, when I see good."[20] Indeed, in 1771, speaking of the Conference then, one of the preachers said, "Mr Wesley seemed to do all the business himself." But John Wesley ensured that it was a body of people, and not an individual, that inherited his power and authority, and today the Conference is the Methodist Church in Britain's central authority. Questions of power and the flow of power in a connexional church might be a fruitful topic of

20 John Wesley, "Minutes (Leeds, August 12 etc., 1766)," Q. 29, in *The Methodist Societies: The Minutes of Conference*, ed. Henry D. Rack, *The Bicentennial Edition of the Works of John Wesley* (Nashville: Abingdon Press, 2011), 10:329.

more rigorous reflection. It was clear from the consultations that fed into the 2017 report on connexionalism that power was commonly perceived to be something others had—usually the disembodied "connexion"—and individual members, Local Churches, ministers, office holders, representatives, Circuits, even the Conference may feel themselves powerless to bring about the change they would like to see.

Conclusion

In the Methodist Church in Britain, connexionalism therefore is, and always has been, in flux. At different times this has prompted us to reexamine both our understanding and practice. Although realistic about its imperfect expression and the plethora of challenges, the Methodist Church continues to affirm its importance, and I finish with the conclusion to the 2017 report:

> The Conference has been greatly encouraged by the affirmation of connexionalism and by the evidence of the effective application of the connexional principle demonstrated in the responses to this consultation. In embracing the persistent and dynamic tension between the local and the wider community, the connexional principle prompts us to face the challenges and hard work of living in relationship with others. Where isolation, individualism and suspicion impair relationships, such a witness to other ways of being can offer life-giving possibilities. In emphasizing relationships of mutuality and interdependence, the connexional principle helps us to reveal something of the love and nature of God. Although working out the practical implications of being a connexional Church in the twenty-first century is challenging (as it was in the eighteenth, nineteenth and twentieth centuries), the Conference is confident that the Methodist people have the resources and the determination to undertake this task. Above all, we affirm our confidence in God, who calls us into connexion, and sustains us in relationship.[21]

21 The Methodist Conference, *The Gift of Connexionalism*, §16.

Bibliography

Beck, Brian E. "Reflections on Connexionalism." In *Methodist Heritage and Identity*, 45–66. Routledge Methodist Studies, edited by William Gibson. Oxford: Routledge, 2018.

Best, Thomas F., and Günther Gassmann, eds. *On the Way to Fuller Koinonia: The Official Report of the Fifth World Conference on Faith and Order.* Geneva: WCC Publications, 1994.

Wesley, John. *The Letters of John Wesley.* Vol. 8. Edited by John Telford. London: Epworth Press 1931.

———. *The Methodist Societies: The Minutes of Conference.* Edited by Henry D. Rack. Vol. 10 of *The Bicentennial Edition of the Works of John Wesley.* Nashville: Abingdon Press, 2011.

Documents

The Methodist Conference. *Called to Love and Praise*, 1999.

———. *The Gift of Connexionalism.* 2017.

———. *The Constitutional Practice and Discipline of the Methodist Church.* 2017, Standing Order 500.

———. *The Constitutional Practice and Discipline of the Methodist Church.* 2017, Standing Order 302.

In the Nigerian Context

The Very Rev. Dr. Chinonyerem Ekebuisi

Introduction

Connexionalism is identified and defined in terms of belonging, mutuality, and interdependence. All Christians are essentially linked to one another; within the Methodist Church Nigerian experience, no local church is or can be an autonomous unit complete in itself, and this is expressed in apt structures of oversight, balancing authority and subsidiarity. Through lived experiences and circumstances, the Methodist

Church Nigeria has adopted and demonstrated the connexional principle within its unique structure. These principles of connexionalism have remained fundamental to its self-identity, to its experience, and to its understanding of the church. This sense of belonging, although expressed and experienced in many different ways, is demonstrated in the evolving history of the Church.

Since the twentieth century, the connexional understanding of the church in Nigeria has faced challenges, such as the cost, ease, and risk of traveling within a large country like Nigeria; it is difficult to sustain a church that is built on a closely integrated committee system in a big developing country already divided along ethnic and political lines. Since its autonomy in 1962, the Conference has wrestled with social and political questions in relation to issues of human identity and belonging, seeking to work out how to live together as members of diverse communities with sometimes competing needs, values, and priorities. These questions have led the Conference to adopt a unique structural expression of connexionalism, which this chapter will attempt to document and demonstrate.

Early Beginning of Methodist Church Nigeria

Methodism began in Nigeria through the activities of two brands of British Methodist Missionary Societies. The first Society to arrive was the Wesleyan Methodist Missionary Society on September 24, 1842. The Primitive Methodist Missionary Society later arrived in 1893 through Equatorial Guinea. Following the 1932 amalgamation and unification of these two Missions in Britain, their activities and achievements in Nigeria were joined to form what later became known as Methodist Church Nigeria. Mercy Oduyoye explains, "When the churches of the Primitive Methodist Missionary Society and the Wesleyan Methodist Missionary Society in Nigeria came together, they did so by instruction from above. . . . From London, Methodist East and

West of the Niger, built up by two different British Methodist traditions, were thrown together to become Methodist Church Nigeria."[22]

Chief Kanu Offonry and Rev. Ike Godwin also record,

> Until 1962, there were two Methodist districts in Nigeria. The first was the Western Nigeria District, which was established by missionaries of the Wesleyan Methodist Church. The second was the Eastern Nigeria District, which was founded by the Primitive Methodist missionary society. No direct link whatsoever existed between the two Nigeria Districts except that they were both administered by the British Methodist Society operating from 25 Marylebone Road London. The situation was in no way changed by the 1932 unification of the various factions of Methodist Church in Britain.[23]

Autonomous Status

Methodist Church Nigeria became an autonomous Conference on September 28, 1962. Rev. Leslie Davison, BD, then president of the British Conference, inaugurated the Nigeria Conference after the signing of the Deed of Foundation and declared the Conference duly constituted. Autonomy did not change the structure of church governance. The Societies and Circuits remained, grouped under seven district synods. The Western District with headquarters in Lagos was divided into three Synods: Lagos, Ibadan, and Ilesha. The Eastern District, with headquarters in Umuahia, was divided into three: Calabar, Umuahia, and Port Harcourt. The work in northern Nigeria, formerly under Lagos, was classed as a district with headquarters in Jos. Over and above these was the Conference. The minister and the catechists were in charge of the Societies. Superintendents, who presided over the

22 M. A. Oduyoye, *The Wesleyan Presence in Nigeria: An Exploration of Power, Control and Partnership in Mission* (Ibadan, Nigeria: Sefer, 1992), 130.

23 Kanu Offonry and Ike Godwin Chukwuezuo, *Most Rev. Dr. Rogers Uwadi: The Compelling Story of a Colossus in The Methodist Church Nigeria* (Owerri, Nigeria: New African Publishers, 1999), 55.

quarterly meeting, headed the Circuits, and the districts were under the chairmen who presided over the synods. The Conference area, comprising all the Methodist churches in the whole country, was presided over by the president.

In giving the Methodist Church Nigeria its autonomy, the Deed of Church Order was patterned after the constitution of the British Conference, and the president had to change every five years or be reelected, but at each annual meeting, the Conference, by ballot, had to designate a qualified person to be president designate with the intent that he would become the president if his designation was confirmed at the next annual meeting.

Just five years after the autonomy, Nigeria experienced a destabilizing civil war that lasted for three years, from 1967 to 1970. Coincidently, the war followed the already-existing fault lines in the church, north and west on one side of the war while the east remained on the other side. The hostilities, suspicions, and bitterness in the nation spilled over to the Church and greatly affected the young Conference. First, there was the problem of lack of communication between the Conference Office in Lagos and the war-torn areas in the East, leading to a total collapse of administration. The General Purpose Committee (GPC) that met in 1967 during the early years of the civil war received a memorandum from the Eastern sector requesting the creation of Area Conferences. That same memorandum was supported by the Western sector that met before the 1972 GPC with these words:

> That this meeting has carefully considered the memorandum from the "Eastern Sector" of the Methodist Church Nigeria, as well as the memoranda which came into being as a result of it. That the meeting has given due recognition to the current problem of the East with regards to inter states and ethnic relations (a problem which is as a result especially of the last civil war in Nigeria) and considered how this might affect an "Eastern Sector" Area Conference if created. That, nevertheless, for the good of Methodist Church Nigeria for the effective prosecution and promotion of God's work by the church, the creation of Area Conference is the only effective answer to our current predicament. The meeting

> therefore recommends to G.P.C. that the principle of the creation of Area Conferences be accepted; and that the mechanics of this be worked out by a committee to be set up immediately, with a view to placing a definite resolution before the 1972 conference.[24]

The GPC, however, reaffirmed its unshaken belief in one Methodist Church for Nigeria. The committee considered, however, that in view of the nature of the country, its size, the channels of communications, the cost of travel, recent political events, and the tensions that now exist and may continue to exist, there is an urgent need for a review of the constitution of the Church, which was designed on the basis of a closely integrated committee system but which had now proved unmanageable. This discussion was on the front burner when the same 1972 Conference elected Professor Emmanuel Bolaji Idowu as the president of Conference on October 14, 1972.

Professor E. Bolaji Idowu Reforms

The Rev. Professor Bolaji Idowu was a leading advocate of theology that bears the stamp of original thinking and meditation of Africans, before his election as president of the Conference. Among modern African theologians, Idowu is seen as a great apostle of Indigenization, having devoted two books to the subject. In 1965, he published *Towards an Indigenous Church* through Oxford University Press.[25] This book was his first scholarly contribution to the delicate and urgent task of building a living church in Africa. At the All Africa Conference of Churches in 1963, he presented a paper, which he later published in *The Selfhood of the Church in Africa*.[26] In these two works, he advocated for a religious consciousness that was inherently African. Also, during the

---

24 M. M. Familusi, *Methodism in Nigeria, 1842–1992* (Ibadan, Nigeria: NPS Education Publishers, 1992), 143.

25 E. Bolaji Idowu, *Towards an Indigenous Church* (Oxford: Oxford University Press, 1965).

26 E. Bolaji Idowu, *The Selfhood of the Church in Africa* (Lagos: Methodist Church Nigeria Press, 1970s).

seventh International African Seminar, organized by the International African Institute in Accra, Ghana, in April 1965, he presented a paper, "The Predicament of the Church in Africa."[27]

Idowu, in his argument, stressed the necessity to replace foreign ideologies when he contended that they cause spiritual sterility in the lives of African churches. He pursued this idea further while he was writing the introduction to the book *Biblical Revelation and African Beliefs*.[28] These ideas formed the bulk of his thesis in that work. Idowu came to the seat of the president of Nigerian Methodist Conference already aware of what he wanted to do. The necessity and urgent need to replace the European complexion of the Church loomed so large in his heart that immediately after his election he said,

> We must undertake the review of our constitution in a way that would reflect and emphasize that ours is an autonomous church in Nigeria. There is a task of ordering the life of the Church in such a way that she will minister effectively and adequately to the needs of our people in their native context, here we are faced with the delicate but urgent undertaking of the indigenization of the Church, which embraces a thorough review of our liturgy. Reconciliation throughout Nigeria is a necessity laid upon us. This will take our spiritual and moral energy—but it is the work into which we have been called and we must fulfill our assignment.[29]

In his first address to the 1973 Conference, he recognized that the Church that came into being in 1962 was made up of two separate bodies, which until then had had little relational contact with each other, each of them having come into being because of two separate missionary activities, determined by two different modes of evangelism

27 E. Bolaji Idowu, "The Predicament of the Church in Africa," in *Christianity in Tropical Africa*, ed. Christian Goncalves K. Baeta (Oxford: Oxford University Press, 1968), 417–40.

28 E. Bolaji Idowu, "Introduction," in *Biblical Revelation and African Beliefs*, ed. Kwesi A. Dickson and Paul Ellingworth (Maryknoll, NY: Orbis Books, 1969).

29 Methodist Church, Nigeria Conference, *Minutes* (Methodist Church, Nigeria Conference, 1972), 11–12.

organized according to two varied ecclesiastic patterns. Each of the two bodies also happened to embrace several ethnic groups each with its own particular orientation, traditional or political. According to Idowu, the tragedy of the power struggles in the past eleven years of the Church's life had caused the Church to waste her spiritual energy so much that she had been rendered insensible to the years that the locust has eaten, hence the title he gave to his 1973 address to Conference, "The Years That the Locust Has Eaten." He posited that Methodist Church Nigeria must be really and truly a living Church, a Church that has a recognizable identity, a Church with an image worthy of her status, a Church effective in her witness and ministry, a Church with life and work that demonstrate an unmistakable Spirit power.[30] To him, a Church that is to be effective in service must be equipped with the Spirit and must manifest that fact outwardly in her expressional activities.

On the image of the Church, he discussed several issues. Regarding the Constitution, he raised the question of what kind of Constitution the Church needed as an autonomous Church, if it is to be truly autocephalous. Further, it had become clear to him that there was an urgent call for the overhauling and the reorganization of the structure of the Church and of the ordering of her ministry. Regarding the liturgy, he averred, "We are in Nigeria and must be faithful in ministering to the spiritual needs of Nigeria worshipers through radical changes in our liturgy and with this we can stop the drift of our people to other places of worship where they are going in their hundreds because they feel that there, their spiritual needs are better answered."[31]

Regarding the staffing of the Church, he said that there was little doubt that the spiritual life of the Church was at a rather low ebb, and the people who were either staying away or deserting the Church were doing so simply as a consequence of the fact that, as hungry and thirsty

---

30 E. Bolaji Idowu, "Restoring the Years That the Locust Has Eaten" (presidential address, Representative Session of Methodist Church Nigeria twelfth annual conference, November 20, 1973) (Ibadan, Nigeria: Oluseyi Press, 1973), 5.

31 Idowu, "Restoring the Years That the Locust Has Eaten," 6.

sheep, they were looking up to the Church in vain for nourishment. He asserted a major reason for this—acute shortage of trained, dedicated staff in the Church. The number of ministers was detrimentally too few, and those few were overworked—so overworked that they had little time for study and meditation.

In that address, he pointed to the need for the Church to reorganize in a way that will give dignity of form and content to its life, the need to consider carefully and adopt every measure that will make the Church effectual, as well as respectable within the cultural setting in which it is situated. He proposed the setting up and building of the District headquarters. He found as abnormal the practice whereby a chairman stayed wherever he was when elected as a chairman and at the same time functioned as the superintendent of a Circuit or Circuits and minister in charge of a congregation in addition to being the pastoral and administrative head of a District.[32]

As a follow-up to his Conference address, he organized a retreat at Asaba from February 1st to 3rd, 1974. During the retreat, those meeting considered matters relating to liturgy, the structure of the Church, and the ordering of the ministry. His address to Conference formed the basis of the retreat's deliberation. On the structure of the Church, which was made up of the Society, Circuit, District, and Conference, he suggested the Local Church in place of the Society, Circuit still remained the Circuit, Diocese in place of the District, a new structure named Archdiocese, and finally the Conference.

At the retreat, he further called on participants to consider whether Methodist Church Nigeria as presently set up was as effectual as she should be and in what way the organizational pattern might affect its effectiveness. The question has come up again and again as to why we should not change the titles of the hierarchy of our Church. The next was the superintendence, the chairmanship, and the presidency, which he saw as ephemeral offices. The office bearer could be sacked from that position at the whims and caprices of a collection of "influential" persons, who could sway or dominate the meeting, which constitutionally held the fate of the office in its hands. He posed the question

32 Idowu, "Restoring the Years That the Locust Has Eaten," 8.

whether this ordering gives grace and dignity (ecclesiastical and spiritual) to the ministry in our Nigerian cultural setting. He suggested that in the context of Africa, the congregation sees the minister as a priest. This is consonant with the African background. He argued that once an African ceases to see his minister as a priest, the minister's position has been emptied of any dignity or virtue. Perhaps this is one of the contributing factors that have resulted in the way that Methodist ministers are regarded or treated as messengers or houseboys in certain quarters. Has it not been said again and again—and quite loudly too—that "the minister is our servant; we employ him and can 'sack' him at any time"?[33] Finally, he suggested the adoption of the designations of deacon, priest, presbyter, bishop, archbishop, and patriarch. The bishops, the archbishops, and the patriarch will hold their office until they retire. Comparing the old and the suggested new order he said,

> The advantage of a nonpermanent, ephemeral office is that the holder of the post tends to be careful in his doings and dealings, especially if he is a person eaten up by love of office for its own sake: power is not left in the hands of one person for too long [because] "power corrupts and absolute power corrupts absolutely" . . . Besides, a situation is created in which dirty ecclesiastical politics will thrive, a situation also in which it is easy for every other minister—especially the unscrupulously ambitious—to see himself annually as competitor for the office with the result that no end of mudslinging, uncooperative attitude, waste of spiritual and emotional energy on the part of certain colleagues, as well as of the person in office, go on behind the scenes. For me, the real disadvantage is that a person who really has something to offer, by God's grace, the edification and expansion of the Church may find it frustratingly impossible to plan ahead, since his tenure of office is uncertain or, worse still, at the mercy of his followers. Such a person, if he is wise, will only go on in faith and prayers

33 Idowu, "Restoring the Years That the Locust Has Eaten," 8.

do the best that he could for the moment, while refraining from placing his trust in man.[34]

Idowu said that Methodism in Nigeria had unwittingly taken something of the marked element of the Eastern Orthodox Church without consciously working out its implications. The position of the president of the Methodist Church by definition is higher than that of an archbishop. The archbishop is limited in his jurisdiction, whereas the presidency of the Methodist Church covers the whole of the Conference area. It is even higher than that of the presiding bishop of American Methodism. Since the president is the head of the whole Church and not an ad hoc chairman of Joint Conference, this rank is that of the traditional patriarch or pontiff. Finally, Idowu called on Methodist Church Nigeria to face the consciousness of the inadequacy within or the pressure of external circumstances to make up its mind and establish its choice with regard to the ordering of the ministry. He finally presented his suggestions: "The pattern, which is emerging by evolution, is that of Patriarch, Archbishops, Diocesan Bishops, Presbyters, Ministers or Priests and Deacons. It seems to me that nothing less than this will meet our situation in a country of this size, in a competitive age." At the end of the three-day retreat, participants came up with resolutions and recommendations, which they recommended to the 1974 Methodist Church Nigeria Conference.

Resolution 1

That the Conference Committees on the Life, Work, Faith and Order of Methodist Church Nigeria, here assembled in retreat at the Rural Training Centre Asaba, having given prayerful consideration, under the guidance of the Holy Spirit:

1) Recognized the need to reappraise the organization of the Methodist Church Nigeria for the purpose of promoting the work of God in the Methodist Church Nigeria.

2) Realized that the present set-up has tended to reflect a lower status on the ministry of the Methodist Church Nigeria,

34 Idowu, "Restoring the Years That the Locust Has Eaten," 15.

not only on the part of the public at large, but also, has constantly tended to embarrass, and has often made our members accept the inferior status attributed to our ministry.

3) Recognized that the desire to give a new, true image reflecting the true status of the Methodist Church is widespread through the conference area.

4) Recognized that the Methodist Church Nigeria, after twelve years of autonomy and autocephaly and over one hundred and thirty years of existence, the time is overdue for reappraisal.

5) Realized that the present nomenclatures of President, Chairman, Superintendent used in describing our ministry do not reflect their true place and function in the Christian Church.

Do resolve and they hereby resolve to recommend to the Conference of the Methodist Church, Nigeria that the time has come for a change suitable to the ecclesiastical stature and reflecting the nationwide image of our Church, and our place in the tradition of the Christian Church, within the guidelines of the Holy Scriptures, and under the continuous tuition of the Holy Spirit.

Resolution 2

That Episcopacy in its scriptural and ecclesiastical connotation be adopted by the Methodist Church Nigeria.

Resolution 3

That the following titles, which are in scriptural and ecclesiastical traditions, be adopted: Deacon, Priest, Presbyter, Bishop, Archbishop and Patriarch.[35]

The *Asaba Retreat Document*, containing the above resolutions, was widely circulated free of charge among members of the Church with the request that in keeping with the Methodist practice, it should be discussed at all levels—Societies, Circuits, and District Synods—and that views and suggestions emanating from this discussion be passed through the usual channel back to Conference. The reports from the

35 *Asaba Retreat Document* (1974) circulated to members after the retreat.

Societies, Circuits, and District Synods revealed the fears of the members. Idowu wrote another document to further explain the proposal and allay the fears of the members. In his words:

> I hear that there is need for further explanation on the proposal for the Ordering of the ministry. I had thought that the published Asaba paper was sufficiently self-explanatory. The explanation, as I believe, is to allay the fears of our people about the misconception of Episcopacy, which translated into practice, has been bedeviling the Church not only in Nigeria but almost throughout Africa. I share our people's concern with considerable sympathy.[36]

He directed the chairmen of Districts, superintendents of Circuits, and all ministers to inform all the people that the Constitution, which was now under preparation, included these ideas:

> The authority of Methodist Church Nigeria is vested in Conference and not in the hands of any single person, and not in the Ordained Ministry. Methodist Church Nigeria believes and maintains firmly that the Church is made up of the whole people of God, ordained and lay. The hierarchy of Patriarch, Archbishops, Bishops, Presbyters, Priests and Deacons, is administrative and functional and shall operate as agreed and decided by Conference and prescribed in the new Constitution. Its purpose is for effective administration and effectual image of the Church in a country and continent, where the designations currently used by us do not convey sufficient meaning and have been partly the reason for the disregard with which our Church is being treated.
>
> There is no title that we are adopting now that is not biblical or historically ecclesiastical. We are, in fact, taking a departure in the right direction, from the biblical or historically ecclesiastical titles. We are, therefore, bringing ourselves back into time with biblical and historically ecclesiastical ordering of the ministry. A high-powered committee will be set up to address itself to the

---

36 E. Bolaji Idowu, *Methodist Church Nigeria: Church Structure and Ordering of the Ministry* (Lagos: Graphic Press, 1974).

task of nominating under Conference Order the new ordained officials according to the proposed reordering.[37]

The Fourteenth Annual Conference, held at the University of Calabar from September 2nd to 12th, 1975, adopted the new Constitution. The sitting Conference, by a unanimous vote, declared January 20, 1976, as "The Appointed Day." The president was elected the patriarch. The Conference areas were divided into four Archdioceses, and the archbishops were named. So were the Dioceses created and the Bishops nominated. The corresponding lay presidents, including two women, also were nominated. The Conference then adjourned to reconvene from January 16th to 26th, 1976. The Appointed Day was held at Methodist Church of the Trinity, Tinubu, Lagos. The president (patriarch-elect), read the deed of the New Constitution Reform Order, and the twenty trustees (ten ministers and ten laypeople) appointed by the Conference signed it. The Bishop Prince Taylor, chairman of the World Methodist Council, preached the historic sermon. The patriarch and all other nominated archbishops and bishops were subsequently invested.

The adoption of this 1975/1976 Constitution created a crisis that divided the Church into two factions. Some members opted to remain with the 1962 inherited Constitution while others accepted the new Constitution. After eleven years of the division, in January 1987, the laity of the two factions in Lagos Diocese passed a resolution of fusion and inaugurated a fusion committee. The work of this committee brought about the Sagamu Assembly of all Methodists from all over the country in July 1989. The Assembly, presided over jointly by the patriarch and the president, appointed a Constitution Review Committee to produce a new Constitution. The Draft Constitution was submitted to the resumed Assembly in October 1989, which was then sent to all Dioceses of Methodist Church Nigeria for study and comments. The Assembly decided to hold joint Conference in Sagamu on March 1–2, 1990, to consider the comments. The joint Conference met as agreed and, after making all necessary amendments based on the comments on the draft Constitution, which included the change of the title from

37 Idowu, *Methodist Church Nigeria*, 2.

patriarch to prelate, the establishment of the Men's Fellowship, and the creation of the lay session of Conference that would be meeting simultaneously with the ministerial session, adopted the new Constitution.

On the decision of this joint Conference, a service of reunification was held on Sunday, March 4, 1990, and on May 23 and 24, 1990, the joint Conference ratified the new Constitution after the agreed-upon amendments had been corrected. The service for signing the 1990 Constitution was held on Wesley Day, May 24, 1990.

The Present Status of the Church

On July 4, 2003, the General Purpose Committee of Methodist Church Nigeria, in full realization of the urgent need to further reposition the Church to cope with the challenges of the twenty-first century, set up a committee called the Strategic Planning Team (SPT). The team was to examine where the Church was, where it is now, where it hopes to be, and how to get there. After several months of research, studies, interactive sessions, and retreats, the SPT came up with a report that identified some problems and weaknesses and then proffered solutions. The recommendations of the team were critically and exhaustively considered and then adopted after necessary amendments by the Thirty-Ninth/Fourth Biennial Conference, which was held at Kaduna in August 2004. The Conference therefore came up with setting the vision of the church—"To be the largest and most spiritually vibrant church in Nigeria"—and the mission—"To consistently win more souls for Christ, develop spiritually fulfilled members and remain very active in serving humanity." They also observed that the weak headquarters of Methodist Church Nigeria had not helped the Church to achieve the right level of cohesion and positioning for vibrant growth. The Conference therefore accepted to reorganize the structure of the Church in order to strengthen the connexional system and make it more unified. Three directorates that would report directly to the prelate therefore were created. They are:

1. *Directorate of finance and administration:* This is headed by a bishop, who is also the secretary of Conference, and he oversees the general administration of the headquarters, interchurch relations, staff matters, management of Conference funds, and organizing the biannual conference.
2. *Directorate of evangelism and discipleship:* This is headed by a bishop and shall be responsible for liturgy and spiritual development, coordination of ministerial training, and coordination of preaching plans and other literatures of the church. He also will supervise the various organs of the church.
3. *The directorate of planning, research, and services:* The directorate coordinates the expansion programs of the Church, logistics and investment monitoring, health care and welfare institutions, and educational and investment institutions.
4. *Conference Connexional Council:* This is made up of the prelate, the Conference lay president, archbishops, archdiocesan lay presidents, and the Conference secretary; the bishop of evangelism replaced the GPC. This Committee is responsible for the day-to-day supervision of the church.[38]

At the end, Conference directed that a new Constitution should be put in place to reflect the new vision of the Church. The committee for reviewing the existing Constitution was given terms of reference, which included reexamining all the suggestions made so as to build on the current trust of the Church. The Fortieth/Fifth Biennial Conference at its Representative Session held at IBOM Hall, IBB Way, Uyo on August 2–10, 2006, ratified and adopted the new 2006 Constitution.

The 2006 Constitution ensured that the practical expressions of connexionalism in belonging, mutuality, and interdependence were maintained. The missionary dynamics, enabling the effective deployment of resources in the service of God's mission with the Conference area, were upheld. A committee of the whole Conference is saddled with the responsibilities of stationing Conference agents. Even with the

38 Methodist Church Nigeria Constitution 2006, ch. 4 ¶183–84, ¶177–78, ¶160.

adoption of Episcopacy, the ordination, preferment, ministerial discipline, and election of bishops are still the sole duties of Conference. Uniquely within Methodist Church Nigeria, bishops and archbishops are translated from one see to another, unlike in other traditions; a Methodist bishop is not excluded from the itinerant ministry. Methodist Church Nigeria as a national Church still maintains the itinerant ministry—wherever they are most needed—an acknowledgment that the ministry as a whole is at the disposal of the entire Connexion.

Relationship is at the heart of connexionalism. Being connected involves hard work: sometimes expectations of support are not met; sometimes churches fail to look beyond themselves to see how they might support and encourage others. Being in relationship is profoundly challenging. The challenge is compounded because contemporary society tends toward a dominant culture in which personal choice and the rights of the individual are emphasized over commitment to others. The twenty-first-century crisis of urbanization is putting a great deal of stress on the principles of connexionalism. We now have rich Dioceses, Circuits, and Local Churches. Many ministers are no longer willing to leave the urban, wealthy, and influential stations to serve in less influential stations. Again, in terms of funding, some of the very rich Local Churches are not disposed to using their resources to help the Connexion. Relationships are sustained and a sense of belonging strengthened through time, attention, and commitment. The idea of connexionalism being a system in which the strong help the weak and in which wider resources and experience can be made available to smaller congregations is quickly dying off. Connexionalism therefore has pastoral, evangelistic, and apologetic resonance in a world craving genuine and meaningful relationships, and it offers a hopeful alternative to a society that can seem individualistic and consumer focused.

The overall governing authority of Methodist Church Nigeria is still vested at Conference in session. The Council of Bishops does not have powers to legislate on behalf of the Church; their recommendations still come to Conference for ratification. The Archdiocesan Councils, Diocesan Synods, Circuit Councils, and Local Church Councils all represent the Conference and derive their powers from Conference.

Conclusion

Connexionalism in its eighteenth-century usage referred both to the circle of those connected to some person or group and to the relationship itself. This description of the Wesleys' movement, retaining its distinctive eighteenth-century spelling, has endured for nearly three hundred years. Connexionalism has been elaborated theologically, expressed in hymns and liturgies, justified in debates, and articulated in the constitutions and polity of the Methodist people in Nigeria as we have seen. Implicitly and explicitly, it has also shaped, and been lived out in, the faith, practice, and assumptions of generations of Methodist people in Nigeria. It is a way of being Christian, which Methodist Church Nigeria shares with other Conferences across the globe. Connexionalism challenges us to a broader understanding of belonging, inviting us to see our experience of being a church as reaching beyond those whom we meet week by week, to other Methodists elsewhere, offering the opportunity of increased connection with other people and the world.

Bibliography

Familusi, M.M. *Methodism in Nigeria, 1842–1992.* Ibadan, Nigeria: NPS Education Publishers, 1992.

Idowu, E. Bolaji. *The Selfhood of the Church in Africa.* Lagos: Methodist Church Nigeria Press, 1970.

———. *Towards an Indigenous Church.* Oxford: Oxford University Press, 1965.

———. "The Predicament of the Church in Africa." In *Christianity in Tropical Africa*, edited by Christian Goncalves K. Baeta, 417–40. Oxford: Oxford University Press, 1968.

———. "Restoring the Years That the Locust Has Eaten." Presidential address. In *Methodist Church, Nigeria Twelfth Annual, Held at Hoare's Memorial Methodist Church.* Ibadan, Nigeria: Oluseyi Press, 1973.

———. *Methodist Church Nigeria: Church Structure and Ordering of the Ministry.* Lagos: Graphic Press, 1974.

Oduyoye, M. A. *The Wesleyan Presence in Nigeria: An Exploration of Power, Control and Partnership in Mission.* Ibadan, Nigeria: Sefer, 1992.

Offonry, Kanu, and Ike Godwin Chukwuezuo. *Most Rev. Dr. Rogers Uwadi: The Compelling Story of a Colossus in The Methodist Church Nigeria.* Owerri, Nigeria: New African Publishers, 1999.

Documents

Asaba Retreat Document, circulated to members after the retreat (1974).
Methodist Church, Nigeria Conference, *Minutes* (Methodist Church, Nigeria Conference, 1972).
Methodist Church Nigeria Constitution 2006.

In the United Methodist Church

Bishop Kenneth H. Carter Jr.

Introduction

I begin by noting the complexity of this assignment. Some of those reading this will have an intense interest in the changes occurring and anticipated in The United Methodist Church, and many of those will have defined positions related to these changes. Many others will have less knowledge or interest, simply because it is outside their own context and sphere of professional responsibility. I will try not to make assumptions in this chapter, instead attempting simply to describe where we are.

This is my third Oxford Institute. I participated as a pastor in 2007 and as a newly elected bishop in 2013. One of my consecration vows was to seek unity of the church. Very soon after the beginning of my service I was asked to serve as one of three moderators of our global process related to LGBTQ (lesbian, gay, bisexual, transgender, and questioning or queer) identity and the unity of the church. And soon after that I was asked by my episcopal colleagues to serve a term (2018–2020) as president of our council of bishops. I have found myself in the midst of the process of change occurring in our global (Africa, Europe, Philippines, US) denomination.

I want to begin by noting three important dates:

- **1968**: The formation of the UMC from the Evangelical United Brethren and Methodist Churches
- **1972**: The introduction of the language in *The Book of Discipline of The United Methodist Church* that homosexuality is incompatible with Christian teaching[39]
- **2004**: The acceptance of the Ivory Coast Annual Conference into The United Methodist Church with one million members—approximately the size of the Virginia, Western North Carolina, North Georgia, and Florida Annual Conferences in my own jurisdiction

We have found ourselves at an impasse over understandings of human sexuality, and this has tested the unity of our church. And so we come to a next date: May 2016.

Our General Conference meets once every four years, as delegates to a global General Conference—half laity, half clergy—and we spend less than one hour on the topic of human sexuality. In Portland, Oregon, at the 2016 General Conference and by a very slim majority, the delegates voted to establish a study commission. There is a criticism of study commissions, but the alternative is not to study, simply to meet for a brief time, and whoever has the most power in an up-or-down vote wins.

By a slim vote a study commission was established. It was referred to as a "pause for prayer." In July 2016, the executive committee of the Council of Bishops met in Chicago. I was elected one of three moderators of the Commission on a Way Forward, along with Sandra Steiner Ball of West Virginia and David Yemba of the Congo.

---

39 This phrase is found in the Social Principles, ¶161 (G) in *The Book of Discipline of the United Methodist Church 2016.*

Organizing

Our first task was to name the members of the Commission, but then someone noted that we should take a further step back and identify the *mission, vision, and scope* of the work. This is the key sentence: "The Commission will design a way for being church that *maximizes the presence of a United Methodist witness in as many places in the world as possible*, that allows for *as much contextual differentiation as possible*, and that balances an approach to different theological understandings of human sexuality with a desire for *as much unity as possible*."[40]

After defining the mission, vision, and scope, we composed the members of the Commission. We wanted diversity that looks like our global church, and we wanted men and women committed to finding a way forward. We ended with thirty-two persons: one-third laity, one-third clergy, and one-third bishops; approximately 30 percent of the members were from Africa. Bishops would not vote on the work of the Commission, which would be given to a called General Conference, but they would be the ones who would lead Conferences through any changes.

In the Commission there are persons from four continents, with theological differences, from urban and rural areas, younger and older, gay and straight, professors, administrators, pastors, youth ministers, campus ministers, lay leaders, large-church pastors. There is Korean, Hispanic, African American, Filipino, European, and African representation.

A decision we had to make was whether we would include persons identified with renewal and advocacy groups, such as Reconciling Ministries (RMN) and Good News. We made the decision to include them. And so we have had the board chair of RMN and Confessing Movement, for example.

---

40 "Commission on a Way Forward: About Us," The United Methodist Church, accessed April 2, 2020, http://ee.umc.org/who-we-are/commission-on-a-way-forward-about-us.

The Work

The key part of the work early on was to build trust among a group of people who had good reasons and experiences not to trust each other. They had been harmed by each other, and they had done harm to each other. And so we worked on relationship-building and trust.

At the heart of this was a book titled *The Anatomy of Peace* by the Arbinger Institute.[41] The book focuses on how we live with a heart at war or a heart at peace. When we have a heart at war, we see others as obstacles to what we want or as vehicles for what we want. When we have a heart at peace, we see them as people. A heart at war exaggerates our differences. A heart at peace sees what we have in common. In addition, *The Anatomy of Peace* talks about collusion and escalation of conflict.

We wrote covenants with each other. It was real, it was emotional and raw, and at the end of our first meeting we gave everyone the invitation to leave with honor. We were not there to represent groups or constituencies. We were there to try to find a way forward.

We planned nine meetings over seventeen months. The first few meetings were about building trust, working together, knowing each other. And along the way the Commission members were ready to work on models or plans for a way forward that might be given to the Council of Bishops and the called General Conference.

I mention that we listened to each other. We also listened to the Church. We have had an open framework for receiving documents, ideas, and testimonies. To speak personally, once I was asked to serve as a moderator I removed myself from some other commitments and responsibilities. In this season of my life, if I were not working with the Florida Conference, I would be working on this. And so I have spoken at several seminaries (at Duke University, Emory University, Claremont, Southern Methodist University, Boston University), in several Annual Conferences (among them Holston, Arkansas, California-Pacific, Tennessee, Western North Carolina), with institutional leaders

41 The Arbinger Institute, *The Anatomy of Peace: Resolving the Heart of Conflict*, 2nd ed. (Oakland: Berrett-Koehler Publishers, 2015).

(such as the Duke Endowment and the Texas Methodist Foundation), in some local churches (like First United Methodist Church in San Diego, California, and Duke Memorial in Durham, North Carolina), and with the general secretaries of The United Methodist Church and a coalition of advocacy group leaders. Other Commission members have done similar work.

One significant conversation was with The United Methodist Church College of Bishops on the African continent. This was a two-day experience of listening to their own context and reflecting on colonialism and how United States divisions are imported to that continent.

The Report

The final report, shared with the church in July 2018, included three plans: a Traditional Plan, which retains the language that homosexuality is incompatible with Christian teaching and heightens accountability at all levels of the Church; the Connectional Conference Plan, which includes three churches under the umbrella of a larger connection or communion, with more loosely defined relationships; and the One Church Plan, which removes the language about human sexuality while including protections for traditionalists that would prohibit them from being forced to conduct wedding services or receive ministry from practicing gay persons.

Two key concepts in the plans are *contextualization*, already noted in the mission, vision, and scope of the Commission on a Way Forward, and *convicted humility*. The latter term was defined by a small working group from our Committee on Faith and Order, which included Sandra Wheeler and Edgardo Colon-Emeric, and, from the Commission on a Way Forward, Bishops Scott Jones, Greg Palmer, and me.

"Convicted humility" was defined as

> the recognition that our members hold a wide range of positions regarding same sex relations and operate out of sincerely held beliefs. They are convinced of the moral views they espouse, and seek to be faithful to what they see as the truth God calls the

> church to uphold. It remains the case that their views on this matter are distinctly different, and in some cases cannot be reconciled. We pray the exaggeration of our differences will not divide us. We also recognize and affirm that as United Methodists we hold in common many more fundamental theological commitments, commitments which bind us together despite our real differences. These also have implications for how we understand and express our disagreements, and for what we do about them. Therefore, we seek to advocate a stance we have called convicted humility. This is an attitude which combines honesty about the differing convictions which divide us with humility about the way in which each of our views may stand in need of corrections. It also involves humble repentance for all the ways in which we have spoken and acted as those seeking to win a fight rather than those called to discern the shape of faithfulness together. In that spirit, we wish to lift up the shared core commitments which define the Wesleyan movement, and ground our search for wisdom and holiness.
>
> We remain persuaded that the fruitfulness of the church and its witness to a fractured world are enhanced by our willingness to remain in relationship with those who share our fundamental commitments to scripture and our doctrinal standards, and yet whose views of faithfulness in this regard differ from our own.[42]

Additional key values in the plans are separation or space and unity. How much separation do we need? How much unity is possible? This goes back to the mission, vision, and scope.

The plans were translated into the four official languages (French, Portuguese, Swahili, and English) of our Church in the summer of 2018.[43] We have important ministries in Korean and Latinx contexts, and these communities are also receiving the report in their churches.

---

42 Commission on a Way Forward's Report to the General Conference (report, May 2018), 7–8, http://s3.amazonaws.com/Website_Properties/council-of-bishops/news_and_statements/documents/Way_Forward_Report_-_Final_-_ENGLISH.pdf.

43 Links to all the versions may be found here: "Way Forward Report Released in All Four Official Languages of General Conference," The United Methodist

The work was finally placed in the hands of the delegations to the called General Conference, held in St. Louis, Missouri in February 2019.

Reflection

I was a pastor for twenty-eight years, and my relation to this work is shaped in part by the shepherding role of episcopacy. Two resources have been helpful. The first is Donald Miller's work on *StoryBrand*.[44] He insists that every great story has a main character. In this story, the main character is not The United Methodist Church, or the Council of Bishops, or the Commission. So who is the main character?

- The traditionalist pastor who has sacrificed to build a strong church
- The lesbian who has been a part of the United Methodist Church her whole life
- The young adult clergy who wonders if there will be a church to serve in
- The African Christian who wants to continue to do life-saving work

There is significant anxiety and even fear. It is worth noting that in each story there is a fear.

- The pastor wonders if all of life's work will be diminished because of conflict.
- The LGBTQ person wonders if this was ever really her church.
- The young adult clergy wonders if there will be a way to express ministry.
- The African leader wonders if the resources will be there to continue.

Church, July 31, 2018, https://www.umc.org/en/content/way-forward-report-released-in-all-four-official-languages-of-general-confe.

44 Donald Miller, *Building a StoryBrand: Clarify Your Message So Customers Will Listen* (Nashville: HarperCollins Leadership, 2017).

There are multiple main characters in this story. A second resource is the TED Talk "The Danger of a Single Story" by the African storyteller Chimamanda Adichie.[45] We do not have one story. We are a global church with twelve million members on four continents. There are many main characters and multiple compelling stories.

Thus, how can we write a *Book of Discipline* for multiple stories? A clue is in our *Book of Discipline (2016)*, Paragraph 165, on pacifism and just war. One of my professors, Tom Langford, briefly referred to this in an address to the Council of Bishops in 1999. Kendall Soulen of Emory has written more recently about this. The only other place where the word *incompatible* appears in our *Book of Discipline* is in relation to war.[46] The words *conscience*, *honor*, *respect*, and *extending the ministry of the church* are prominent in this paragraph, acknowledging disagreement.

This past year I did some work at Harvard Law School in their program on negotiation. One of the learnings I took from the program is that it is very difficult to negotiate values, for example, between traditionalists and progressives. There is no splitting the difference. Kendall Soulen has noted that there are two primary frames involved here: one is orthodoxy and heresy, and the other is liberation and oppression. And neither frame can compromise.

My question is whether our Church can include both; said in a different way, I do not assume that human sexuality is a church-dividing issue.

In conclusion, I am very traditional in my theology, which is to say I am generously and unashamedly orthodox in my convictions. I believe in the Scriptures and the creeds. I am also led to believe that because of these convictions, I want the church to be open to all people, the grace of God is for all people, the ministry of the church is for all people. I have been blessed by the courage and gifts of LGBTQ

---

45 Adichie, Chimamanda Ngozi, "The Danger of a Single Story," July 2009, TED video, 18:33, https://www.ted.com/talks/chimamanda_ngozi_adichie_the_danger_of_a_single_story?language=en.

46 This word is found in the Social Principles, ¶164 (I), in *The Book of Discipline of the United Methodist Church 2016*.

members of our churches, and I have known more closely LGBTQ persons who are on the same journey of holiness that I am on. At the same time, I have been nourished by the traditionalist streams of theological reflection in our church. And, in my reading of a book like Tom Langford's *Practical Divinity*, I believe we have had multiple streams of theological resources in our Church since the beginning, and in that work he speaks especially of American Methodism.[47]

These convictions and commitments ground my motivations to seek the unity of the church, for the purpose of finding a way forward. This unity is not a given. It is the work we do, and it is described in Ephesians: we are "bearing with one another in love" and "making every effort to maintain the unity of the Spirit in the bond of peace" (4:2–3, NRSV).

We are grateful for your prayers as we seek a way forward in this season in the life of our Church.

Postscript

The report of the Commission on a Way Forward was taken up by the called General Conference in 2019, which chose in contrast to adopt a traditional plan. The voting was marked by some documented voter irregularities. The response across the Church was one of lament from different places, and this unease led to a vision of Bishop John Yambasu of Sierra Leone for renewed conversation. This resulted in the Protocol of Reconciliation and Grace through Separation, which was crafted into legislative form for the 2020 General Conference. This General Conference would be delayed until 2024 because of complexities related to the global coronavirus pandemic in a Church that exists in forty nations. The Church continues to explore, struggle, and discern its future as a connection amid a world that is increasingly fractured.

---

47 Thomas A. Langford, *Practical Divinity: Theology in the Wesleyan Tradition*, rev. ed. (Nashville: Abingdon Press, 1998).

Bibliography

The Arbinger Institute. *The Anatomy of Peace: Resolving the Heart of Conflict*. 2nd ed. Oakland: Berrett-Koehler Publishers, 2015.

Langford, Thomas A. *Practical Divinity: Theology in the Wesleyan Tradition*. Rev. ed. Nashville: Abingdon Press, 1998.

Miller, Donald. *Building a StoryBrand: Clarify Your Message So Customers Will Listen*. Nashville: HarperCollins Leadership, 2017.

The United Methodist Church. *The Book of Discipline of The United Methodist Church 2016*. Nashville: The United Methodist Publishing House, 2016.

The Broken-Open Church: When the Church Gets Broken, the World Gets Mended

Peter Storey

Closing Service at Wesley Memorial Methodist Church, Oxford, August 19, 2018

Isaiah 58:1–14, 2 Corinthians 5:14–20, Mark 2:1–10

This past week we have been very privileged. We have listened to erudite and outstanding papers about everything Wesleyan. John and Charles Wesley have been dissected and reassembled every which way, and the remarkable story of the evangelical revival has been microscoped and analyzed once more. As we returned to these subjects yet again, I sensed some desperation, as in, "Why can't we do today what they did then?" and "What secret of theirs have we overlooked?" And I can hear Mr. Wesley saying dryly, "Well, you haven't yet written a paper on my horse. Surely you realize there could have been no revival without it? That horse took me out of the church's bubble, into the real world."

This was a wonderful week, but let's concede that it was spent in a bubble. There's a real world out there that wouldn't make head or tail of most of what we've been talking about. The challenge as you go home now is surely how to help aspiring preachers discover what it means to minister in that world.

This sermon has been edited and updated since it was preached to allow for reference to more recent events. The substance remains unchanged.

Which Is Why Our Gospel Today . . .

Here are five friends. One is paraplegic, and the others feel deeply for him. You could say they are intercessors; they may not know what that word means, but long before they carry him with their hands, they have carried him on their hearts. That's the beginning of intercession, but it's not the end: intercession comes to life in action. So, our four faithful friends lift up their heart burden—their paralyzed mate—and bring him to Jesus.

Well, they try! The trouble is the church gets in the way.

The crowd filling every nook and cranny in that house is there to hear Jesus "speaking the word to them." You could say that *they are doing church,* and there's nothing wrong with that, except that when our four friends get there, everybody has their backs turned and nobody lets them in.

Nearly sixty years of ministry have taught me that having our backs turned to the world may be the church's most practiced posture.

Which is why, on that long-ago day in Capernaum, however important it was to do church with Jesus, to listen to his teaching, and to do all the stuff churches do, *it was time for more important things to intrude.* Our four heroic saints determine that if a preoccupied church has its back to the world, the pain of the world will have to hack its way in.

You all look politely preoccupied doing church with me right now. Imagine if we began to hear the clomp of heavy boots on *this* roof, followed by the sound of pickaxes and other heavy cutting tools right above us, and bits and pieces of wood and plaster began to drop down on our heads. Some of us would begin to shift out of the way, and in spite of the congestion of a moment ago, a space would appear miraculously in front of me. We look up, and there, peering down on us, are four grimy faces covered in dust and sweat, each bearing a triumphant grin. One of them shouts down, "So you thought you could keep us out?" and then, "Watch out, preacher! Here comes some work for you!"

Real intercession is much more than knowing about the world's pain; it is about feeling it so deeply that we have to act, and we shouldn't be surprised if compassion for excluded, wounded, and hurting persons results in some damage to church property. Mother Teresa used to pray, "O Lord, break my heart so wide open that the whole world falls in." That can be painful—it can cause damage.

Let me tell you about a church I know. The Central Methodist Mission (CMM) in Johannesburg is South African Methodism's cathedral, but in my years there, our congregations were often defiant protesters, our visitors were police with guns and batons, and our incense was the scent of tear gas. This is because CMM spoke out against apartheid and gave sanctuary to people resisting its terrible oppression. Then, in the years after I left, CMM offered a different kind of sanctuary: more than two thousand refugees from Robert Mugabe's terror in Zimbabwe found refuge there. They were in every space: each night they stretched out on the pews and floors to sleep, they cooked there, they ate there, some gave birth there, others died. It was not a "nice" place anymore. It stank, and *doing* church the traditional way was difficult; CMM was *being* church in a broken-open way.[1]

Two thousand refugees sleeping for years in a prestigious downtown church didn't make the Methodists popular. I struggled with the idea myself, and when I visited, it angered and hurt me to see the massive damage done to this gracious building. I could feel its agony: it was almost as if it had absorbed into its very walls the travail of its new, lost, and frightened inhabitants.

But Jesus wasn't hurt or surprised when something like this happened to *his* church. The people saw a disruption, but Jesus applauded great faith—faith that freed him to act. Neither would John Wesley have been unduly disturbed by what happened in Capernaum or Johannesburg. Once Wesley engaged the world in the wide-open air, "disruptions" like this were common. We've been reminded this week of his instruction that works of mercy should take precedence over

1 The story of CMM's long tradition of sanctuary is told in Christa Kuljian, *Sanctuary—How an Inner-City Church Spilled onto the Sidewalk* (Auckland Park, South Africa: Jacana Media, 2013).

works of piety and that if we're doing church—even if we're holding out our hands for the sacrament—when a deep human need intrudes, we should leave the bread and wine and attend to our neighbour's pain.

So, however I felt about the damage those poor people were doing to CMM, I had to reckon with this story in Mark 2 as well as Wesley's instruction, because—and here's the thing—*When the church gets broken, that's when the world gets mended.*

Let me go further: Only *when the church gets broken-open* can *the world be mended.*

Maybe we church people need to get real about what is more important to God, the church or the world? *I've no doubt that God's vote is for the world,* and there's some good Scripture to back that up.

- It was into the *world* that the Word came in human flesh (John 1:14).
- It is the *world* that "God so loved that God gave . . ." (John 3:16, NEB).
- It is the *world* that God in Christ is busy reconciling to God (2 Cor. 5:19).
- It is into real cities and regions and to the *ends of the earth* that Jesus sends his disciples (Acts 1:8).
- On the day of Pentecost, the Holy Spirit blew the disciples out of their upper-room sanctuary *into the world*, and the church was born on the streets of Jerusalem (Acts 2).
- It is the "*whole created universe* that waits with eager expectation for the children of God to be revealed" (Rom. 8:19, NEB).
- It is the *kingdoms of this world* that must become "the Kingdom of our Lord and of His Christ" (Rev. 11:15, NKJV).

So if the God we worship is a world-engaging, world-affirming God, if Scripture is about God's love affair with this messy, hostile, fallen, and broken world, then the call to engage it is a nonnegotiable. In fact, *maybe the only time we are truly being the church is when we are engaging the world*; the rest is at best a dress rehearsal and at worst playing with ourselves. That's what the prophet told us in Isaiah 58. Let me offer a simple paraphrase: God says, "this religious stuff you're doing just doesn't move me—not until you get broken open and start doing something about my world."

Wesley and his Methodists got close to seeing this. In a world where so many religious people pride themselves in being right, the Methodists were more concerned with being good. They put loving action ahead of religiosity—and so should we.

Two other factors made the Wesleyan revival not just a soul-saving exercise, but a nation-transforming movement. They were *location* and a *three-letter word.*

First, location: When John Wesley changed location and turned to the poor, something happened to him: in the process of regularly sharing their humble homes, their meager crust, their heavy burdens and terrible degradations—and marveling at their newfound trust in God—he found he had arrived at Jesus's home address. When that happens, you cannot remain unchanged. The result was that this starchy high churchman got broken open himself. On the one hand, awe at the discovery that being with the poor was as much a channel of God's grace as receiving the bread and wine at the Eucharist. On the other hand, blazing indignation at the way the comfortable looked upon the poor: "So wickedly false," he cried, "so devilishly false, is the common objection: 'they are poor only because they are idle.' "

When I was relocated to make my ministry among the thousands of people of a Cape Town ghetto called District 6[2]—where the government was determined to forcibly remove every one of them because of the color of their skin—*I got broken open too.* The pain of those people and their faith changed me. I was not only baptized into a community of courage and grace, but I felt a holy indignation at this trampling of God's little people, the poor. I had to be different because I found myself located where Jesus lived.

---

2 District 6 was an inner-city area in Cape Town that the apartheid regime declared to be a "White Group Area," forcibly removing some sixty thousand people of color.

There is no rediscovery of the "secret" of the Wesleyan revival without migrating the church's priorities and resources away from institutional survivalism and relocating them where Wesley spent most of his time and energy—with "the least of these."

And then that three-letter word: We've used a lot of long words this week. But the Wesleyan word that brought tears of joy to the poor of England, the word John Wesley preached in St. Mary's Church down the road from here just weeks after his Aldersgate experience, was much simpler and far more dangerous. It was the word *all.* That word started a quiet revolution because it had social implications beyond those even understood by Wesley. The nineteenth-century political scientist Moisei Ostrogorski spoke of the political influence of the leaders of England's Evangelical Revival: "They appeal always and everywhere from the miserable reality to the human conscience. They make one see the man in the criminal, the brother in the negro." He declared that they had "introduced a new personage into the social and political world of aristocratic England—*the fellow man* [*sic*]." That fellow man, Ostrogorski predicted, "never more will leave the stage."[3] Indeed, this new honoring of *all* men and women, valuing human dignity above position and property, led to the birth of both the British Trades Union movement and the Labour Party. Two hundred years later in South Africa, Wesleyan convictions about an *all*-including God would challenge Methodists in an apartheid society shaped by Calvinist exclusionism.

Remember those days? When the whole world looked on my country with disbelief and disgust because of what we were doing to people? I have two abiding memories.

The first was that we had to choose what really mattered. We could turn our backs on the injustices that apartheid was perpetrating and go on playing church—and many Christians did just that—or we could recognize, as Jesus showed in Capernaum, that playing church while

3 Moisei Jakovlevich Ostrogorski, *Democracy and the Organization of Political Parties*, trans. Frederick Clarke (London: Macmillan, 1902). Originally published as *La Démocratie et l'Organisation des Partis Politiques.* Quoted in J. W. Bready, *England: Before and After Wesley—The Evangelical Revival and Social Reform* (London: Hodder & Stoughton, 1939).

people suffered was the supreme sin of the religious. Apartheid denied the core of God's reconciling intention for all humanity (2 Cor. 5:14–21), and if we were silent, our very identity as church was at stake.

My dad used to say, "Everything begins in theology and ends in politics," which is why, as leader of South Africa's Methodists in 1957, he confronted the apartheid regime: "The government's view," he declared, "is that while one white man [*sic*] and one black man are friends, apartheid will have failed; the Church's view is that so long as one white man and one black man are not friends, the Church will have failed. We are therefore diametrically opposed. We will not place the church at the disposal of the state."[4] *Convictions like that broke us open*. We had to decide, and our decision led us into nearly forty years of struggle and disruption.

The second memory is about you and your solidarity. You never left us. You recognized that our sickness might be yours too. Christians in the United Kingdom, Europe, and the United States—and all over the world—stood with us. When we were weak, you challenged us; when we faltered, you were there carrying us back into the struggle.

In the early 1980s, the South African Council of Churches was put on trial before a government tribunal set up to destroy it. It was a lonely time. Desmond Tutu and I were each interrogated for more than twenty-one hours.[5] But neither can we forget the day when we heard a scraping of chairs, and into the public gallery of that tribunal came representatives of the World Council of Churches, the World Alliance of Reformed Churches, the National Council of Churches in New York, the World Methodist Council, the World Lutheran Federation,

---

4 Clifford K. Storey, address on the occasion of his induction as President of the Conference, Methodist Church of South Africa Annual Conference, October 1957, in *The Methodist Churchman*, October 1957, pp. 4 and 13.

5 Bishop Desmond Tutu, "The Divine Intention" (presentation by Bishop D. Tutu, General Secretary of the South Africa Council of Churches to the Eloff Commission of Enquiry, September 1, 1982) (Braamfontein: South Africa Council of Churches, 1982). Peter J. Storey, *Here We Stand* (submission to the Commission of Enquiry into the South African Council of Churches by the Rev. Peter John Storey, President of the SACC, March 9, 1983) (Braamfontein: South Africa Council of Churches, 1983).

the EKD in Germany, and others. They had left their work all over the world and flown to South Africa, literally breaking into that tribunal and demanding to make their witness. They took the stand and declared that "when you attack the South African church, you attack the Church of God everywhere. You will not prevail."

So many of your churches around the word allowed themselves to be broken open for us in sick, sinning South Africa, and in the end the purveyors of apartheid did not prevail. South Africa began a journey of forgiveness, healing, and reconciliation.

But the disease was not blotted out. My South African colleague Professor Dion Forster was right when he delivered the Fernley Hartley Lecture two days ago in this church: we cannot yet talk about a post-apartheid South Africa, nor should we speak of a post-apartheid world.[6] My country was not the last outpost of racism, discrimination, and the oppression of the poor; rather, we were the foreunners of a worldwide epidemic that is now crashing around us all. There is a global form of apartheid abroad today, and we dare not ignore it. Great democracies are being taken over by government-driven hate.

What might this gospel story be saying in the world of Trump's wall and Boris's Brexit? We've tiptoed round those issues this week, but in private conversations many have metaphorically wrung their hands in despair. Most of all I sense that too many of us see the wall and Brexit as purely political issues, to be solved by a next United States election or some miracle negotiations in Brussels. But remember, *everything begins in theology before it ends in politics!*

These and other populist movements are a backward slide into the worship of the destructive idols of nationalism, pride, and fear: of walls and drawbridges, of the arrogance of whiteness and the fear of "otherness." We South Africans know these signs; we've been there, we've done that! We are witnessing a "re-fracturing" of humanity. These withdrawals into apart-ness—and you can add the tragic prospect of a

6 The 2018 Fernley Hartley Lecture was "An Understanding of Christian Perfection as African Christian Humanism in the Methodist Church of Southern Africa," delivered by Dion Forster, Head of Department, Systematic Theology and Ecclesiology, Stellenbosch University, South Africa.

United Methodist Church ceasing to be united—contradict the words of Paul when he says that the mandate to reconcile rather than alienate comes from God: "All this is from God, who reconciled us to himself through Christ and gave us the ministry of reconciliation: that God was reconciling the world to himself in Christ, not counting people's sins against them. And he has committed to us the message of reconciliation" (2 Cor. 5:18–19, NIV).

If that is true, then God is pleading with us not only to introduce people to Jesus, but to be in the forefront of God's struggle to bring divided humanity together. *If we cannot do that, we have no word for the world.* We can talk about conversion and we can talk about holiness and piety until the cows come home, but if we cannot demonstrate how alienated humans can be brought together to find one another, we are mere sounding gongs and clanging cymbals.

It follows that if we don't see the tragic divisiveness of Trump and Brexit—yes, and the sad scandal of a looming "Sexit" in The United Methodist Church—as essentially moral and spiritual problems rooted in retrograde theology, we are as blind and oblivious as that church congregation in Capernaum long ago. Some of us who come from the countries that Donald Trump dismisses with an expletive find it hard to believe that the church in America remains more preoccupied with issues of sexuality than with the immoral abuses of power he is perpetrating. We have also waited to hear God's church on the British side of the Atlantic say unequivocally and together, "How can you with a Christian conscience place your nationalist jingoism above one of the greatest experiments in peace-building that the world has seen, a Union that has turned the enemies of centuries into friends and neighbors, and saved Europe from war?"

So, the question this old gospel story leaves us with is whether we will continue to think our job is to keep doing church in the old, safe way while the world—that God loves more than us—goes deeper into sickness and death, or whether we might find the courage of those four faithful friends who refused to let the church remain undisturbed, or the magnificent discernment of a Wesley who said, "It's the *world*, not the church; that's my parish," or maybe we might even come to live out a paraphrase of the words of a wizened little Albanian nun named Teresa and pray, "O Lord, open up your *church* so wide that the whole world can fall in."

Chapter Bibliography

Forster, Dion A. "Revival, Revolution and Reform in Global Methodism: An Understanding of Christian Perfection as African Christian Humanism in the Methodist Church of Southern Africa." *Black Theology* 17, no. 1 (2019): 22–39. https://doi.org/10.1080/14769948.2018.1554328.

Kuljian, Christa. *Sanctuary—How an Inner-City Church Spilled onto the Sidewalk.* Auckland Park, South Africa: Jacana Media, 2013.

Ostrogorski, Moisei Jakovlevich. *Democracy and the Organization of Political Parties.* Translated by Frederick Clarke. London: Macmillan, 1902. Originally published as *La Démocratie et l'Organisation des Partis Politiques.*

Bready, J. W. *England: Before and After Wesley—The Evangelical Revival and Social Reform.* London: Hodder & Stoughton Limited, 1939.

Storey, Clifford K. Address on the occasion of his induction as President of the Conference, Methodist Church of South Africa Annual Conference, October 1957. *The Methodist Churchman*, October 1957.

Storey, Peter J. *Here We Stand.* Submission to the Commission of Enquiry into the South African Council of Churches by the Rev. Peter John Storey, President of the SACC, March 9, 1983. Braamfontein: South Africa Council of Churches, 1983.

Tutu, Desmond. *The Divine Intention.* Braamfontein: South African Council of Churches, 1982.

Index

Lightning Source UK Ltd.
Milton Keynes UK
UKHW010645090223
416681UK00006B/1384